PAYING FOR MASCULINITY

PAYING FOR MASCULINITY

Boys, Men and the Patriarchal Dividend

MURRAY KNUTTILA

FERNWOOD PUBLISHING
HALIFAX & WINNIPEG

Editing: Jessica Antony
Cover design: John van der Woude
Printed and bound in Canada

Published by Fernwood Publishing
32 Oceanvista Lane, Black Point, Nova Scotia, B0J 1B0
and 748 Broadway Avenue, Winnipeg, Manitoba, R3G 0X3

www.fernwoodpublishing.ca

Fernwood Publishing Company Limited gratefully acknowledges the financial support of the Government of Canada through the Canada Book Fund, the Manitoba Department of Culture, Heritage and Tourism under the Manitoba Publishers Marketing Assistance Program and the Province of Manitoba, through the Book Publishing Tax Credit, for our publishing program. We are pleased to work in partnership with the Province of Nova Scotia to develop and promote our creative industries for the benefit of all Nova Scotians. We acknowledge the support of the Canada Council for the Arts, which last year invested $153 million to bring the arts to Canadians throughout the country.

Canada   Canada Council   Conseil des arts   NOVA SCOTIA   Manitoba
         for the Arts   du Canada

Library and Archives Canada Cataloguing in Publication

Knuttila, Kenneth Murray, author
Paying for masculinity : boys, men and the patriarchal dividend / Murray Knuttila.

Includes bibliographical references and index.
ISBN 978-1-55266-824-5 (paperback)

1. Patriarchy. 2. Masculinity. 3. Male domination (Social structure).
4. Sex role. 5. Men. 6. Boys. I. Title.

GN479.6.K68 2016   305.235'1   C2016-904979-5

CONTENTS

ACKNOWLEDGEMENTS

It is difficult to offer adequate acknowledgements for a project many years in the making; however I have many people to thank. Raewyn Connell and the manner by which she welcomed me to the department she was building at Macquarie University many years ago set me on an intellectual trajectory from which I have, thankfully, never recovered. Her groundbreaking *Gender and Power* was hot off the press and I quickly realized I would never see social class in the same way. Her impact on this field has only grown.

Colleagues at the University of Regina offered encouragement and insight over many years, and I thank them. More recently, my department and other colleagues at Brock University have been extraordinarily welcoming to a recovering senior administrator and this I much appreciate. It is good to be back.

I really should list Wayne Antony as a co-author because of his encouragement, patience and support for this project; however that may excessively implicate if not taint him. Fernwood remains a beacon in a darkening moment in Canadian publishing and we are all indebted to them. Thanks also to Jessica Antony for her copy edit and to Deb Mathers and Beverley Rach for their production work.

A large crew including Wendee Kubik, Erin and Lee Knuttila, Laine Gabel, Germaine Tourond and Andre Magnan have tried unfailingly and even partly successfully to help me think clearer, and to them I extend my most heartfelt thanks. Then there are the reasons for trying to make the world better — Maëlle, Pascal and Rose Lea — who constantly leave me speechless in wonder and hope!

I, of course, am solely responsible for any and all of the errors and misinterpretations herein and for any offence taken.

INTRODUCTION

THE GOOD,
THE BAD
AND THE UGLY

What are we to make of men and boys? Perhaps the title of Sergio Leone's 1966 movie, *The Good, the Bad and the Ugly*, aptly describes how men and boys sometimes behave, how we are perceived and are we are represented. Clearly there are good men, bad men and ugly men (not in appearance but obnoxious, ill-mannered or unpleasant). This book is part of ongoing attempts to find a route to better explain and understand boys and men and, perhaps, why we are good, bad and ugly. Boys and men present many perplexing paradoxes, enigmas and contradictions. I speak of the fact that men, and sometimes boys, commit the vast majority of murders, yet the majority of lives lost by firefighters and emergency workers attempting to protect and save lives are also men. Men occupy most positions of power and authority in many major social institutions, yet men also often suffer loneliness, feelings of isolation and the lack of intimacy and close friendships. There is evidence that male newborns are more sensitive and emotionally attuned to disruptions in their social and physical environment, yet boys are typically the perpetrators of physical bullying.

What then are we to make of these paradoxes, puzzles and enigmas? There is certainly no shortage of punditry, analysis, opinion and academic discourse on the matter. As we shall see, there is a too-common belief that this is just how boys and men are, simply capable of being good, bad and ugly and prone to switching demeanours with little notice or provocation. While such a facile "explanation" may be acceptable for those only interested in superficial description, it is inadequate for those really wanting to better understand boys and men. Surely we can do better than "that's just they way it goes." The need for a more robust understanding and explanation of the behaviour of boys is brilliantly demonstrated in Rob Reiner's magnificent 1986 movie, *Stand By Me*. The final scene in which characters Gordie Lachance and Chris Chambers are saying good-bye ("See ya later" ... "Not if I see ya first" and the obligatory tap on the arm) is a demonstration of human love, not to be debased with any implication of carnality, just human love. Contrast this scene with the actions of teenagers and young adults, represented by Ace Merrill (Kiefer Sutherland), who are bullies verging on psychopaths, and you are left with one question — what happens that makes loving boys into violent thugs? Surely we are not content with "it just happens."

What are we to make of 46-year-old Arland Williams Jr. who died on January 13, 1982, in Potomac River in Washington after the crash of an Air Florida plane? Mr. Williams survived the crash and like a number of other passengers was found in the icy water of the river. Rescue crews arrived immediately and began lowering life lines from helicopters and pulling survivors from the water. Each time he caught a lifeline Mr. Williams passed it to another passenger as he continued to tread water. When the rescuers returned for him Mr. Williams had perished. How do we square this sort of conduct with those men (and boys) who were involved in the mass killings and organized rape in Srebrenica during the summer of 1985, or those who seem to delight in recording and broadcasting their mass executions? Surely we are not content with "it just happens."

What these sorts of anecdotes point to is the complexity of understanding human behaviour, including that of boys and men. An interesting feature of the contemporary world is our propensity to seek and utilize simply answers to complex problems. The complex behaviours of boys and men have, for example, been reduced to male instincts, male hormones, the male brain or some supposedly evolutionary propelled drive to promulgate our genes into the future. What such "explanations" lack is an appropriate understanding of the complexities of the human personality and behaviour, particularly with regard to the social construction of our character. If for no other reason than the fact that human survival at the most basic level is dependent on the presence of other humans, we must put the behaviour of boys and men in an historical and social context if we are to understand anything about them. Moreover, we need to ensure that we have an appropriate intellectual and conceptual toolkit with which we can begin to try to unpack the complexities of the lives of boys and men. Such tools must permit an understanding of the individual lives and actions of boys and men — "agency," to put it in sociological terms — and the larger historical and social structural context.

We know that explaining a phenomenon is profoundly different than merely describing it. Moving beyond description of boys and men requires analytical tools, concepts and a framework capable of enhancing our understanding. I will argue that such a framework can be based on C. Wright Mills' notion of the sociological imagination. In *The Sociological Imagination* (1959) Mills laid out an approach to understanding ourselves and the behaviour of others that focuses on the intersection of biography and history. Mills argued that placing our life story (our biography) in the context of the society and historical periods that shaped, molded, influenced and conditioned that biography enhances self understanding. He further argues that we must be able to simultaneously understand the society and historical period in a logical way through which our biography moves, discerning its essential elements, characteristics and dynamics. It is this capacity to link our self/biography to its historical and social context that Mills termed "the sociological imagination."

The task that Mills set before us, with its potential reward of greater self understanding and a greater capacity to understand those around us, requires us to systematically approach two different aspects of the human condition: 1) the individual human social agent or us as individual beings in the world; and 2) the social structure, our society and the historical periods through which we move in our lifetime. In short, we need to approach understanding ourselves as social agents and the social structures and processes of which we are a part in a dynamic, coherent and systematic manner.

It turns out, however, that this task is not as easy as it sounds, in part because of the very nature of reality and how we go about understanding the world around us. Peter Berger (1963: 23) points out one of the problems we face in this astute observation: "It can be said that the first wisdom of sociology is this — that things are not what they seem." This is, in fact, not just the first wisdom of sociology.

To be successful in our search for a degree of self understanding, achieve an improved capacity to understand others, better understand the nature and dynamics of our society and hopefully help create the foundation for a better, more equal society, we must, to return to Berger, figure out what is really going on with boys and men in our patriarchal capitalist society. And just how do we do this? I am a sociologist and therefore my answer is we begin by systematically utilizing appropriate modes of thought and conceptual frameworks to enhance our sociological imaginations, even though the task is complex.

PREVIEWING A CONCEPTUAL TOOLKIT

Before we can actually begin the search for a better understanding of boys and men in contemporary society we need to understand the pivotal role played by the concepts, ideas and assumptions that we bring to the task. I, for instance, will proceed on the basis of the fact that humans are cultural creatures and our behaviours must be understood within the context of the social structures that we, as active social agents, create. However, we must also acknowledge that we exist as individual agents who cannot be reduced to social structures. For those who ask if it is really necessary to restate these social constructionist assumptions, I remind you of the continuing importance of the ideology of biological determinism, as illustrated by the remarks Canadian Chief of the Defence Staff Gen. Tom Lawson who told the CBC in 2015 that sexual harassment in the military can be understood in terms of men's "biological wiring" (CBC News Online 2015). So it seems as if the processes by which the human self or personality, including the masculine self, is created, constructed, moulded and formed remain misunderstood and contested. Among the lessons learned from the last several centuries of psychology, social psychology, anthropology and sociology is the fact that human behaviour and societies are diverse and often radically different. Given this fact, those arguments that reduce the complexities of human behaviour to simple causes are clearly untenable. What we require instead are a variety of approaches and conceptual tools that properly place human personality in its larger context as a point of departure as we seek to increase our understanding.

In the pages that follow I will make an argument in favour of understanding gender as a form of social practice, not mere character or personality traits. We will come to see that understanding gender as a form of social practice points to the multiple complex modes of doing gender in what I will call different gender orders. Masculinity, I will argue, is a form of gender practice, but in the sense of a singular masculinity. Further, I will argue that gender must be studied in its historical and social contexts. It then follows that I see Western masculinities as the historical products of a patriarchal gender order, connected to and conditioned by the political economy of Western capitalism.

Even though we will come to understand gender as a mode of social practice embedded in a particular gender order, and masculinity as a particular mode of gendered practice, this book focuses on a particular form of masculinity represented by the concept of hegemonic masculinity — a form masculinity that predominates in a gender order such as patriarchy. Relations of (male) domination and inequality are inherent to patriarchal gender orders and such relations generate benefits, which I will refer to as the patriarchal dividend, which accrue, in varying degrees, to males.

As a form of practice, hegemonic masculinity does not come naturally to boys and thus they must taught to be(come) practitioners. Hegemonic masculinity and various elements of the patriarchal dividend have unfolded historically. This historical backdrop includes shifting manifestations of the patriarchal dividend as the labour market and familial relations evolved. Work and family lives are among the most important arenas of activity for most humans in contemporary society, and therefore are central sites in which gender relations play out. It is also within the workplace and shifting familial relations that contemporary forms of gender relations took shape and were consolidated over the past several centuries.

Establishing and maintaining hegemonic masculinity is often precarious and its practice and maintenance take effort and work and often come at a high cost. Such is the case in all systems of domination and inequality. As a result, social control is necessary, resulting in the use of manipulation, misrepresentation, deception (including self deception) and violence in order to establish and maintain hegemonic masculinity and its associated dividends.

Although hegemonic masculinity and the patriarchal dividend necessarily mark the existence of an unequal and oppressive gender order embedded in an economic order that also necessarily implies a class structure, there are defenders and protectors. Both the high costs of the dividend and the extent to which patriarchy and the practice of hegemonic masculinity share an elective affinity with social interactions and behaviours are typical of capitalism and market competition. Given the high costs of engaging in and practising hegemonic masculinity and the high costs of the inherent inequalities in patriarchal capitalism, men need to be challenged to rethink these costs and engage in considering alternate modes of practising masculinity. At the individual level, given the inherent power of the human agent to consider and reflect on the costs and implications of our actions, and given the flexibilities and options that are often available in terms of how we practise masculinity, we need to think carefully and humanely about our actions. At the social structural level we need to think critically about the possibility of alternatives to the modes of behaviour and social action required to maintain the structural dynamics and embedded interests of patriarchy and corporate capitalism. Before we begin the elaboration of this framework we must explore the view of science that informs this work and how we use concepts.

CRITICAL REALISM: WHAT IS REALLY GOING ON

In this book, I explicitly use an approach commonly called analytical dualism, which is embedded in a critical realist understanding of science in the tradition of Roy Bhaskar (1944–2014) and elaborated by Berth Danermark et al. (2002) and Margaret Archer (1995; 2000; 2007; 2013). The focus of a critical realist approach is on the mechanisms that cause or explain events, as opposed to merely describing events. In the spirit of Berger's warning, it follows that the essential task of social science is to delve beneath the surface appearance of events and uncover what is really going on. Flowing from Mills's insight, it is clear that we must recognize, analyze and understand the independence, powers and properties of both the individual agent and her or his biography, and the social structure and history within which that biography unfolds. In Archer's words, "both humanity and society have their own *sui generis* properties and powers, which makes their interplay the central issue of social theory for all time" (2000: 17). That is, structure cannot be made dependent on agency nor agency reduced to structure because "distinctive properties and powers pertain *sui generis* to both structures and agents" (Archer 2000: 87).

AGENCY AND STRUCTURE

Agency and structure are the most basic level, the foundation for understanding the behaviour of men and boys. This clear ontological, epistemological and conceptual foundation is important because of the ever-present tendencies toward simplistic arguments and explanations. Perhaps it is out of a desire for a measure of security in a complex world, or perhaps it is because powerful interests often encourage simplistic thinking, but we seem to live in an age that seeks simple answers. One form of simplistic thinking is what we might term essentialism. Essentialism is a form of understanding and explanation that, as the name implies, assumes that most phenomena possess or are characterized by some core or essential attribute that mark them, make them what they are, and that without which they would be something different. An essentialist argument might claim, for example, that humans are by nature competitive. When seeking to explain competitiveness the explanation is simple — that is how we are, plain and simple. Alternate simplistic explanations might involve something more sophisticated, as is the case with bio-logical determinism. A biological determinist might argue that there are certain innate or inherent biologically based imperatives that produce complex behaviours, as in the notion that somehow there is a biologically based drive to reproduce our genes that leads to the sexual and reproductive tactics that humans employ. In a sense, all such arguments are reductionist in that they attempt to reduce complex phenomena to simple elements and then in turn use the character of those simple elements to describe the whole. All such arguments typically see the whole as merely the sum of the parts.

HUMAN SOCIAL AGENCY:
BIOLOGICAL BUT NOT BIOLOGICALLY DETERMINED

I will attempt to develop a more adequate and complex understanding of humans, although I begin with a mundane fact, human beings are biological creatures with certain basic biological or physiological needs that must be satisfied if we are to survive as individuals and as a species. At the most elementary level these include matters such as food and nutrition, water, shelter, security and sleep. Further spe-cies needs include the necessity of biological reproduction and the early care and nurturing of infants. Although scholars such as Abraham Maslow (1943) have postulated a wider range of other needs related to the psychological and spiritual dimensions of humans, for the present purposes we need not belabour the point, other than noting that we have a number of basic needs that must be addressed and problems that must be solved if we are to survive as individuals and as a species.

Although like many other life forms we have core or basic needs, humans are different in one important way — we lack a substantial repertoire of instinctual behaviours sufficient to allow us to address our needs and solve our basic survival-related problems. Many life forms, particularly more complex animals, possess unlearned and genetically transmitted problem-solving behaviours that facilitate survival; however, humans do not seem to possess such complex instinctual behaviours. The question then becomes: how have we survived, prospered and come to dominate the planet as we do? The answer, interestingly, lies in our physiology and a unique combination of physiological and biological characteristics. These include our erect posture, prehensile hands and opposable thumbs, relative longevity, large and complex brain, flexible voice mechanism, long and significant dependency in infancy and slow maturation, flexibility of solutions to our needs and drives and constant sex drive as opposed to definite mating seasons or periods.

While other creatures also possess some of these characteristics, we alone possess all of them and, as a result, in the absence of a strong reservoir of instinctual behaviours, we have developed and honed the ability to think and then act so as to meet our needs and solve our problems. We have perfected the development of tools, and learned how to engage in complex social problem- and need-solving behaviours. We use our brains and hands and our ability to reason, remember and communicate to build complex systems of knowledge and tools to solve our needs and address our problems. Further, we use our ability to communicate to transmit this knowledge from one generation to the next. In short, we have developed social solutions or behaviours to address our core needs and problems — we developed culture. Thus we might say that a defining characteristic of humanity is our transformative capacity, our ability to engage in deliberate social action and forms of labour so as to meet our needs and solve our problems through the transformation of nature as opposed to merely availing ourselves of what nature provides.

Two further comments on the physiological characteristics of the human species are in order. First, there is the sex differentiation of humans as female and male. As we shall see, the matter of sex differences is not as simple as might first seem; nevertheless for now we note humans possess a sex-differentiated physiology, and since humans are not capable of parthenogenesis, species reproduction and continuance requires the existence of both females and males. An additional important biological fact with regard to humans is the importance of our large and complex brain organ. The human capacity to reason, think, reflect and remember has been instrumental in the development of human social relationships, patterns of behaviour and institutions. These intellectual powers, particularly recall and memory, generate an essential component of every human culture and society — an accumulated and complex "stock of knowledge." Depending on the society and the historical period this stock of knowledge contains a great many diverse elements ranging from myths and folklore to the intellectual legacy of the society's science, religion, art, literature, common sense and more.

There is much in our society's stock of knowledge that bears on issues relating to men and boys; however, in line with Archer's comments above regarding the necessity of understanding both agency and structure, the manner by which an individual both accumulates and utilizes such stocks of knowledge is far from simple and determinate. Sociologists are occasionally accused of losing agency, or the individual, to culture and structure. The value of analytical dualism lies in the insistence that, to repeat Archer's words, we always understand that human agents always have "distinctive properties and powers" and thus their actions and social practices always maintain an element of choice and intentionality.

SOCIAL STRUCTURE

Humans engage in a wide range of social activities in order to solve our problems and satisfy our needs. We know that these behaviours and actions tend to become the "way of doing things," more-or-less fixed, routinized and patterned, or, as sociologists say, institutionalized. Used in this manner an institutionalized behaviour is not so much about a place or building, but rather behaviours that become habitualized, regularized, patterned and organized; that is, structured. Over time relationships and interactions between institutions and clusters of institutions (what we call "institutional orders") become patterned into societies or social structures.

Most human societies contain a variety of institutions and institutional orders. Among the multiple fields of human practice and social behaviour are those relating to the satisfaction of our material needs (for example, food, clothing and shelter). Sociologists typically refer to those as economic institutions or, collectively, the "economic order." Those institutionalized behaviours cannot either logically or empirically be conceived of as occurring outside a wider complex web of human activities relating to other individual and species-wide needs and problems. Thus, human societies contain some form of institutional arrangements relating to biological reproduction and childcare (family or the familial order); cultural transmission and enhancement (education or educational order); social or collective decision making (the polity or political order); those social practices associated with the human penchant for spirituality and asking ultimate questions (religion and religious institutions); and patterns of behaviour relating to relationships between women and men (gender order), to name a few. We know, at a very high level of abstraction, that the myriad ensembles of social activities, arrangements, organizations, groups and institutions that typically are the components of a social system tend to coalesce as a totality that exists across time in a particular locale or space and develops in relations with other societies.

Since I will be referring to the notion of levels of abstraction throughout this book, a reminder is in order. Whether or not we are aware of it or not, we are constantly thinking about and discussing the world at different levels of abstraction. When an economist talks about how the market works, or a psychologist explains the symptoms of narcissism or a sociologist explains the nature of a bureaucratic institution, she typically is operating at a high level of abstraction, that of the market, narcissism or bureaucracies in general. At such a high level of abstraction we seek to explain, document and outline the general or abstract features and characteristics of the phenomenon in order to provide a guide or framework to allow us to better understand a particular market (the Canadian market), or a particular patient (Murray's narcissism) or a particular bureaucracy (Canada Revenue Agency, or CRA). We are able to understand the complexities of the Canadian market, Murray's narcissism or the CRA because we have this high-level guide or map. When we move to a lower level of abstraction, we concretize our concepts and frameworks, modifying them as necessary in order to explain the more complex real world. Ultimately we might want to move to an even lower level of abstraction, the nature of market dynamics in a city or province, or the way Murray's narcissism results from his life as an academic or the dynamics of a particular CRA office, our analysis gets even more detailed, but we are able to make sense of the complexities of daily interaction because we have the higher level concepts and framework to guide our thinking and understanding. Awareness of the level of abstraction at which we are operating is important because it bears on the nature of the concepts and our expectations in terms of what they can and cannot explain.

MOVING ON

We know the world is complex and that it often presents itself in a way that might lead us to assume that on the basis of first impressions we immediately understand it. Heed the words of Berger and the lessons of the critical realism and never assume that "what you see is what you get"! We know that humans are social creatures that exhibit a profound sense of agency. Despite the fact that social and historical circumstances are of fundamental importance in shaping our biographies, we have individual biographies that mean we can never be reduced to the status of cultural dupes acting without volition and will. We also know that the way we crack open appearances and get to the discussion of causal mechanisms is through the engagement of appropriate conceptual frameworks. In the first chapter I will begin to introduce what I think are the key concepts for understanding contemporary boys and men.

CHAPTER 1

TOWARDS CONCEPTUAL CLARITY
Sex and Gender and Much More

If boys and men are paradoxes, puzzles and enigmas, perhaps we can make them less paradoxical, puzzling and enigmatic by systematically studying and analyzing them. Critical realists tend to argue that the world appears paradoxical, puzzling and enigmatic because we confuse what *seems* to be going on with what is *really* going on. As a critical realist utilizing an analytical dualist approach, I assume that conceptual clarity is a necessary prerequisite for getting at what is really happening. The core concepts that open the door to the paradoxes, puzzles and enigmas include sex, gender, sex roles, masculinities, patriarchy and the patriarchal dividend. Since these are complex and often contested concepts we will have to consider the history and evolution of concepts such as gender, sex roles and masculinity. Additionally, we will have to consider several different approaches with regard to the connection between sex and gender, and the individual and social dynamics by which certain individuals become boys and how boys then become men.

Given that the topic at hand is boys and men, the obvious starting point is a definition of our subject matter. I will begin with a simple question: What are boys and men? The answer to this question leads unavoidably to the subject of sex differences, a matter that might seem simple, but actually is very complex.

SEX DIFFERENCES

I suspect that for many people the notion that there are two sexes is common sense, and the possibility of there being multiple sexes seems counter-intuitive, not to mention just plain wrong. The notion that human sex differences are binary (two) with humans being either female or male is a core component of so-called common sense knowledge in many societies. However, the world is often not what it seems to be. Advances in biology, generics, reproductive medicine and many other fields have produced new knowledge regarding human physiology, including matters relating to sex differences. In particular, new research suggests that there are three important biological bases for differentiating females and males: genes, hormones and brains (Wade 2013: 278). In regards to the genetic component, there are three types of influence: 1) sex-linked differences (different chromosomes); 2) sex-limited differences (shared genes that are only expressed when in a male or female body such as the gene governing lactation that men also have); and 3) sex-influenced differences (genes that produce different outcomes in males or females, including the gene for balding, which women also have but is usually not expressed) (Wade 2013: 280).

Anne Fausto-Sterling (1993) is among the most important scholars in the study of sex differences. She identified three major sexual subgroups for humans falling outside the strictures of traditional binary thought: 1) those born with an ovary and a testis; 2) those with testes along with some female genital structures but no ovary; and 3) those with ovaries and some male genital structures but no testis. Elsewhere Fausto-Sterling notes that while some estimates for the number of transsexual people are as high as 4 percent, she suggested 1.7 percent (2000b: 51). In a more recent work she discussed how a wide range of environmental factors influence and complicate cell and gene expression during the development of a zygote from embryo through fetal and neonate status. She notes that during this complex process it is possible to speak of numerous sexes, including chromosomal sex, fetal gonadal sex, fetal hormonal sex, internal reproductive sex, genital sex and finally brain sex (2012: 4–5, 10).

An important aspect of sex differences is the fact that humans are incapable of parthenogenesis (asexual reproduction), meaning that biological reproduction requires the performance of distinctive functions by both females and males. Much has been made of this fact throughout human history, with the implications still a matter of much debate and discussion. While acknowledging that the notion of sex differences is often worrisome with regard to social equity and non-oppressive relations, the total neutralization of those sex differences, "if it were possible, would correspond to the end of the human race. The human race is divided into two *genres* to ensure its production and reproduction" (Irigaray 1993: 22, emphasis in original). However, acknowledging different functions in the reproductive arena does not mean we succumb to biological determinism in terms of personality or character, nor does it provide any basis for understanding or postulating what sorts of social behaviours are related to sexual activity or the meaning attached to pregnancy, birth, motherhood, fatherhood, parenting, childcare or household organization (Lerner 1986: 42).

Species reproduction aside, another issue that emerges from a consideration of sex differences relates the larger question of the social division of labour. Ann Oakley (1972: 156) studies this matter and concluded: "To sum up, then, we can say that the chief importance of biological sex in determining social roles is in providing a universal and obvious division around which other distinctions can be organized. In deciding which activities fall on each side of the boundary, the important factor is culture." Heidi Hartman (1976: 141) adds: "The existence of a sexual division of labor is a universal of human society, though the exact division of tasks by sex varies enormously." Kuhn and Stiner (2006: 953) agree: "Anthropologists have long recognized that the division of labor by gender and age is a universal property of small-scale human societies," suggesting that most researchers "seem to have implicitly accepted the notion that some sex or gender roles crystallized very early in human evolutionary history." However, a sex-based division of labour does not necessarily imply social inequality, indeed in many cases it did not, as in early band societies (Leacock and Lee 1982: 159–160).

BEYOND TWO SEXES: CIS, INTERSEXUAL, TRANSSEXUAL AND TRANSGENDER

The final paragraph of Anne Fausto-Sterling's (2012: 123) important book *Sex/Gender* begins with this sentence: "Of all of the points emphasized in this book, the one that needs most urgently to seep into people's ways of thought is that bodies are not bounded." She goes on: "To understand sex and gender we have to study how sensory, emotional, and motor experiences become embodied." Given what what we know about the human non-binary body and the advocacy work of groups such as the Intersex Society of North America, we must recognize the importance of intersex people and of protecting their rights to pursue the gender practices of their choice regardless of the particulars of their body structures.

It is important not to confuse intersexual with transsexual. Transsexual refers to an individual whose gender practice and identity do not align with their assigned sex. A person with those physiological attributes and characteristics that define her as female, but whose self-identity is that of a male, is considered to be transsexual. The emergence of organized movements to recognize the civil, legal and social rights of transsexual people has radically changed the sex and gender landscape, although the struggle for simple things such as social space is ongoing (Westbrook and Schilt 2014: 49–51).

Whereas transsexuals may live out their lives doing gender in a manner that is exceptional to their physical bodies, some individuals determine that in fact something about their body is out of synch and they choose to synchronize their physical body and their preferred gender. Such a synchronization or adjustment typically involves medical intervention, often in the form of hormone treatments and/or surgical interventions. The result is the emergence of a transgendered person, a transformed person who will then typically engage in a new life trajectory that is informed by their newly chosen sex. The growing number of first-hand accounts illustrate that the decision, at whatever age it is made, to become true to oneself is of course liberating but also politically complicated and subversive to the gender regimes because it "dramatically expresses the mutability and historicity of gender" (Connell 2010: 18).

As our understanding of basic biology expands and we finally move away from simplistic binary thinking, Fausto-Sterling's reminder of the importance of understanding that bodies are not bounded takes on new meaning. Perhaps it is our biological fluidity in matters relating to sex that has generated so much confusion with regard to the question of gender. I note in passing that in the context of the evolving conceptual environment that increasingly cis, or cisgender, is used to refer to those people whose physical bodies match the gender identity and practices prevalent in their social situation.

In sum then, I will follow in the lead of Fausto-Sterling, who, after reviewing the multiple uses of the words "sex" and "gender," stated that when she is speaking of the body she will use the term sex, but that she will use the term gender when referring to the social implications of sex: "An individual therefore, has a sex (male, female, not designated, other); but they engage with the world via a variety of social, gender conventions" (2012: 7). In this quote Fausto-Sterling introduces the next concept that we must begin to deal with, gender and the social, political, cultural, economic and personal implications of sex difference.

GENDER: EARLY CONCEPTUAL CONFUSION

Gender is a word we regularly encounter, for example, when filling out various bureaucratic and other forms and we are often asked to identify our gender; however, far too often we are offered two options — female or male. Obviously there is a need to devote some time and space to better understand the concept of gender.

Prior to the late nineteenth century the word gender was used largely in the context of grammatical studies (Scott 1986: 1053). Anthropologists such as Margaret Mead studied and described the relationship between what they called biological sex, social roles, institutional organization, and behaviours; however in her 1935 classic study, *Sex and Temperament in Three Primitive Societies*, she referred to "temperament" and not gender. Ann Oakley (1972: 16) offered a new understanding of gender. She notes that sex is typically based on some biological criteria and gender "is a matter of culture: it refers to the social classification into 'masculine' and 'feminine.'" She also warns about overstating biological differences, suggesting there is a tenuous relationship between biological sex and gender and thus contributing to our understanding of gender as a social process. Rubin Gayle (1975) used the term "sex/gender system" to direct attention to the need for a new mode of analysis of these issues; however, she did not really clarify the meanings of the terms.

Katharine Blick Hoyenga and Kermit T. Hoyenga (1979) suggest that there are eight different ways of defining gender, including chromosomes, gonads, hormones, internal sexual organs, external genitals, rearing history, identity and roles/behaviour. The fact that there was a considerable lack of clarity with regard to the concepts is further illustrated by a promise made, but not fulfilled, by J. Richard Udry (1994: 561):

> Before I finish, I want to give you an integrated theory of gender. Since current usage is so inconsistent, we need a good definition. Gender is the relationship between biological sex and behavior; a theory of gender explains that relationship. A gendered behavior is one that differs by sex. (1994: 561)

Udry's conflation of sex and gender in his search for a biological theory of gender partly explains why a scholarly journal such as *The Journal of Applied Physiology* determined that the issue of conceptual confusion surrounding sex and gender had to be explicitly addressed. Torgrimson and Minson (2005) note that all articles the journal published between 1960 and 2004 misused "gender" because they were not about gender, but rather about the physiological differences commonly associated with the concept of sex. The authors suggest a definition that was to become quite commonplace, noting that when studying humans, "sex should be used as a classification according to reproductive organs and functions that derive from chromosomal complement" (786), while gender refers to self-image and institutional representation based on the individual's presentation.

In 1994 Caplan and Caplan summarized the conventional wisdom of the era: "We shall use sex to refer to the biological sex of the individual—whether a person is born physically female or male." As for gender, they note:

> We shall use gender to refer to the social role of being a woman or being a man. Gender means "being feminine" or "being masculine," standards

that look different in different societies. Gender is composed of a whole list of features that the society in question labels as appropriate for, or typical of, one sex (but not the other, or more than the other), including feelings, attitudes, behavior, interests, clothing, and so on. (1994: 4–5)

It could be said that achieving a distinction of some form between sex and gender was an important step in understanding the nature of each; however, progress in understanding the world is not always that easy. Standing in the way was a clear understanding of the relationship between sex and gender, or put otherwise, sex and social behaviour. This very question had, of course, occupied philosophers, theologians, political leaders, religious leaders and many others over virtually all recorded Western history, at least since Homer created the *Odyssey*. Although the philosophers of Greece and Rome, the Christian theologians who followed, not to mention the thinkers of the so-called Enlightenment had much to say about sex, gender, women and men, we will only comment on relatively recent thought on the matter. My point of departure in this regard is one of the most important and controversial twentieth-century thinkers whose work is often associated directly with the issue of the relationship of sex to gender — Sigmund Freud. Although we leave the discussion of gender at this point, our work in this regard is not over. I will return to an historical overview of the concept and conclude with an appropriate definition.

SEX ROLES

The early difference between a social science and sociological approaches to understanding the relationship of sex to the social behaviour we have been calling gender is the emphasis sociologists place on the social environment and social learning. As North American and Western sociology was emerging, much of the emphasis on social learning coalesced around the concept of social roles. Social roles were broadly understood, as the name implies, as an expected behaviour like a stage role in a play. For example, the author of the play writes the script, an actor learns the script and then plays out a role. In early sociological thought the analogy held that society provides the script in the form of norms, values, beliefs and expectations, and humans learn the script and play the roles. The normative orientations and value systems of an advanced industrial society are complex, and complications, so it was argued, were the role structures. Among the important roles in the repertoire of roles were those associated with sex and gender.

The question of sex-based social behaviour was of central concern to one of the founders of U.S. sociology — Talcott Parsons. The concept of role figured prominently in the structural functionalist sociology that dominated the Western world in the era after the Second World War, with sex roles representing an important type of role. Parsons examined the various social functions of the family, arguing that in order for the family to function properly there must be role specialization. He further argued that there were the two essential and different sets of sex-based roles within what he called the normal family form that was for him the nuclear family. Parsons maintained that expressive roles involved internal family activities centred around caring, nurturing, emotional support, family integration and group harmony — the private sphere. On the other hand, instrumental roles were external to the family and connected the family to the larger society. Instrumental roles involved leadership, achievement, securing resources to maintain the family and identifying and accomplishing goals — the public sphere. Parsons links expressive roles to females and instrumental roles to males, making a sex-based distinction between the private and public spheres of activity. According to Parsons, the family was an essential agent of socialization and thus children would be socialized within the family into what he saw as appropriate sex and gender roles. Boys in the family would typically see their fathers performing instrumental roles and through socialization they would come to internalize these roles and their associated behaviours. The same process would result in girls finding their social role models, their mothers, performing expressive roles. In short, Parsons and his colleagues put the concept of role, including sex roles, front and centre in sociological analysis, thus paving the way for the development of the notion of the male sex role.

The Male Sex Role

It might be said that the 1960s and 1970s were the golden age or heyday of sex role theory. In terms of its analytical value, all was not clear, as Edward Thompson and Joseph Pleck (1987: 25–26) note an ambivalence between the "male sex role," which describes the characteristics men are perceived to actually have as opposed to the "male role" as a more ideal set of culturally valued attributes.

And what of the actual nature or the content of the male sex role? Numerous descriptions of the male sex role emerged between the 1950s and the 1970s, summarized into four main themes:

1. No Sissy Stuff: The stigma of all stereotyped feminine characteristics and qualities, including openness and vulnerability.
2. The Big Wheel: Success, status, and the need to be looked up to.
3. The Sturdy Oak: A manly air of toughness, confidence, and self-reliance.
4. Give 'em Hell: The aura of aggression, violence, and daring. (David and Brannon 1976: 12)

These four themes encompass much of what was to become, and for some still remains, the stereotypical male sex role across much of the Western world. Scholars have summarized this role as focusing on "success/power/competition, restrictive emotionality, and restricted affectionate behaviour between men" (Good, Dell and Mintz 1989: 295). The male child is instructed to avoid "womanly things" and further "is told that he is supposed to be rugged, independent, able to take care of himself, and to distain 'sissies'" (Hartley 1959: 460).

In the efforts to summarize the male role, consistent themes include achievement, antifemininity, suppression of emotions, level-headedness and independence or being self-contained (Thompson and Pleck 1986). William Snell (1986: 443–444) set out to study the main features of the lives of men and their values and expectations, concluding that a "multidimensional measure of the masculine role" was required, thus the Masculine Role Inventory was born. His research supported three elements of the inventory: restricted emotionality, inhibited affection and a preoccupation with success. Snell (1989: 751) subsequently utilized the Masculine Behavior Scale, finding four important self-reported behavioural tendencies among men: restricted emotionality, inhibited affection, success dedication and exaggerated self-reliance. The amalgamation of all of this research can be summarized in the following seven traditional male role norms: "Avoiding femininity, restrictive emotionality, seeking achievement and status, self-reliance, aggression, homophobia, and non-relational attitudes toward sexuality" (Levant 1992: 380).

The distinction between a cultural ideal and the actual behaviours of boys and men began to attract the attention of scholars who were not satisfied with general descriptions such as these and who wanted to add an element of scientific rigour to the field. And nothing added the appearance of scientific rigour like measurement. As a result, a flurry of measuring, quantifying and scaling followed, building on the general popularity and widespread use of personality testing in general.

Scaling Male Sex Roles

While personality testing has a long and varied history, the business took a quantum leap (perhaps even forward) in the twentieth century. The work of Alfred Binet and his efforts to develop tests and scales to measure intelligence in the 1900s is among the best known examples. Much debate and discussion ensued regarding IQ and its measurement, nevertheless the notion that various personality traits or characteristics could be tested, measured and scaled became a part of the military, educational and corporate landscape as military recruits were screened, students streamed and newly founded human resources departments sought to match employee skills and traits with jobs (Gregory: 2000). Throughout the twentieth century a wide range of different tests ensued, including the Minnesota Multiphasic Personality Inventory, the Wechsler Intelligence Tests, 16PF Questionnaire, the Wechsler Adult Intelligence Tests, the Meyers Briggs Type Indicator (MBTI) and the California Psychological Inventory.

When these various tests did address issues relating to sex and gender, the treatment tended to be simplistic and based on the assumption that sex and gender differences could be represented as positions on a continuum. In an examination of a number of the personality tests — including the Attitude-Interest Analysis Test, the Minnesota Multiphasic Personality Inventory, the Guilford-Zimmerman Temperament Survey and the California Personality Inventory — researchers concluded that "each provided a single masculinity-femininity score locating an individual somewhere on a continuum from extremely masculine to extremely feminine" (Martin and Finn 2010: 34). This aspect of personality and other similar tests came under critical scrutiny from scholars who argued that "one recurring question that is reflected in varying terminology ... is whether M-F is a single bipolar dimension or whether there may not also exist two separable dimensions of masculinity (M) and femininity (F), either in addition to or instead of the M-F dimension" (Constantinople 1973: 389).

Sandra L. Bem (1974) addressed these concerns and changed the landscape with her Bem Sex-Role Inventory, which attempted to address the issue of a single continuum with femininity on one end and masculinity on the other by listing an inventory of three different types of traits, namely those that are typically masculine, feminine and neutral. Bem provided, however modestly, a critical note with regard to the potentially harmful impact of adherence to traditional sex roles. After noting the importance of investigators moving away from focusing on traditional roles she ends with this observation: "In a society where rigid sex-role differentiation has already outlived its utility, perhaps the androgynous person will come to define a more human standard of psychological health" (162). These concerns were echoed by researchers linking the tendency of binary or bipolar notions of gender to the instrumental-expressive distinctions found in Parsons, making a case for the inclusion of androgyny as a distinctive role (Kelly and Worell 1977).

These concerns notwithstanding, the latter part of the last century witnessed a variety of efforts to develop personality, behavioural and character-trait scales explicitly addressed to male behaviour and masculinity. Among these was the Brannon Masculinity Scale developed by Robert Brannon and Samuel Juni in 1984. It was based on the four themes I noted above that classified men and male behaviour on the basis of their propensities with regard to avoiding femininity, concealing emotions, being the breadwinner, being admired and respected, toughness, the male machine, and violence and adventure (Thompson et al. 1992: 587–89). Additionally, scholars summarized seventeen different scales that were developed to measure various aspects of masculinity (Thompson, Pleck and Ferrera 1992). If the number is surprising, they actually excluded several, so clearly social scientists were very busy in this field.

In a review of fifteen years of research in the field, including a discussion of the Male Role Norms Inventory (MRNI), researchers conclude that the MRNI is "a useful tool for measuring endorsement of traditional masculine ideology ... and for examining the relationship between social location/individual difference and cultural context variables for the endorsement of traditional male gender roles" (Levant and Richmond 2007: 141). While noting variations among men, they added a word of warning relating to a series of potential attitudinal problems such as racism and sexist that are associated with strong endorsement of the so-called traditional male sex role (2007: 142). One overview identified two issues among the studies and scales (Thompson et al. 1992). First, after focusing on eleven different measures of masculine ideology and those studies in particular that identify character traits, personality attributes and behaviours, researchers identified the existence of a strong masculine ideology, the violation of which is stressful to many men (1992: 602). The second issue they noted was the presence of some studies that, based on their view of "'masculinity' as a socially constructed gender script," examined "ideologies and institutions involved in maintaining different masculinity standards." In this regard they note that many of the studies have focused too much on one particular notion of masculinity or one particular masculine ideology at the expense of recognizing other ideas about masculinity (Thompson et al. 1992: 576). I will explore the implications of this notion of multiple masculinities below.

BEYOND SEX ROLES

The notion that living according to the strictures of traditional sex roles was problematic in a number of ways for both women and men became an important issue in the early days of what is called Second Wave feminism. One of the issues addressed by Second Wave feminism was related to various dimensions of the oppression of women and girls caused by the actions and behaviours of men and, sometimes, boys. The essays in Joseph Pleck and Jack Sawyer's 1974 *Men and Masculinities* chronicle the negative implications across many aspects of the lives of boys and men as they attempt to live in accordance with traditional masculinity, including the tendency for fathers to be too absent, the lack of intimate friendships and the tendency of men, through their dedication to work, to sometimes support and bolster oppressive institutions, all of which limit the emotional and social options for men.

Joseph Pleck (1984) developed a more theoretically informed set of concerns with regard to the impact on men and boys of living under the auspices of the sex roles characteristic of what one might call a post-war Western gender model. In *The Myth of Masculinity*, Pleck sets out to critically study what he calls "male sex role identity" (1984: 1) and the impact of men trying to live up to the expectations of that role. Stated as a series of propositions, he notes the difficulties that many men and boys have when it comes to living up to these expectations, difficulties that result in, among other things, the risk of failure, loss of psychological adjustment, hypermasculinity, negative attitudes toward women and difficulties in school performance (1984: 18–26). In order to address the obvious fact that the traditional male sex role was not conducive to individual or social well-being and stability, Pleck went on to develop a new concept in an attempt to explain the circumstances of males. He called the new approach the "sex role strain (SRS) paradigm" (1984: 133). He documents some of the reasons for and implications of sex role strain, noting that the felt need to try to maintain the breadwinner role can leave men with feelings of inadequacy, insecurity and stress leading to aggression and conflict (160). Pleck continued to defend roles as an appropriate analytical approach, while updating his approach to place more emphasis on what he saw as three essential forms of strain experienced by men: discrepancy, trauma and dysfunction-related strain (13–17), all of which can result in males feeling shame over their failures (121–22).

As impressive as was the work of hosts of scholars and researchers in documenting the attitudes of men and women with regard to the various components of the male sex role, substantial criticisms emerged, criticisms that were to result in arguments in favour of an alternate research agenda and a redefinition of the concept of gender and a move away from sex role theory. The criticism can be understood, in part at least, as a disconnect between the efforts of academics and researchers to construct elaborate scales of personality traits, attitudes and beliefs about sex and gender and the massive social changes underway during these decades.

The immediate post-war era witnessed the emergence of sexuality studies as a recognized field of medical and academic study. In the field of medicine, Alfred Kinsey's *Kinsey Reports* were among the first high-profile studies of post-war human sexuality; however, it was the work of William Masters and Virginia Johnson that drew the public's attention to a variety of issues surrounding the physiology of sexual intercourse and sexual behaviour. Although their studies tended to focus on the physiology of sexual activity, their book *Human Sexual Response* sold 300,000 copies in two months, resulting in Masters and Johnson appearing on the cover of *Time* magazine. This was also the era when Dr. John Money and the Gender Identity Clinic at the Kinsey Institute at Johns Hopkins University were active and gaining much publicity with their application of medical and surgical interventions in the field of sex and gender reassignment.

In June 1969 a brutal police raid on a predominantly gay nightclub, the Stonewall Inn, in New York City resulted in a riot, hastening the emergence of the gay liberation movement and making gay and lesbian rights a public issue concern. Concurrent with all of these developments was the emergence of what we know as the Second Wave of feminism or the women's movement, a multidimensional political, cultural, social and educational movement and campaign seeking to address the many manifestations of sex- and gender-based oppression, inequality and injustice. All of this put the issues of sex and gender in the public arena in a way like never before.

BEYOND SEX ROLES

In 1987 Tim Carrigan, Bob Connell and John Lee offered a devastating critique of sex-role theory while suggesting a new approach. First, in terms of sex role theory, they point out the incapacity of role theory in general and sex role theory in particular to address central issues that were emerging out of the political dynamics of the day — the nature of power, social change and the possibilities of a more egalitarian gender order. The authors put it this way: "'Sex role' research could, and did, wobble from psychological argument with biological assumptions, through accounts of interpersonal transactions to explanations of a macro-sociological character, without ever having to resolve its boundaries" (1987: 72). On the question of social change they noted: "As social theory, the sex role framework is fundamentally static," noting that when it does address change it does so in an inadequate manner (78–79). They also note the incapacity of sex role theory to address social relations. Because it focuses on differences, role theory and sex role theory in particular miss a central issue:

> The result of using the role framework is an abstract view of the differences between the sexes and their situations, not a concrete one of the relations between them ... The political effect is to highlight the attitudes and pressures that create an artificially rigid distinction between men and women and to play down the power that men exercise over women. (Carrigan, Connell and Lee 1985: 79)

A few years later, Michael Kimmel's (1991; 2004) critique of the notion of sex roles includes the fact that it shifts responsibility from men and their actions to the roles they are supposedly forced to play. Additionally, he notes that the so-called male and female sex roles suggest "a single monolithic entity, a 'role' into which all boys and all girls were placed as opposed to recognizing the variety of different masculinities and femininities that vary with class, ethnicity, age, region and so on" (2004: 91). In addition, focusing on roles and sex roles ignores power and power differentials and the fact that gender is inherently a relational matter, while assuming that only individuals are gendered, thus ignoring the wider institutional nature of gender dynamics (91).

It is important to note that the criticisms of role theory and the sex role approach emerged in an intellectual environment in which the traditional definition of gender noted above was itself under systematic questioning. As it turned out, the critique of not only sex role theory, but of how gender was defined, made it possible to develop a much more robust understanding of gender, and a much deeper critique of the existing sex and gender relations.

GENDER: THE EVOLUTION (AND REVOLUTION?) OF A CONCEPT

By 1987, scholars began to argue that the traditional academic understanding of gender was inadequate, particularly with regard to the issue of power. They proposed a more dynamic concept of gender: "gender is not a set of traits, nor a variable, nor a role, but a product of social doings of some sort" (West and Zimmerman 1987: 129). Further they stated that "gender itself is constituted through inter-action." This approach suggested that doing gender was a dynamic process because "displaying gender must be finely fitted to situations and modified or transformed as the occasion demands" (135) since "a person's gender is not simply an aspect of what one is, but more fundamentally, it is something that one *does*, and does recurrently, in interaction with others" (140, emphasis in original). Moreover, power is a part of doing gender because social performances are always subject to evaluation (145–46). Two decades later the continuing strength of this argument was to move the discussion away from the emphasis on socialization, making gender more dynamic (Deutsch 2007: 107). However, this approach still did not go far enough — more attention needs to be directed to undoing, that is, resisting gender. Nevertheless, these arguments marked an important shift in attention.

A year prior to this conceptual shift, Joan W. Scott generated considerable debate focusing the importance of gender for historical analysis that strikes a similar chord. The core of Scott's (1986: 1067) definition "rests on an integral connection between two propositions: gender is a constitutive element of social relationships based on perceived differences between the sexes, and gender is a primary way of signifying relationships of power." With regard to the issue of power, she notes that "gender is a primary field within which or by means of which power is articulated" and further "as an objective set of references, concepts of gender structure percep-tion and the concrete and symbolic organization of all social life" (1069). In 2010 Scott reviewed the core questions that gender as an analytical tool had opened up, concluding that "it is gender that produces meanings for sex and sexual difference, not sex that determines the meaning of gender," and that this opens the possibility for gender to become a more critical concept (2010: 13).

One of the most important contributions of the era was Raewyn Connell's *Gender and Power* (1987: 140), in which Connell makes her understanding of gender clear, noting it "means practice organized in terms of, or in relation to, the reproductive division of people into male and female." She explicitly points out that gender was not to be seen as some simple sex-based dichotomy: "It should be immediately be clear that this does not demand an overriding social dichotomy. Gender practice might be organized in terms of three, or twenty, social categories" (140). She also refers to gender as a "linking concept," linking various social practices to childbirth and parenting, and further, as a "process rather than a thing" (140). Connell also introduces two related concepts, gender order and gender regime. For Connell, a gender order refers to the overall patters of gender in a society, or in her words "the structural inventory of an entire society," while gender regime is used to describe the "structural inventory of a particular institution" (99). In subsequent work she is clear about gender and physiology: "Gender is social practice that constantly refers to bodies and what bodies do, it is not social practice reduced to the body" (2000: 27). The strength of the approach is apparent in that Connell applies the definition in a manner that allows an understanding of the gender projects of boys and men by focusing on relations of power, productive relations, cathexis (desire and emotions) and systems of symbolism. The notion that gender as a complex social practice manifests in human productive relations (labour and the allocation of tasks), in the distribution of power and in the playing out of and satisfaction of desire and emotionality (in a Freudian sense) is a constant theme in Connell's work (1995: 71–76)

In *Masculinities,* one of the most important books in the field of critical men's studies Connell (1995: 71) provides an expanded definition:

> Gender is a way in which social practice is ordered. In gender processes, the everyday conduct of life is organized in relation to a reproductive arena, defined by the bodily structures and processes of human reproduction.

She goes on to again note that reference to the reproductive arena does not imply any notion of a simplistic association of gender and biology that is characteristic of biological determinist approaches.

To the extent that these scholars challenged the conventional understanding seemed radical, others, including Christine Delphy and Judith Butler, pushed the boundaries even further. Delphy (1993: 3) argued that the conventional understanding of the relationship between sex and gender is fundamentally wrong because existing definitions of gender have "continued to think of gender in terms of sex: to see it as a social dichotomy determined by a natural dichotomy." The error is further compounded, she argues, by the fact that "we now see gender as the *content* with sex the *container*" (3, emphasis in original). The problem is the fact that the categorization of humans by sex has generated a hierarchy that posits male as dominant, female as subordinate; sex has become a marker of a social division or position in a hierarchy. To understand this marker as somehow being related to further distinctions, such as those between masculine and feminine, is to compound the misunderstanding.

In 1988, writing in the *Theatre Journal*, Judith Butler distances herself from the conventional position regarding gender when she notes that "gender is in no way a stable identity or locus of agency from which various acts proceed; rather it is an identity tenuously constituted in time—an identity instituted through a *stylized repetition of acts*" (1988: 519, emphasis in original). In this short statement she previews what were to become key themes: the notions of gender as performance, stylized, constituted and not fixed but prone to repetition (2004: 113–14). As she put it in *Gender Troubles*: "Consider gender ... as *a corporeal style*, an 'act,' as it were, which is both intentional and performative, where '*performative*' suggests a dramatic and contingent construction of meaning" (2004: 113, emphasis in original).

Thus far we have seen gender morph from being synonymous with sex, to sets of traits, characteristics and attributes, then as social behaviours, practices and performances with the emphasis on doing gender as opposed to being gendered. Our understanding of gender is deepened by focusing on the institutional context of gender, defining gender as "a system of social practices within society that constitutes people as different in socially significant ways and organizes relations of inequality on the basis of the difference" (Ridgeway and Smith-Lovin 1999: 192). This approach illustrates how the inequalities that arise from gender as a system of social practices come to shape interaction and behaviour across all major institutions. The workplace is a special case of the impact of gendered social practices as manifested in sex-segregated workplaces and the differential levels and types of social capitals that women and men bring. What this means is the tendency of males and masculine behaviour to more easily assume positions of leadership and authority and control, a tendency that can disadvantage women with whom they might be peers or even competitors in a workplace (1999: 196–198). The idea that gender is best understood as a system of social relations is subsequently taken up by Ridgeway and Correll (2004: 510), who begin their discussion by noting: "There is increasing consensus ... that gender is not primarily an identity or role that is taught in childhood and enacted in family relations. Instead gender is an institutionalized system of social practices for constituting people as two significantly different categories, men and women, and organizing social relationships of inequality on the basis of that difference." They also noted that, "like other multilevel systems of difference and inequality such as those based on race or class, gender involves cultural beliefs and distributions of resources at the macro level, patterns of behavior and organizational practices at the interactional level, and selves and identities at the individual level" (510–11). Focusing on cultural beliefs and the omnipresence of sex and gender in everyday lives, they draw attention to what they call hegemonic values and their role in constructing identities and in maintaining the existing "age old gender system in Western societies," albeit with the necessary changes to ensure its continuance (522).

The theme of gender as a social institution is also present in Patricia Yancey Martin (2004). Martin reviews various definitions of a social institution, establishes a lengthy list of criteria (twelve in all) and then proceeds to argue that gender meets all of her criteria. What is worrisome about the argument is a tendency toward reification as illustrated by her seeming endorsement of claims about gender establishing expectations, ordering social processes and being willingly incorporated into identities: "In my judgment, gender qualifies as an institution, showing itself as institutional as any other social phenomenon" (2004: 1261). Barbara Risman and Georgiann Davis (2013) develop the notion of gender as a social structure, more precisely, as a structure of social stratification. They developed an approach to gender that integrates agency (voluntaristic theories) with structuralist theories. This tactic allows them to approach gender at the levels of the self, social interaction and the institutional (2013: 744). Such an approach ensures we pay attention to the embodied reality of every human agent as having been shaped and moulded to a significant extent by their social environment without making them into "cultural dupes" while necessitating ongoing attention to the dynamics and power of social structures.

Other scholars view gender partly in the context of the concept of gender regime, emphasising femininity, while developing an approach to gender that is explicitly relational. It is useful to see gender as a core organizing principle of virtually all human relations and as having cultural and material manifestations. Gender, in this way, manifests itself across three dimensions of human existence: the self or individual, the cultural or interactional and the institutional or social (Budgeon 2014: 319). Therefore, the ideas and notions we have regarding gender are ever-present in all daily interactions, meaning that "femininities as lived by social actors materialize in the everyday practice of gender at the level of interaction" (Budgeon 2014: 319). The materialization of gender in everyday life in embodied social actors is an important consideration for understanding both women and men. The construction of new femininities, then, requires a dynamic notion of a plurality of genders even in the face of potentially dominant or hegemonic forms of gender practice. Equally important is the concept of gender regime to allow us to understand gender at the societal level (330–31). Kimmel notes the importance of locating individual gender in its historical and social context: "A sociological perspective examines the ways in which gendered individuals interact with other gendered individuals in gendered institutions," thus drawing our attention to the fact that "gender revolves around ... identity, interaction, institution" (2004: 102).

In summary, gender represents historical, cultural and emergent social practices and the associated stocks of knowledge, artifacts, institutional structures and ideological frameworks that arise out of the recognition of sex differences between females and males. While gender may have its origins in activities in the reproductive arena, it also concerns the social practices, characteristics, temperament and relationships of females and males beyond the reproductive arena. Defined in this way, gender is very abstract without reference to any particular mode of social organization or the actual content of the practices, knowledge and beliefs; however, we are not yet ready to move to those levels of abstraction since some further conceptual elaboration is required.

MASCULINITY AND MASCULINITIES

If we assume that gender represents the social practices, actions and behaviours associated with sex differences in those cultural and historical contexts in which sex differences carry behavioural and practical implications, it follows that we may use the concept of masculinity to describe the social practices, actions and behaviours associated with males as a sex category. Put otherwise, masculinity is a concept we use to describe the social practices of men in cultures and historical situations in which females and males exhibit differential social practices.

Given what we know about the complexities and variations in human practice, it follows that there are multiple genders, that is, many ways of being female and/ or male. As Connell (2000: 10) put it, "it is clear from the new social research as a whole that there is no one pattern of masculinity that is found everywhere. We need to speak of 'masculinities,' not masculinity." Elsewhere she writes: "First, there is not just one 'sex role' for boys and one other for girls. There are multiple patterns of masculinity and femininity in contemporary societies" (2002: 77). She notes the need to go beyond merely identifying multiple masculinities: "To recognize more than one kind of masculinity is only the first step. We have to examine relations between them" (1995: 76). Michael Kimmel (2012: 4, emphasis in original) makes a similar point: "What it means to be a man in America depends heavily on one's class, race, ethnicity, age, sexuality, region of the country. To acknowledge these differences among men, we must speak of *masculinities*." Kimmel goes on to discuss a range of manifestations of masculinity across various centuries and decades of American history and American capitalism, which evolved and changed from time of the founding fathers to the economic crisis of the 1999s.

The argument that there are multiple means and modes of performing masculinity does not mean that in any given gender order all modes and means will be equal or equally important. Indeed, a central argument of this book follows on the work of Connell and others who have argued that it is not uncommon that a particular mode or means of performing masculinity emerges as dominant and hegemonic.

Hegemonic Masculinity

While one could attribute groundbreaking significance to many aspects of Connell's work, perhaps no concept is more associated with it than hegemonic masculinity. Carrigan, Connell and Lee (1987: 86) wrote: "What emerges from this line of argument is the very important concept of hegemonic masculinity, not as 'the male role' but as a particular variety of masculinity to which others — among them young and effeminate as well as homosexual men — are subordinated." Later Connell (1995: 37) noted that recognizing "diversity in masculinity is not enough. We must also recognize the relations between different kinds of masculinity: relations of alliance, dominance, and subordination." Hegemonic masculinity is "the configuration of gender practice which embodies the currently accepted answer to the problem of the legitimacy of patriarchy, which guarantees (or is taken to guarantee) the dominant position of men and the subordinate position of women" (Connell 1995: 77). I will pick up the issue of legitimacy later; however, it is important to keep in mind that like all institutional systems that involve relations of domination and power, resistance is always a possibility, hence the presence of ongoing legitimation. For now the task remains to better understand the notion of hegemonic masculinity.

As it turns out, we know something about masculinity as it is practised in many Western societies that is of assistance when it comes to understanding the contemporary hegemonic masculinity because much of the discussion of the male sex role was in fact describing Western masculinity. You will recall the four themes to the male sex role:

1. No Sissy Stuff: The stigma of all stereotyped feminine characteristics and qualities, including openness and vulnerability.
2. The Big Wheel: Success, status, and the need to be looked up to.
3. The Sturdy Oak: A manly air of toughness, confidence, and self-reliance.
4. Give 'em Hell: The aura of aggression, violence and daring. (David and Brannon 1976: 12)

I introduced other summaries of the stereotypical male sex role, including "success/power/competition, restrictive emotionality, and restricted affectionate behaviour between men" (Good, Dell and Mintz 1989: 295); achievement, anti-femininity, suppression of emotions, levelheadedness and independence or being self-contained (Thompson and Pleck (1986); restricted emotionality, inhibited affection, success dedication and exaggerated self-reliance (Snell's Masculine Behavior Scale 1989: 751); and "avoiding femininity, restrictive emotionality seeking achievement and status, self-reliance, aggression, homophobia, and non-relational attitudes toward sexuality" (Levant 2007: 380). To the extent that these descriptors were initially used in sex role theory to just describe apparent character or personality traits, their analytical capacity was limited; however, if we re-deploy these concepts as descriptors of the social practices and ideologies and beliefs associated with hegemonic masculinity, their heuristic value increases.

In 2005, Connell, along with James Messerschmidt, offered refinements to the notion of hegemonic masculinity. On the matter of masculinity they note: "Masculinity is not a fixed entity embedded in the body or personality traits of individuals. Masculinities are configurations of practice that are accomplished in social action and, therefore, can differ according to the gender relations in a particular social setting" (2005: 836). They defend the use of abstract models as analytical tools, and later offer another definition of masculinity: "Masculinity is defined as a configuration of practice organized in relation to the structure of gender relations. Human social practice creates gender relations in history. The concept of hegemonic masculinity embeds a historically dynamic view of gender in which it is impossible to erase the subject" (843). Stated differently, by insisting gender is a form of social practice — not just an abstract set of norms, values or roles — this definition keeps the human actor or subject in the forefront. Accepting that a complex view of power is required and acknowledging the need to be ever-wary of falling back into viewing gender as a set of character or personality traits or social roles, they suggest four areas to best understand hegemonic masculinity: "the nature of gender hierarchy, the geography of masculine configurations, the process of social embodiment, and the dynamics of masculinities" (847).

By identifying the types of issues that the study of men must address (various types of masculinities, locale, the social context and actual male social practices) Connell and Messerschmidt remind us of the importance of understanding that the nature and use of concepts varies depending on the level of abstraction at which we are working. Thus far I have tended to discuss the concept of hegemonic masculinity at a high level of abstraction. Similarly, we are operating at a high level of abstraction when we define hegemonic masculinity as a social practice by which male power and the privileged status of masculinity are expressed and maintained, and in patriarchal society is public, heterosexual, constructed in relation to subordinate males and women, and often expressed as cultural ideals (Connell 1987). At this level there tends not to be actual historical and concrete representations of specific practices and institutional configurations through which domination and subordination are established, maintained and negotiated. Such important detail can only be addressed in the context of an actual gender order or gender regime and historically specific gender relations at the level of an actual social structure. However, it is important when studying the complexities of an actual social formation or society to have a theoretical and conceptual guide to allow us to make sense of the complexities of day-to-day life, and the concept of hegemonic masculinity is potentially such a tool. It is the actual historical application or use of this and other similar concepts that prevents the concept from "collapsing into a character typology" (Wedgwood 2009: 335). That is, hegemonic masculinity is one that dominates women (the high abstraction), but how that actually happens is varied and cannot be completely specified for all men and all societies (actual practice and behaviour).

The argument that gender can be understood at a high level of abstraction in the context of the large-scale patterns of gender practice, or a gender order, is an important step in moving toward applying the concepts (Connell 1987: 99; Connell 2000b: 29). Just as one might undertake an analysis of the relations of production that typify capitalism without specifying how capitalism actually operates in Germany, Australia or America, so too I will use the notion of gender order to draw attention to some of the characteristics of patriarchy. I will be following this approach later when we examine gender relations in particular institutions, or gender regimes. As is typically the case, the use of concepts such as these allows us to make sense of the complexities of individual social relations. I turn now to consider the particular gender order within which we live — patriarchy.

PATRIARCHY

Patriarchy is a contested, complex and difficult topic and itself the singular topic of much thinking and writing. I will present several definitions to illustrate the point. First, from the website of the London Feminist Network (LFN n.d.) an answer to the question "What is patriarchy":

> Patriarchy is the term used to describe the society in which we live today, characterised by current and historic unequal power relations between women and men whereby women are systematically disadvantaged and oppressed. This takes place across almost every sphere of life but is particularly noticeable in women's under-representation in key state institutions, in decision-making positions and in employment and industry. Male violence against women is also a key feature of patriarchy. Women in minority groups face multiple oppressions in this society, as race, class and sexuality intersect with sexism for example.

Gerda Lerner (1986: 239) identifies several definitions, including:

> Patriarchy in its wider definition means the manifestation and institutionalization of male dominance over women and children in the family and the extension of male dominance over women in society in general. It implies that men hold power in all important institutions of society and that women are deprived of access to such power.

Learner (1986: 36) notes, however, that such a definition should not be taken to mean that women are totally powerless, because indeed her volume documents important instances of women struggling to resist and overcome domination.

In modern English there are three different meanings attached to the word "patriarchy": 1) the ecclesiastical power of men; 2) the legal power of men over wives and children; and 3) feminist inspired notions (Bennett 2006). In terms of feminist-inspired definitions, patriarchy is a "familial-social, ideological, political system in which men — by force, direct pressure, or through ritual, tradition, and language, customs, etiquette, education, and the division of labour, determine what part women shall or shall not play, in which the female is everywhere subsumed under the male" (Rich in Bennett 2006: 55). Patriarchy can also be defined "as a set of social relations which has a material base and in which there are hierarchical relations between men, and solidarity among them, which enable them to control women ... Patriarchy is thus the system of male oppression of women" (Hartman 1976: 138). Feminist scholar bell hooks (n.d.) writes: "Patriarchy is a political-social system that insists that males are inherently dominating, superior to everything and everyone deemed weak especially females, and endowed with the right to dominate and rule over the weak and to maintain dominance through various forms of psychological terrorism and violence."

There are of course many more definitions; however, it is important to note that there are significant arguments against utilizing the concept at all. Many of these approaches are unable to understand the multiple forms of oppression operative in advanced capitalism. Some scholars advocate for a more intersectional approach:

> "Kyriarchy" is a neologism coined by Elisabeth Schüssler Fiorenza to denote interconnected oppressing systems in which a person or a group of people might be dominated or oppressed in some relationships but privileged in others. Kyriarchy is the intersectional extension of the concept of patriarchy, but one that does not rely on the inherent dualism of the sex/gender distinction. Kyriarchy encompasses sexism, racism, homophobia, trans phobia, classism, ableism, cissexism and other forms of hierarchical structures that has been institutionalised or/and internalised. The currently very popular term "intersectionality" is the study of these intersections of oppression and domination. (Rosbech 2013: n.p.)

While many important changes have taken place in terms of the situation of women, nevertheless "it is still meaningful to describe western societies such as the USA and Britain as 'patriarchal'" even though the concept of patriarchy has somewhat fallen out of use (Bryson 1999: 515). Although there exist continuing patterns of gender inequality, it is important not to define patriarchy as a system because system analysis too easily slips into a tautology giving patriarchy an internal dynamic, that is, we assume that patriarchy is an agent with an agenda and priorities of its own rather than a concept we use to explain the social actions of human agents (Bryson 1999: 321). The concept should not be abandoned, but rather just used with caution (322).

It is also important to understand the danger of using the concept of patriarchy as the basis of circular reasoning when it is postulated as the explanation of gender relations (Pollert 1996). This is particularly the case when patriarchy is conceptualized as a system with its own logic and dynamics, meaning that patriarchy is suggested as the explanation of certain patterns of gender relations such as male domination; however, such a claim does not explain what drives patriarchy. If patriarchy is a system, what are its internal mechanisms that explain the gender relations associated with it? A circular argument ensues when we simply claim, without explaining why, that certain gender relations are inherent in patriarchy, that is, male dominance is a characteristic of patriarchy and this explains male dominance. Among the ways to avoid such circularity is to ensure careful differentiation of the levels of abstraction at which concepts are used and to use the concept of patriarchy as a descriptive aid in the context of the interplay of various social forces in actual historical social structures (Pollert 1996: 653–54).

Taking all this into account, patriarchy descriptively refers to a gender order in which men are dominant and masculinity tends to be esteemed, and in which major social institutions, practices and ideological frameworks tend to support, legitimize and facilitate male and masculine domination and the oppression and exploitation of many women and the concomitant devaluation of femininity. This notion of patriarchy does not include or preclude other forms of domination or oppression, be these based on class, ethnicity, race, age or other mechanisms. The use of the term patriarchy to refer to a gender order implies rejection both of biological determinism and the notion that every individual man in a patriarchal gender order is in a dominant position or every woman automatically in a subordinate one.

PATRIARCHAL MASCULINITY

We know that gender represents one form of social practice and that masculinity represents one form of gender practice. We know that gender order refers to an ensemble of gender practices with particular characteristics and that patriarchy describes a particular gender order in which males are dominant. Thus, within a patriarchal gender order there will be particular characteristics of masculinity as a form of gender practice. These practices will vary within patriarchy, and within Western patriarchy, and even more concretely modern Western patriarchy and even more specifically the practice of masculinity in twentieth-century North

America, Australia and Western Europe. Understanding gender in this way allows us to begin to look at some more concrete manifestations of gender practices, that is, how male social practices operate and their history, characteristics, ideological dimensions and institutional manifestations.

We know that for reasons yet to be disclosed, Western hegemonic masculinity has tended to be focused on male status, power, control and domination. We know that patriarchy is a system of male privilege, power, control and domination. That Western patriarchal masculinity would be virtually indistinguishable from what we have been calling hegemonic masculinity is thus not a surprise. What is missing in all this are causal mechanisms, motives if you will.

PATRIARCHAL DIVIDEND

Systems of domination and subordination, by definition, involve an unequal distribution of costs/inputs and benefits/rewards. Patriarchy as a system of male domination means that benefits will tend to accrue to men: "One of the central facts about masculinity, then, is that men in general are advantaged through the subordination of women" (Carrigan, Connell and Lee 1987: 90). Even though relations between different types of masculinity and some men who participate in alternate gender practices are complicit, "the overwhelmingly important reason is that most men benefit from the subordination of women, and hegemonic masculinity is centrally connected with the institutionalization of men's dominance over women" (1987: 94). This is the "patriarchal dividend."

In *Masculinities*, Connell (1987: 79) discusses hegemonic masculinity: "Yet the majority of men gain from its hegemony, since they benefit from the patriarchal dividend, the advantage men gain from the overall subordination of women." She then further elaborates: "Men gain a dividend from patriarchy in terms of honour, prestige and the right to command. They also gain a material benefit" (82). Connell elaborates somewhat on the manifestations of these elements of the patriarchal dividend, noting that the material benefit is obvious from any comparison of income levels of men and women. Other manifestations are apparent by examining how men hold positions of power in major institutions such as the state, and what she calls the "cultural disarmament" of women by many definitions of femininity as dependent or weaker. Additional manifestations of the dividend are found in patterns of violence and the daily patterns of social interactions (82–83).

Moreover, in the context of considering the unequal distribution of resources, it is important that we reverse our thinking in terms of sex and gender inequality and rather than defining women in relation to men, we "turn the equation around and consider the surplus resources made available to men" (Connell 2002: 142). To elaborate:

I call this surplus the *patriarchal dividend*: the advantage to men as a group from maintaining an unequal gender order. The patriarchal dividend is reduced as gender equality grows. Monetary benefits are not the only kind of benefit. Others are authority, respect, service, safety, housing, access to institutional power, and control over one's own life. (Connell 2002: 142, emphasis in original)

Thus far I have introduced a series of concepts and drawn on extensive literature that has been developing over more than a half century to arrive at an understanding of the complexities of sex, gender, the ins and outs of role theory, gender as social practice, masculinity and social practice, multiple masculinities, hegemonic masculinity, patriarchy, patriarchal masculinity and the patriarchal dividend. Many if not all of these concepts remain contested and debated; however, there is empirical and theoretical support for the ways I have connected the dots. Given the foundational role that the notion of hegemonic masculinity plays in what follows, I do want to, however, recognize some concerns.

CRITIQUES OF HEGEMONIC MASCULINITY

Given the importance of sex and gender relationships in our lives and the complexity of the concept of hegemonic masculinity, as one would expect there have been significant criticisms and voices of caution. One of the most systematic critics identifies a series of serious defects in the notion of hegemonic masculinity:

- Focuses too much on the notion of men seeking material advantage.
- Is excessively structuralist thus ignoring or downplaying the human subject or agent.
- Overplays the extent to which heterosexual men act with intentionality.
- Lacks specific details as to what hegemonic masculinity actually is in terms of behavioural content.
- Provides too little room for resistance and alternate masculinities. (Whitehead 2002: 92–94)

Additionally, the concept of hegemonic masculinity has often been employed in a narrow manner and, some argue, tends to ignore the class element of oppression, and lacks clarity as to whether it is about cultural representations, or institutions or gender practices (Hearn 2004: 58–59). Others are critical of the use and overstatement of the notion of hegemony, originally described by Italian Marxist Gramsci. For those not familiar with Gramsci, he used the concept to describe a situation in which a dominant class presents their interests and world view as the only possible, natural, sensible way of understanding the world, thus winning the approval of subordinate classes and their support for the system. Gramsci saw such ideological and cultural mechanisms of control as part of an ongoing struggle in which total hegemony is not achieved and in which intellectuals play an important role both for and against the dominant class and their efforts to establish hegemony. The adoption of the concept is argued as problematic for a number of reasons, including an overly stated sense of the extent to which domination is total, hence an inadequate recognition of resistance and the overall role of intellectuals (Howell 2006; ch. 3 and 4). Critics also argue that there is a tendency to understand hegemonic masculinity as an ideal typical singularity that impedes political action geared to social justice and the tendency to ascribe too much controlling power to hegemonic masculinity.

In response to these and other criticisms (Clatterbaugh 1998; Donaldson 1993; 2001), Connell and Messerschmidt (2005) defend the concept while offering some revisions. They reject the claims that the concept is essentialist, noting that it is premised on gender as practice and relational and not just character traits (836–37). Similarly, they reject the argument that it is structural determinist since gender relations must ultimately be understood in historical contexts. While they acknowledge that it is necessary to avoid simplistic notions of social relations, their main point is to offer suggestions for revising the concept, acknowledging that hegemonic masculinity only really comes to life when used in conjunction with particular societies located concretely in their historical and geographical contexts.

Other critics point to "slippage" and to the "singular monolith" contained in hegemonic masculinity (Beasley 2008: 97). Slippage suggests there is a degree of inconsistency in a concept that is sometimes understood as a political mechanism, as in leadership of men, while at other times it is used as a description of a certain kind of manhood and still at other times as a descriptor of some actual men (2008: 88). Singular monolith refers to the failure to see these inconsistencies and continue to use the concept without providing an adequate explanation of how the concept is being used. However, it is clear that at more concrete levels of analysis, the claims of this apparent slippage evaporate because as concepts are expanded and developed as we move to more concrete levels of analysis — for example, examining the modes and forms of practising hegemonic masculinity among farmers in Wagga Wagga, Australia, as opposed to accountants in suburban Sydney — we might well be examining political mechanisms, forms of manhood and referring to actual men. This does not mean the concept is flawed; it just means we are applying it to analysis at a lower level of abstraction and, by necessity, broadening and expanding its meaning and identifying salient elements of this form of practice in a concrete setting. A far-reaching critique of critical men's studies argues that it focuses too much on concepts such as hegemonic masculinity and for losing sight of the fact that male domination also means that some men also dominate other men (Schwalbe 2014:

31–33). The claim that the notion of multiple masculinities somehow diminishes or makes some men "lesser" does not follow because, I would argue, we can and should develop an understanding of different mores of practising masculinity that do not necessarily place them in some type of hierarchy (34). I read this critique as a call to essentially abandon abstract concepts as unproductive for critical realist science (also see Lusher and Robins 2009).

Hegemonic masculinity refers to a particular configuration or ensemble of gender practices and relations typical of a patriarchal gender order, and which publicly exhibit the domination of male heterosexuality through cultural, material and ideological mechanisms. The mechanisms involved, the benefits and costs involved and the implications for boys, men, girls, women and the world in general, vary widely.

MOVING ON

The ideas and concepts I have dealt with in this chapter are among the most contested and debated in the social sciences, among the most talked about in the talk-show world, among the most challenging in theological circles and perhaps the most argued about within intimate relationships. I moved us from the apparent but erroneous naturalness of a two-sex schema to the slightly more complex notion of sex and sex roles. The valiant efforts to add quantitative dimension to our understanding of sex roles by developing various types of scales might be seen as part of the confusion that necessitated moving beyond the focus on sex roles and gender as traits, to gender as social practice. The influence of the work of R.W. Connell on our understanding of sex and gender became more important as the argument progressed. Having arrived at an understanding of gender as a form of social practice, we were in a position to explicitly see masculinity as a particular form of gender practice and hegemonic masculinity as a particular form of masculine gender practice. Moving on, we will draw on our understanding of the human self and the gender order in order to examine boys and how they come to learn masculinity in a patriarchal gender order.

CHAPTER 2

ACQUIRING GENDER

In Chapter 1 I discussed the development and evolution of some concepts that we can utilize in addressing the paradoxes, puzzles and enigmas that seem to characterize boys and men. Beginning with what was once deemed to be the simple reality of physiological sex differences, we followed the convoluted history of the notion of gender into several decades of sex role studies, then male sex role studies, replete with multiple efforts to add a scientific hue through establishing scales that measure compliance to a male sex roles. The re-emergence of a new wave of feminist critiques of the prevailing nature of sex and gender relations across the West, dare I say, engendered attention to issues of inequality, power, control and oppression. In this context, gender began to be redefined as social practice, something that is done and not just sensed as an identity. The successes and contributions of critical feminist analysis to understanding sex and gender relations required a reappraisal of the notion of the male sex role and associated notions of masculinity, paving the way for a more adequate understanding of masculinity as social practice and the recognition of multiple masculinities. As the oppressive character of patriarchy was more and more exposed, the centrality of masculinity (in its various forms) to various forms of oppression became apparent, as did the obvious connection between patriarchal and class oppression. The end result was the elaboration of new conceptual frameworks that identified hegemonic forms of masculinity, the many faces of masculinity within patriarchal gender orders and the benefits and dividends that accrue to many men as a result of those forms of social practice.

Prior to exploring some concrete forms of what we know are multiple masculinities and the benefits and costs to boys, men, girls, women, the environment and society in general, we need to consider how it is that males acquire masculinity. In the simplest possible form, the question is how does the unambiguously male infant become a boy then a man? That is, how does he acquire the agency, the personality and the character that practices masculinity? Stated otherwise, how do males acquire the characteristics, behaviours, attitudes, overall sense of "Self" or personality that drives, generates, facilitates, allows and even requires us to engage in those social practices we call masculinity? Needless to say, such a complicated question is not easily answered, nor would one expect it to be answered without controversy and debate. We need, however, to make an effort if we are to grasp the complexities of the human male social agent.

The fields of psychology, social psychology, child development, sociology, psychoanalysis, neuropsychology, endocrinology, philosophy and others contain an array of efforts to explain what I would call the acquisition of gender or personality formation. I will however limit the discussion to a few approaches that continue to have public presence, are historically significant and/or offer what I think are fruitful possibilities. We begin with perhaps the best known of all who have addressed the issue, Sigmund Freud.

SIGMUND FREUD

Sigmund Freud (1856–1939) understood the human personality to be closely linked to the physical body and various physiological processes. The body, Freud suggested, must be understood as an energy system, subject to biological and physiological forces and processes that govern all life forms (Freud 1933: 90–92). As a result of our biological and physiological processes, the human body is prone to developing various types of need-related tensions. For example, normal metabolism requires periodic ingestion of food and liquids in order to supply the muscles, organs and tissues with nutrients. When the body requires more food or liquids, tensions associated with hunger or thirst emerge, stimulating instincts. As utilized by Freud, instinct has a unique meaning in that it is not an identifiable behaviour or action, but rather a psychological representation of a source of tension. As Duane Schultz (1975: 315) explains, "Freud's term in German, Trieb, is best translated as driving force or urge," that is, the driving force of the human personality. Freud identified two very different sorts of instincts, one directed toward life, pleasure and reproduction, the other relating to our unconscious desire to have all tensions removed, a condition only possible with death. The tensions back and forth between these contradictory instinctual forces are among the forces that characterize human existence. Life and death (sometimes referred to as eros and thanatos) manifest themselves variously in our capacity to be kind, generous and loving or, when driven by thanatos, selfish, aggressive, hostile and even war-like.

The elementary component of the human personality — the id — is present from birth. The id is the component of the human personality that is acutely aware of the needs of the body and the tensions that emerge from normal physiological processes. When nutrition is required, for example, the id signals the need to act; however the id is limited in its capacity to satisfy needs because it seeks to reduce tension only through the primary processes of fantasy and wishful thinking. If nutrition is required the id indicates hunger, but cannot direct behaviour in the real world, since it can only engage in fantasies, wishful imaginary thoughts about food or whatever would satisfy the need causing the tension.

Reliance only on the id to satisfy needs and address tensions associated with nutritional needs would result in starvation and death because the id is oblivious to reality and relies only on, in this case, fantasies about food. Freud suggests that humans overcome the limitations of the id through the development of the second component of personality, the ego. The ego engages in secondary processes and the reality principle, and puts the organism into contact with the real world. The ego works out realistic plans and actions to secure real satisfaction to needs, thus reducing tensions. The problem with the ego is that it acts only in a purely prag-matic, direct and self-interest-driven manner, that is, it lacks any sense of morality or ethics to guide it. It will essentially direct us to do anything that we can get away with in order to address the tensions the id has identified. This is a problem because a world dominated by ids and egos would be a classic case of jungle warfare, survival of the fittest in a world without security or safety. Despite the occasional outbreaks of conflict and war, this is not our world because, as Freud explains in *Civilization and Its Discontents* (1982), we are saved from this fate because of the third component of the personality: the superego. The superego introduces values, moral codes, rules, regulations and controls, thereby making society, social exist-ence, civilization, progress and a moral and ethical life possible by constraining and holding the ego back from immediate gratification. The id signals tensions related to thirst and the ego may direct me to steal water or do whatever is necessary, but the superego constrains the ego with the assurance that it will not necessarily die of thirst and can wait until water is available, thus making civil interaction and society possible. Society's values and norms then become the individual's, imposed on the ego through the operation of the superego, understandable as equivalent to our conscience (Hall 1979: 31–35).

Central to Freud's approach to personality is the importance attached to chang-ing sources of tension and differing modes or means of tension reduction that emerge as a human being develops. Freud suggests that all humans pass through a series of similar developmental stages that are related to differing sources of ten-sion and concomitant relief possibilities. For about the first year of life energies are focused on the oral cavity because hunger is the major source of tension, and food the major mode of tension reduction. Beginning at about age 2, awareness of the bodily functions associated with waste removal from the body and tension reduction becomes more focused on the anal cavity during toilet training. While the manner by which tension reduction occurs in the oral and anal stages is important, Freud argues, for certain aspects of subsequent personality development it is the third state that is important for the task here — understanding boys and men.

Around age 3 there is a change in the primary source and locus of tension as sexual energy becomes important. The phallic stage brings significant differences in the development of females and males based on physiological differences, particularly genitalia. At this point in life the male child will have noticed he has a penis and he will have noticed that the penis is a source of pleasure and tension reduction. The emergence of sexual energies and tensions directs his attention to the most available object of sexual gratification, typically the mother. Given that the mother figure has been the source of nourishment, comfort, security and love since birth, such attraction is understandable. The emergence of sexual energy, however, radically complicates the situation because while the male child begins to desire his mother he is also aware of another figure that actually sexually possesses the mother: the father figure. The male child begins to fear his competitor, the larger and more powerful father figure, and begins to also fear that his father will become jealous and harm him. This fear becomes focused on what the male child sees as the offending organ in this sexual drama, his penis. This fear manifests itself as castration anxiety as the male child fears the father will remove his capacity for sexual activity through castration. The male child resolves the situation by renouncing his attraction to the mother, repressing all sexual thoughts and modeling his behaviour on that of the father, identifying with the father, so one day he too may possess a woman like the mother figure. This entire business is known the Oedipus Complex, named after Oedipus Rex, the central character of the Greek tragedy of the same name, which tells the story of a man who, without knowing what he has done, kills his father and later marries his mother (for more detail see Freud 1965: lectures xxxii and xxxiii).

Owning to their different genital structures, the process is quite different for the female child, a process often called resolution of an Electra Complex:

> Girls too go through an Oedipal stage, Freud supposed, but with far different results. Whereas the boy worries that he might be castrated, the girl, after seeing a penis for the first time, worries that she already has been castrated. As Freud described it, "When she makes a comparison with a playfellow of the other sex, she perceives that she has 'come off badly' and she feels this is a wrong done to her and a ground for inferiority" ... She is, to say the least, angry that she lacks the marvelous male organ and has an inferior clitoris. She blames her mother for this deprivation, rejects her, and seeks to displace her in the father's eyes. She becomes daddy's darling. (Tavris 1984: 180–81)

Having resolved these issues, the human child enters a period of latency in which the personality characteristics formed during the oral, anal and phallic stages mature and develop. The onset of puberty ushers in the last major development stage, the genital stage, at which time the personality characteristics forged throughout childhood develop even further, now in the context of the emergence of adult sexual beings. During the developmental process individuals will develop a number of what Freud calls defensive mechanisms to deal with the anxiety that is an inevitable part of the human condition.

Freud explicitly notes that prior to the emergence of the phallic stage there are few sex-based differences in the developmental trajectories of females and males; indeed he notes a significant degree of bisexuality inherent in both sexes (Freud 1965: 100, 104). As was noted above, the emergence of sexual energies and tensions associated with the phallic stage launches males and females on different trajectories. Focusing on the male child, there are several important dynamics as boys resolve their Oedipus Complex.

First we note that a male child's attachments to his mother will remain lifelong; however, it is repressed and controlled out of fear of the father. The father figure is a rival and, although the boy may feel jealousy, this is overtaken by fear, particularly fear of castration. In order to address the obvious anxiety the boy is experiencing he represses his sexual attachment to the mother, distances himself from her and the femininity she represents and identifies with the father. For simplicity's sake one might say he imitates instead of identifies with because the boy begins to fashion his personality and behaviour after that of the father so as to someday make himself attractive to a woman just like the one possessed by the father.

Although there is no universal pattern, because the superego is developing, several possible courses of development emerge as a result of social interactions and contexts. First, it is clear that the character of the father figure with whom the boy is identifying will be a significant factor in the character, personality and behaviour of the child. As is the case with the precise prescriptions and proscriptions provided by the superego, the particularities of the model with which the boy is identifying will vary with the concrete and empirical circumstances of the child. For example, a boy with a forceful and dominant father or role model will have a tendency to take on those characteristics and emulate his father in later life, and, likewise, a meek and withdrawn father would serve as a different behavioural model. Thus, although the process of identification is deemed to be universal, the particular form of masculinity that provides the role model that the boy is identifying with will vary, accounting for some individual personality differences. Second, depending on the dynamics and extent of the boy's efforts to separate and distance himself from the mother in order to remove the threat of castration, he may subsequently develop feelings of scorn and the need to demonstrate mastery over women. The boy's flight or separation from the mother and the repression of his sexual interest and affections may result, if there is overcompensation involved, in the boy and later the man denigrating and devaluing women and those traits and behaviours associated with femininity. A last potential reaction of the male child relates to his reaction on first seeing the genitalia of a girl. The logic of a Freudian analysis might well have the male child view the girl as inferior, lacking as she does his much-valued penis. Should this reaction be strong it would be deemed to carry forward into later life and impact the individual's interactions and attitudes toward females in general.

It is clear that a Freudian view of human personality development, its dynamics and the similarities and differences between females and males is complex. To say that these and other aspects of the work of Freud were and are controversial and contested is to commit a gross understatement. However, his ideas and positions were important and often served as a point of departure for other theorists, including those associated with feminist theories.

RETHINKING FREUD

Although Freud's work was subject to criticism from the moment of its publication, many scholars have sought to revise aspects of his thought and recast some of his ideas in the context of a feminist understanding of childhood development. Among those who have sought to retain, yet radically revise, certain elements of Freud was Juliet Mitchell. Mitchell (1967) encouraged those with a Marxian bend to rethink how we understand both material production (the production of the goods and services we need to survive) and biological reproduction of the species (socialization and care of young and dependent children) and how we understand sex and gender. Her initial major attempt to utilize Freud came in 1989 with *Psychoanalysis and Feminism*, in which she considers and reconsiders many tenets of the thought of Freud and his followers.

While there were many others, some of the tasks Mitchell set out were taken up by Nancy Chodorow. The notion that male and female children take different developmental tacks, particularly after reaching the genital stage, is a common assumption in Freudian thought. Chodorow suggests a different understanding of how the process of gender differentiation unfolds and its implications.

Although Chodorow's focus tends to be on females and certain aspects of mothering, she has some important observations with regard to the psychological and gender development of boys. Given that the background to this work is a "debate" with Freud, there is a certain biological presence in Chodorow's work, although it is by no means a biological determinist argument.

Chodorow places significant emphasis on the role of mothering. While acknowledging the biological roles mothers play in reproduction — they give birth and in the early period of a child's life typically provide nutrition, safety and comfort — Chodorow understands that much of the post-natal care is cultural and historical. Nevertheless she is interested in the implications of the fact that so much childcare for both female and male children is provided by females. In breaking with the classical Freudian understanding of the role of sexual attraction by boys and the subsequent Oedipal conflict and the mother's apparent privileging of the boy because of his possession of more valued sex organs, Chodorow emphasizes the close personal, indeed intimate, relationship that develops between the caregiving mother and both female and male children. The dependent and vulnerable infant, both female and male, naturally develops a sense of intimacy with the mother but because of their physiological similarities mothers and daughters come to identify more closely with each other than do sons and mothers.

In typical patriarchal families, the father or male figure is absent a great deal of the time and typically is not very actively involved as a caregiver. The absence of the father, often both physically and emotionally, means that boys spend much more time with their mothers, who continue to provide immediate care, nourishment and comfort of all kinds. As the boy grows and develops he learns that he cannot identify with the physiologically different mother, but rather he realizes that he should identify with the father. The problem is, however, the father as a model is typically absent, causing difficulties for the boy to establish a stable, ever-present model with whom he might identify. Nevertheless, the boy works hard at differentiating himself from his mother, adopting and incorporating into his character whatever manifestations of masculinity are available. The process could be viewed from another angle as essentially a rejection or repression of his feminine characteristics or perhaps the feminine in general. In a sense the boy must seek out and emulate, identify with, absorb and incorporate masculine gender behaviours and roles in an effort to establish his identity as non-feminine. Girls, on the other hand, will continue a relationship with the mother based in large part on uninterrupted identification with the feminine, not both a conscious and unconscious rejection of it.

Freudian thought and the Freudian legacy remain both contested and important when we consider issues relating to sex, sexuality and gender. While Freud's understanding of the relationship between physical sexual differences and personality and character are complex, there are a host of other thinkers who have argued for a much more straightforward, indeed simplistic relationship founded largely on some dimension of biology.

THE BIOLOGY OF GENDER:
HORMONES, BRAINS AND SEX

One of the most popular approaches in many public narratives regarding how we can best understand human personality and development is both mistaken in fact and ideologically driven. Perhaps its popularity is owed to the fact that it is simple and confirms some so-called "common sense" notions of human behaviour. The approach I speak of is diverse in its focus, although there is a common thread that locates explanations of complex human behaviours and characteristics in some dimension of our basic biology. As we will see, some argue human behaviours are simply about brain structure, while others look to hormones and even sex-specific instinctual reproductive strategies. I will begin by examining an argument that suggests that differences in hormones and brain structures explain the complex human behaviour that humans exhibit.

Doreen Kimura's work illustrates the position that sex hormones are among the most important factors in the physical organization of the brain and subsequently in behaviour. Kimura (2002) argues that the presence or absence of hormones such as estrogen and testosterone at various stages in life impact various sex-differentiated intellectual abilities and cognitive functions such as spatial task skills, mathematical reasoning, spatial skills, motor movement abilities, perception, verbal skills, memory, fine motor skills and even the capacity to remember landmarks. The implication is that such apparent differences influence a range of complex social behaviours. Carina Dennis (2004) agrees, declaring that human brain is "The Most Important Sexual Organ" in the prestigious journal *Nature*. Likewise, Marian C. Diamond (2003) argued that there is a relationship between the physical characteristics of the brain and sex- and gender-specific behaviours. The political implications of her position are clear in that she suggests that once we understand the physiological basis of some behaviours we will be in a better position to accept them, be patient and acknowledge that they are inevitable. Simon Baron-Cohen (2003) studied female and male brains, concluding that everything from the work we do, to the clothes we wear, to our levels of aggressive behaviour and even to the magazines we look at in airports is fundamentally hard-wired into our sex-determined brains.

Despite the relentless repetitions of these sorts of arguments and the beliefs about sex and gender they support, the issues they raise remain hotly contested. For example, Kenji Kansaku et al. (2000) looked at sex differences in brain lateralization, the apparent differences in the extent to which females and males use the different sides of their brains, and found differences in how language is processed, while Iris Sommer et al. (2004: 1850) "found no significant sex difference in functional language lateralization in a large sample of 377 men and 442 women."

On the matter of intelligence, as defined by the result of typical IQ tests, there are literally hundreds of contradictory studies. Richard Lynn's (1994: 257) claims to have found that, "among adults, males have slightly higher verbal and reasoning abilities than females and a more pronounced superiority on spatial abilities. If the three abilities are combined to form general intelligence, the mean for males is 4 IQ points higher than the mean for females." On the other hand, Scott Barry Kaufman (2012: n.p.) found that, as far as sex-based intelligence was concerned, the "lesson is that Flynn's international comparative data really shows little innate difference in intelligence as defined by IQ test scores and that differences are linked to differential social experiences." As for hormones and brain structures, Ward (2013) notes the differences are not radical or even significant in that both males and females typically have all the various human hormones, just in different quantities.

In recent years, neuroimaging has added significantly to our understanding of the brain. Phan et al. (2002) performed what they suggest is the first meta-analysis of neuroimaging-based studies of brain regions and emotional activation. While this study did find evidence that "discrete brain regions ... are involved in various emotional tasks" (2002: 344), it did not focus on possible gender differences and the brain. Wagera et al. (2003) did, however, study brain activators, gender and emotion. They saw some sex-based differences in certain parts of the brain, but that the conclusions given are speculative with a number of alternate explanations. The conclusions regarding brain differences and emotions are highly tentative because, having noted the differences, the authors qualify that "neuroimaging differences between males and females do not necessarily imply behavioral or psychological differences, and we stress again that these interpretations are speculative" (2003: 527). Further, they note that "these findings provide evidence that the emotional brain is much more complex than indicated in the simple hemisphere-level predictions of the past, and highlight the usefulness of imaging studies in the generation of more specific hypotheses regarding the brain's role in emotion" (2003: 528). Sometimes lost in all this is a fact that few investigators seem to consider: that all humans could be said to be born prematurely; hence we require months and years of intensive care by other humans simply to survive. The human brain grows at a very rapid pace after birth, tripling and even quadrupling in size in the five years following birth, a period during which nerve cells that compose the brain grow in size and complexity, a growth and development process that is significantly impacted by a variety of environmental conditions (Fausto-Sterling 2012).

If the accounts of the roles of hormones and brain structure in impacting, if not determining personality, including sex and gender behaviours (that is, biological determinism of personality), are accurate and verifiable, then the implications are quite straightforward — just understand the physiology of hormones and/or the brain and voilà, sex and gender behaviours are explained. Sociologists and many others do not, however, think that this is the case, as numerous scholars have taken great care to examine and critique this kind of research. For example, Eleanor M. Miller and Carrie Yang Costello (2001) offer a devastating critique of both the evidential basis and logic of various biological determinist arguments. Anne Fausto-Sterling's work (2000a; 1985; 2012) demolishes virtually every aspect of various biological determinist arguments, pointing out that the assumptions that scientists bring to the lab often impact their observations and findings. She points out the important role that early learning plays in impacting the physiological structures of the brain and that it needs to be considered when studying apparently natural biological differences (2012: 63). Fausto-Sterling presents detailed and cogent arguments, as do Miller and Costello, with regard to why we should be cautious when conclusions about human brain function, structure and behaviour are extrapolated from animal — particularly rodent — studies. Fausto-Sterling (1985) documents the complex and symbiotic relationships between the social and so-called natural environment and the manner by which genes are expressed. Her account of the politics of hormone research, including the fairly recent "discovery" of hormones, paints a much more complex picture of the roles of hormones, noting with a degree of irony that although we know and acknowledge that humans are learners, much of the biological determinist literature ignores human learning (2000: 232; see also Paula Caplan and Jeremy Caplan 1994).

Barbara J. Risman and Georgiann Davis (2013: 735) describe the conclusions reached in a recent study of the research on the importance of brain differentiation. With regard to the many studies they examined, they conclude:

> Brain organization research does not pass the basic litmus tests for scientific research: they are so methodologically flawed as to produce invalid results, as they rely on inconsistent conceptualizations of "sex," gender, and hormones. When conceptualizations of one study are applied onto another, findings are not usually replicated. The major deficiency of brain theories of sex differences is that there are few consistent results across studies; they also depend on inconsistent definitions and measurement of concepts, and so lack reliability as well. This research continues albeit mostly in the form of animal research or quasi-experimental data about human beings.

I note in closing that if complex human behaviour were reducible to brain structure, hormone levels or some other simplistic mechanism to understand the world, all we would need to do is study the roles of hormones and the physical structures of the brain and all would be clear. However, the world is just not that simple, since one of the things we know about humans is this: we are learners.

While the role of social learning is downplayed or not explicitly addressed in many of these biologically based approaches, that is not the case in most other, more sociological approaches.

GEORGE HERBERT MEAD

Although the discipline of sociology is not known for its attention to personality development, two of the founding figures of North American sociology are exceptions. The work of George Herbert Mead (1863–1931) and Charles Horton Cooley (1864–1929) provides the basis for an alternate approach to Freud and any and all simplistic biological determinist arguments.

One of Mead's core assumptions provides the basis for the sociological approach to human personality — the inseparability of the human mind, the human self and society. Humans possess, Mead argued, a number of unique characteristics and abilities, including a large and complex human brain organ that makes possible the existence of what he called the mind. It is the mind that provides humans with several unique capacities, including temporal dimension (the ability to understand that events happen sequentially), reflective intelligence (capacity for organized systematic thought and reasoning) and the human capacity for the utilization of complex symbolic communication systems.

For Mead the Self was not just something we possess, it is something we acquire. As he explained: "The self is something which has a development; it is not initially there, at birth, but arises in the process of social experience and activity, that is, develops in the given individual as a result of his [sic] relations to that process as a whole and to other individuals within that process" (1934: 135). The process he refers to involves several distinct stages, each involving more complex bodies of knowledge and the engagement in more complex patterns of social interaction as we pass from playing-acting and pretending to be in certain social roles or positions (such as a teacher or firefighter) to actually interacting in concrete situations in which we must take account of the rules and the actions of other players (going to school and meeting real teachers and other students). Although he used the analogy of a game, the "game" might be going to school or any other interactive situation in which we need to know the social expectations of those around us, or the more formal rules of engagement as it were. The type of social learning that makes human interaction possible is fundamentally dependent on the human capacity to communicate using complex and abstract systems of symbols, as in language. Without some form of symbolic communications the type of learning required to function as a human in the complex social interactions that make up our existence would not be possible.

The Self emerges and takes form through learning about norms, roles, rules, expectations and social situations. While acknowledging the importance of the actor as a physiological being (Mead's somewhat confusing term for his element of our being is the "I"), the Self is very much a social construct. The importance of the social dimension of the Self was the focus of the work of Mead's fellow traveler Charles Horton Cooley, whose notion of "the looking-glass self" remains important. Cooley (1956: 184) argues that the looking-glass self, which he also refers to as the self-idea, has three essential elements or components: "the imagination of our appearance to the other person; the imagination of his [sic] judgment of that appearance; and some sort of self-feeling, such as pride or mortification."

The process is actually quite simple, and when you think about it, it is your lived experience, common and everyday. Assume I interact with someone and in so doing experience or pick up on cues or clues as to how I appear to them in whatever role I am playing. Suppose I am a student and I somehow detect that the teacher thinks I am a dull dolt. Step two involves my sense or imagination that the teacher has a negative judgement of me because the teacher favours bright students and not dull dolts. The last element or step three involves the self-feelings I get from thinking I appeared a dull dolt and that the teacher thinks I am a dull dolt, self-feelings that impact my behaviour. The teacher asks a question and I am not fully confident I know the answer (remember I have done something that made me think that the teacher thinks I am a dull dolt) so I hold back. I don't answer questions in class because I don't want to make myself look even worse. The more I sit quietly while others answer, the more I appear a dull dolt and this might even start to be my self-concept. In some of the literature this process is referred to as a self-fulfilling prophecy. The importance of these dynamics will vary depending on the "other" with whom we are interacting because not all others are equally significant. Depending on our age, level of maturity, social situation and so on there may well be some individuals whose opinion and attitudes are really significant. Think about a parent or caregiver for a four-year-old child as opposed to the self-appointed coach in a pick-up ball team in the park. A parent's attitudes, praise, criticism and overall attitude are vitally important to the child's sense of self-worth and identity, while the guy in the park that thinks he knows how to coach is written off as irrelevant.

In sum, the works of Mead and Cooley have become very important in sociology and virtually all of its subfields. The emphasis on the importance of social interaction as both being reliant on and generative of human symbolic communication is something of standard wisdom in sociology, social psychology and many other disciplines as is the insistence on avoiding either biological or cultural determinism.

TOWARDS AN INTEGRATED APPROACH

Before I outline what I call an integrated approach I draw your attention to the work of Ivan Pavlov, Edward Thorndike and B.F. Skinner and the school of behaviouralism, which argued that the human personality is merely the sum total of one's learning experience. Whether learning experiences involve rewarding, reinforcing or punishing behaviour produced by some stimuli, the approach tends to see the world in stimuli-response terms with little role for the active reflexive mind. The famous claim made by John Watson (1878–1958) is illustrative:

> Give me a dozen healthy infants, well-formed, and my own specified world to bring them up in, and I'll guarantee to take any one at random and train him [sic] to become any type of specialist I might select — doctor, lawyer, artist, merchant-chief, and, yes, even beggar, and thief, regardless of his talents, penchants, tendencies, abilities, vocations, and race of his ancestors. (Quoted in Robertson 1981: 107)

While without doubt we sometimes learn as a result of rewards and punishments, the approach I want to suggest is much more complex, borrowing some insights from the theories or approaches discussed above and referring back to the Introduction, offering a more comprehensive approach that integrates an understanding of both agency and structure. We know that humans are active, intelligent creatures who are inherently social, but not simply reducible to the sum total of our social learning and experiences. Neither are our personality and character the simple outcomes of genes, hormones or pre-programmed instinctual drives. Margaret Archer notes that social scientists tend to make one of two erroneous assumptions about the relationship between human agents and social structures. One error she identifies is understanding humans as possessing common species-wide traits, behavioural tendencies or attributes, as in the case of classical liberals, rational-choice advocates and neo-classical economists, who hold that all humans are inherently and inevitably aggressive and self-interested. The other error at the opposite end of the spectrum is to understand humans as "oversocialized," that is, making society, culture and socialization responsible for most if not all of our character traits, behaviours and personality. Such a position is a culturally determinist, and holds humans to be mere cultural dupes. Neither position understands that we must recognize, analyze and understand the independence, powers and properties of both the individual agent and the social structure.

The approach that I think best offers the possibility of understanding boys and men is predicated on a number of assumptions:

1. As they make their way through the world (to borrow from the title of

one of Archer's many books) humans live their lives in the context of and across three analytically distinct orders of reality: 1) the Natural (the physical world that we, as embodied sexed creatures enter as neonates, inhabit and develop in and that we sense, feel and experience with our bodies and senses); 2) the Practical (the action world of performativity in which, through various stages of maturity, humans act, move, behave and seek to achieve practical objectives); and 3) the Social (the symbolically oriented realm of social and cultural knowledge and action that includes social interaction, self-image, identity, self worth and consciousness, including that related to gender). We live our lives seamlessly in, through and across these orders as embodied practical, self-conscious and reflective actors. It is through practice in each of these orders or realms that we develop and maintain the uniquely human characteristics of possessing a "*continuous sense of self*" and a "*personal identity*," including self-consciousness. (Archer 2000: 9, emphasis in original).

2. Each human exhibits the presence of an ontologically inviolable Self, a sense of Self that we normally hold secure from violation by others, that emerges from our activities in the three orders of human existence. The human Self is emergent, yet with a significant degree of continuity and stability: open to change and related to our experiences, but also with a degree of self-containment. The human Self is emergent throughout the life cycle and not reductive to either biology or society.

3. The ontologically inviolable human Self that makes its way through the world is an emotional being, a fact often ignored in spite of the fact that there are more than around four hundred words in the English language to describe emotions (Archer 2000: 61).

4. As active, reflexive, intelligent, embodied beings, we are constantly engaged in internal conversations or self-reflexivity understood as "*the regular exercise of the mental ability ... to consider themselves in relation to their (social) contexts and vice versa*" (Archer 2007: 4, emphasis in original). The Self, as a motivated agent, is aware of its own subjective motives that are based on "the subject's own reflexively defined reasons, aims and concerns" (2007: 13). We may not typically talk to ourselves in a manner that is audibly apparent to others, but we are in constant conversation.

5. Humans are active actors, meaning we constantly engage in projects as opposed to mere random acts and actions: "Action itself depends upon the existence of what are termed 'projects,' where a project stands for any course of action intentionally engaged upon by a human being" (Archer 2007: 7).

These assumptions provide a way of approaching human personality development that, while acknowledging the contributions of behaviouralism, Freud, symbolic interactionism and feminist critical thought, move beyond the limits of each. We are sensate physical beings, necessarily part of the Natural realm, in which we manifest our humanness as actors in the Practical realm, but governed by our social nature as creatures dependent for our survival on symbolically based self-reflective social interaction. As self-reflective emotional beings we develop and possess a strong sense of Self, normally secure from violation or trespass, that is nevertheless generative and fluid, and always the subject and object of our conversations with ourselves and others. Our actions are typically project-driven and motivated by our reflections, conversations and actions in the Natural, Practical and Social realms.

The realms within which my biography or my Self unfolds and moves are of course constitutive of a social structure itself situated in time, space and locale. While my Self is normally secure from violation or trespass, it is unavoidably bound to time, space and locale. The precise nature of my projects, the resources I bring to bear on those projects, the possibilities and limitations of my actions, the social and collective support or resistance I face and many more such contingencies represent the other dimension of an analytical dualist approach. The options open to an ego, the limitations of the superego, the nature of the interactions that generate the "me" and my significant others are all necessarily social and important to consider when we trace our developmental trajectories.

There is one final qualifier, which is the necessity of understanding both the cultural, linguistic and political context of the self and the individual's personal, subjective and unique psychodynamics, including various emotions, fantasies and defence mechanisms (Chodorow 1995). In a series of clinical case studies of women, the common cultural context of their lives, including patriarchal family histories, does not tell the entire story: "The existence of cultural and social gender inequality does not explain the range of fantasy interpretations and varieties of emotional castings women bring to this inequality" (Chodorow 1995: 539). I take this point seriously and acknowledge that while I will lay out some broad-brush contextual issues that are important, when it comes to explaining why a particular boy or man undertakes a particular action on a particular day, we need the help of those immersed in one-on-one psychodynamic interaction.

MOVING ON

The human Self, our Self, our personality, character and mode of being in the world is an extraordinarily complex phenomenon. In this chapter we have seen this Self, or our being in the world, explained in a wide variety of ways with a wide variety of emphases. Some would have us largely as the product of relatively simple conditioning, or others our character and behaviour largely explainable in terms of hormones, physiological brain structures, the alignment and realignment of instincts and tension-reducing mechanisms across our id, ego and superego. Yet others see the Self largely as a social product impacted by symbolic-based interactions of adjustments to others. There are elements in most of these arguments that are worthy of consideration. However, I do believe that as they stand they miss as much as they grasp. It was this opinion that drew me to consider the emergence of the Self as a biological, practical and social process (Archer 2007).

If we are to understand the Self in these terms, we need now to focus on the other dimension of the analytical dualist approach: social structures. The reflexive Self emerges in the context of its relationships with others in an external natural, practical and social world. The social component of the Self is not everything, but it is important. The performances of the Self, its projects, its identities and much else are emergent properties in which society and social structures are central. In a subsequent chapter we will examine some of the major features of the structural dynamics of contemporary capitalism; however first we will look at the emergence of elements of the masculine self in the lives of boys.

CHAPTER 3

BOYS WILL
BE(COME) MEN

Simone de Beauvoir (1973: 301) famously noted: "One is not born, but rather becomes, a woman." Without in any way diminishing the importance of the observation with regard to the lives of females and women, and at the risk of appropriation, I think the logic is applicable to boys — boys are made and not born. This observation directly contradicts the oft-repeated Latin proverb: "Boys will be boys" (Ammer 2013: 52).

SENSE AND SENSIBILITIES

With due respect for Jane Austen, making infants into boys and then making boys into men involves dispelling some myths about the supposed innate or inborn toughness and insensitivity of males, and the also supposed concomitant monopoly on tenderness and sensitivity by females. We know that neonates exhibit some minor sex-based physiological differences; however, the fact remains that human embryos and neonates are overwhelmingly physiologically similar. On the social and emotional side of the picture, female and male neonates and infants have much in common:

> As every human is born into relationships with other people (otherwise one would not survive), we all begin with an original sense of relational connection. Studies of infants have shown that both boys and girls are also born with a fundamental capacity and primary desire for close, mutual, responsive relationships with other people. Thus, boys are not inherently less capable than girls of being attuned to emotions (their own and others) and responsive within their relationships. (Chu 2014: 5–6)

While there exist similarities, studies involving very young infants have found minor sex-based differences in emotive responses or sensitivity to care. However, boys are more, not less sensitive to certain aspects of the social environment: "Boys appear to be more vulnerable to early parenting effects, but only in association with omission errors (attention) and not with the other cognitive function dimensions" (Mileva-Seitz et al. 2015: 194). "Omission errors" refers to findings that indicate that "boys are also more vulnerable to — that is, they exhibit more behavioral problems in response to — the effects of the early social environment, including family effects such as divorce, marital discord, and maternal depression" (194). This leads to the question of boys' sensitivity: "This is congruent with evidence that boys are more sensitive to familial influences such as marital discord suggested and that boys are more vulnerable to the effects of family discord in general" (202). Another study notes a sex difference with regard to fussiness that seems to be a function of different amounts of certain hormones, but that also relate to the emotional reactions of parents: "In contrast to their more stoic adult selves, infant males are actually the more emotional of the two sexes ... boys are more irritable, more easily distressed and harder to sooth than baby girls" (Eliot 2009: 74).

WHEN BOYS ARE JUST BOYS

When we resort to mindless clichés such as "boys will be boys" as an explanation of the behaviour of boys, it is often based on the assumption that from birth there is something essentially different about boys, usually that they are rough and tough when they emerge from the womb. This is not the case; indeed, we now know that young boys are no less sensitive, emotional and considerate than girls.

Various studies have tended to produce four different types of analyses or understandings of boys in contemporary society. First, are studies that focus on the negative impact of the practices and ideologies of hegemonic masculinity within patriarchal gender orders, as manifested in the "boy code" and its harmful influence "on the social, emotional, and academic well-being of boys" (Way 2011: 44). The second genre tends to use some form of essentialism, either cultural or biological, to produce a narrative of typical boy behaviour as necessarily involving aggression, restlessness, obsession with sex and so on. This approach typically encourages the need to adapt institutions such as schools and parenting styles to these so-called natural proclivities of boys in order to "more effectively respond to boys' 'natural' deficits in the areas of compassion, empathy, and other relational skills and to foster 'safe' environments that permit 'boys to be boys' in its stereotypic sense of the word" (46). The third approach focuses on schools and the apparent contemporary performance crisis of boys in the educational system and the so-called boy-unfriendly environment in schools as illustrated by the lack of male role models in primary school and the apparent needs to adopt different pedagogical approaches for males (48–49). None of these first three approaches addresses "the blunting of boy's and men's capacity for empathy, intimacy, and emotional expression that denies them the very skills and relationships they need to thrive" (50). A fourth approach attempts to "begin to touch on these relational themes and the influence of stereotypes, expectations, and conventions in boys lives" (50). By focusing on relational themes this approach provides a thicker view of culture and the underlying processes that impact the actions and lives of boys (51).

All of these approaches, however, have two common weaknesses. The first is that they "present boys as passive receivers of their biology or their culture or context (e.g., both the immediate and the larger context of negative stereotypes and gender straitjackets)" and thus they ignore boys' resistance to gender prescriptions and proscriptions (51). The second relates to the question of friendships: "they share the assumption that while boys may want friendships, they have difficulty finding or having intimate, 'secret-sharing' friendships" (52).

This extensive research demonstrates that, for many years of their lives, boys do not have difficulty establishing and finding friends, the kinds of friends with whom one has a level of intimacy and secret sharing. Niobe Way's (2011) documentation of the lives and concerns of boys in early and middle adolescence is both heart-warming and gut wrenching. Her accounts brings to mind the last words of Gordie Lachance, the young adolescent character in the 1986 movie *Stand By Me,* who as an adult narrator at the end of the movie muses: "I never had any friends like the like the ones I had when I was twelve. Jesus, does anyone?"

One of Way's chapters, titled "Sometimes You Need to Spill Your Heart Out to Somebody," is replete with stories and comments from boys regarding their deep-felt need to have friends with whom they can have intimate friendships that include sharing their deep secrets. Boy after boy speaks of their desire and need to be able to share their secrets and feelings. Way writes: "Boys repeatedly indicated that intimacy or sharing of secrets is what they *liked most* about their friendships" (2011: 96, emphasis in original). The boys Way interviews fully understood their intense need for a best friend. The boy she calls Paul puts it this way: "My ideal best friend is a close, close friend who I could say anything to…'cause sometimes you need to spill your heart out to somebody and if there's nobody there, then your gonna keep it inside, then you will have anger. So you need somebody to talk to always" (91).

For Michael it is about sharing your innermost feelings and the security of a friend:

> You know on that Christmas day we all slept in this little bed. It was little, we were like squeezing and then we were listening to this cheap radio, my friend got a cheap radio, we were turning it to like a low volume and

listening to songs at like 12:30 at night until like three in the morning, we were not all listening, we were talking about secrets and then that's how I know my best friends. (95)

David describes his best friend:

I think our relationship is wonderful. Because, we like, I can't explain. The feelings that I have for him if something would happen to him I probably won't feel right ... Like when he was sick and I hadn't seen him for like a week and I went to his house and I, and I asked his grandmother what was wrong with him and he was in his room like he couldn't move. So I went in there. I sat for the whole day talking to him. And like the next day he got up and he felt better. (103–104)

It is clear that boys are capable of, nay need, that necessary basic human emotion called love as Justin explains:

[My best friend and I] love each other ... that's it ... you have this thing that is deep, so deep, it's within you, you can't explain it. It's just a thing that you know that that person is that person ... and that is all that should be important in our friendship ... I guess in life, sometimes two people can really, really, understand each other and really have a trust, respect and love for each other. It just happens, it's human nature. (1)

Boys relayed a common theme relating to the need to share secrets: "without friends you will go crazy or mad or you'll be lonely all of the time, be depressed" (97). Way comments on other perceived benefits of having intimate friends: "Sharing secrets, however, was not only necessary to avoid 'going crazy'; it was also helpful for boys to learn problem-solving strategies" (97). Close friends were also important in establishing trust and expressing vulnerability because the world of boys' friendship that Way discovers is very much a world in which "kindness, mutual recognition, and support are central" (103).

That young boys are not stoic, mini-Rambos is illustrated by a report concerning a classroom exercise related to the White Ribbon Campaign. Grade 4 boys were asked what they disliked about being a boy (Bologna 2014; *Telegraph* 2014). One boy provided the following dislikes (spelling from original):

- Not being able to be a mother
- Not suppost to cry
- Not allowed to be a cheerleader
- Suppost to do all the work
- Suppost to like violence

- Suppost to play football
- Boys smell bad
- Having a automatic bad reputation
- Grow hair everywhere

These dislikes mirror the comment made by an older boy to Way: "It might be nice to be a girl because then you wouldn't have to be emotionless" (2011: 61).

Judy Chu's study of boys as they navigate Kindergarten and Grade 1 also tells us a great deal about the emotional lives of young boys. Reflecting on her extensive and intensive times spent with boys she notes: "I observed these young boys to have the cognitive and emotional capacity to exhibit qualities and skills that challenge how boys are commonly thought of and spoken about in the literature on boys' development and in our everyday lives" (2014: 33). Further, she observes: "In contrast to the depictions of boys as being insensitive to emotions and incapable of or uninterested in developing close relationships, the boys in my study demonstrated a remarkable ability to be astute observers of their own and other people's emotions, sensitive to the dynamics and innuendos within their relationship, and keenly attuned to the norms and patterns within their social interactions and cultural contexts" (33).

Chu also examines the processes and dynamics by which some of these sensitivities and emotional characteristics are blunted and repressed. She summarizes her findings regarding the social and emotional intelligence of boys, their openness and honesty in self-expression, and the fact that they are no less capable than girls in terms of "understanding emotions, communicating their thoughts, feelings and desires and negotiating relationships" because they can be "attentive, articulate, authentic and direct in their interactions" (143). However, as Chu notes, something drastic begins to happen and, as a result, "we witness a shift in these boys' relational presence, including ways in which they behaved and engaged with others, through which they appeared to become inattentive, inarticulate, inauthentic, and indirect" (143). Chu notes that there is no doubt what this change is about "the boys' adaptation to the norms of masculine behavior" (143), a process that Chu is careful to note is not just something imposed on the boys, but a process in which they are active participants.

MANNING UP: EARLY SOCIALIZATION

Before tracing a few of the socialization experiences boys encounter, a word of warning. A full treatment of the complexities and nuances of what boys experience, learn, react to, accept and reject at the hands of teachers, peers, family, on the playground, while playing video games and watching television and so on is well beyond the scope of any single volume. Nevertheless, I do want the reader to think about, by way of a few illustrations, some of the gendered proscriptions, prescriptions, representations, messages, practices and norms that boys encounter in their life journey.

We know that gender socialization is truly a lifelong process that begins very early. The issue has been important in the scholarly literature for more than a half-century, as illustrated by the fact that Ruth Hartley's 1959 "Sex-Role Pressures and the Socialization of the Male Child" is still cited. Hartley noted some themes that were to remain important, including the additional pressures young boys feel as a result of the tendency to be subject to negative reinforcement when they violated traditional masculine norms and practices; the importance of fathers and peers; the role conflict that accompanies stifling of emotions; and an accompanying emphasis on toughness that generates unrealistic expectations. Hartley (1959: 463) identi-fied four different modes by which boys handle the pressure: 1) over-striving with hostility against women; 2) over-striving without hostility; 3) give up, possibly with protest; and 4) success in balancing the various dimensions of the male role.

Illustrative of the many, many studies of early child-rearing practices is Melissa Clearfield and Naree Nelson's study of the speech and play patterns of mothers with male and female babies at ages 6, 9, and 14 months. They conclude: "Results indicated that mothers act in different ways, both in speech content and play behavior, toward their boys and their girls" (2006: 134). Further, they note: "More important, the results also support previous findings that parents talk differently with their daughters and their sons, with parents expecting more verbal responses from daughters than from sons" (135). When the child was exploring the room, they found mothers spent more time interacting with their daughters while: "In contrast, the boys were reinforced for exploring on their own, as seen through the levels of interaction and also the high number of comments directed toward them. This might reinforce a sense of independence in boys that is not reinforced in girls" (136). The sense of independence was founded in the tacit approval given to boys as they move away from the parents without parental concern, while girls were watched over more.

Traditional patterns of gender-based socialization continue to hold true when examining the types of behaviours and socialization engaged in by mothers and fathers. Even when fathers were actively involved with a child, "mothers were still more involved than fathers in three out of the four aspects of engagement examined: socialisation, didactic, and caregiving. Differences for socialisation and caregiving in favour of mothers were medium to large. Fathers only reported more frequent engagement than mothers in physical play" (Schoppe-Sullivan et al. 2013: 509). This is not to say fathers are not important, particularly for boys. In fact, there is a "strong and positive relationship between fathers' and sons' sex-role beliefs and expectations," particularly during adolescence (Emihovich, Gaier and Cronin 1984:

861). Using survey data researchers found that while men were increasingly aware of the negative implications of the norms of traditional masculinity, they also were active agents of socialization, transmitting a definition of masculinity about which they may themselves have qualms (863).

There is an extensive literature on parental responses to non-traditional or unconventional gender displays nicely summarized by the very title of Emily Kane's 2006 article: "'No Way My Boys Are Going to Be Like That!': Parents' Responses to Children's Gender Nonconformity." Kane notes significant inflexibility when it comes to boys and learning how to practise gender: "Although some parents did speak of their sons as entirely 'boyish' and 'born that way,' many reported efforts to craft a form of hegemonic masculinity. Most parents expressed a very conscious awareness of normative conceptions of masculinity (whether explicitly or implicitly)" (165). She notes fathers were particularly concerned when it came to nonconformity in gender practice, quoting one father as saying: "I don't want him to be a little 'quiffy' thing, you know … It's probably my own insecurities more than anything. I guess it won't ruin his life … It's probably my own selfish feeling of like 'no way, no way my kids, my boys, are going to be like that'" (63).

PLAYING AROUND WITH GENDER

The importance of gendered toys and gender socialization continues to be a matter of much interest. The stereotypical image of dolls and dish sets being marketed to girls, and action figures, chemistry sets and various "build-it" toys to boys remains a reality. A British-based organization called Let Toys Be Toys maintains an active campaign geared to addressing the issue in the media, schools and in the retail sector. The group is actively working with the a major toy store chain to change the policy of bright pink designated store areas for girls and blue action-figure-dominated areas for boys <http://www.lettoysbetoys.org.uk/>. Major corporations such as Disney are among the important agents of gender socialization, as Carol Auster and Claire Mansbach (2012) demonstrate in their study of the corporation's Internet toy marketing. This study of toy marketing by this omnipresent corporation indicated clear patterns of gender-based marketing of different types of toys based on the color palettes and intended audience. While the finding is not surprising, and their conclusion with regard to the long-term implications of toys and play rather speculative, it is worth noting:

> As a result of learning different skills, children may become more experienced in and more prepared for some occupational fields and future roles and less for others … Children limiting themselves to certain categories of toys may narrow their career interests in the future and contribute to the gender segregation of the occupational structure with women statistically

dominating fields such as nursing and men statistically dominating fields such as engineering. (385)

A variety of other studies make similar points (Wood, Desmarais and Gugula 2002; Auster and Mansbach 2012; Fisher-Thompson, Saus, and Wright 1995; and Sherman and Zurbriggen 2014).

Researchers have also found that the impact of playing with so-called superhero toys on the imagination and creativity "may indeed increase children's creativity and language, cognitive, social, and emotional skills" (Parsons and Howe 2013: 204) simply because such toys typically involve more social interaction, greater use of one's imagination, movement and communication as opposed to more passive and individual-oriented play. An important aspect of socialization is what might be called a self-reinforcement element, that is, once a child has developed a preference for a certain kind of toy or television show they will seek out toys and shows in line with the emergent preferences. Such a pattern of behaviour can lead to a circular argument in which male children play with certain toys stereotyped as male with such behaviour being explained in terms of the child being male without asking fundamental questions about why male children have come to prefer certain toys. Such selective behaviour with regard to toys is apparent by age 3. When shown non-electronic pictures of toys, children rated toys differently in that "'girl toys' were rated significantly uninteresting, while 'both' and 'boy toys' were rated as interesting" (Hull, Hull and Knopp 2011: 560). Judith Owen Blakemore and Renee E. Centers reconfirmed this: "We found that girls' toys were associated with physical attractiveness, nurturance, and domestic skill, whereas boys' toys were rated as violent, competitive, exciting, and somewhat dangerous" (2005: 619).

SCHOOL

Schools are very important sites and agents of socialization. In terms of sheer time, children in most Western countries spend around thirty-five hours a week in school and doing homework. We also know that the ages during which schools are active agents of socialization, from around 5 or 6 to 17 or 18 years, is an extremely important age in terms of physical growth, brain growth, language acquisition and overall personality and character formation.

Amy J. Orr (2011) studied over six thousand kindergarten children in the U.S. She describes one of the essential social functions of the school system: "A primary focus of kindergarten is to prepare children for their role as students." Further, she notes: "a great deal of time in kindergarten classrooms was spent teaching children to be compliant and to unquestioningly follow orders and routines" (2011: 272). She also notes that "education is structured to foster attitudes and behaviors that are compatible with being laborers; therefore, there is a strong emphasis on being obedient and compliant." School is partly about learning routines and gendered patterns of activity and play, the learning of which involves important lessons. Orr puts it this way:

> In general … girls are more likely than boys to engage in stereotypical "female" activities, to exhibit positive social behavior, and to have positive attitudes about school; boys are more likely than girls to engage in stereotypical "male" activities and to have negative attitudes about school. Participation in "female" activities and positive social behavior positively affect grades; participation in "male" activities has no initial direct effect. Positive attitudes positively affect the grades of girls; negative attitudes negatively affect the grades of boys. (2011: 280)

The "hidden curriculum" in schools can have an impact, for example, on the construction of bodies and gender through particular physical activities. Karin Martin stated: "I find that the hidden school curriculum that controls children's bodily practices in order to shape them cognitively serves another purpose as well. This hidden curriculum also turns children who are similar in bodily comportment, movement, and practice into girls and boys—children whose bodily practices differ" (1998: 494). In summary she writes: "a significant part of disciplining the body consists of gendering it, even in subtle, micro, everyday ways that make gender appear natural. It is in this sense that the preschool as an institution genders children's bodies" (510), that is, actually potentially impacting muscle growth and athletic abilities while reinforcing dominant stereotypes regarding sex- and gender-based activity and passivity.

Many school-related activities have a deep impact on boys and girls, such as school drama productions. In one illustrative case, a school drama production was based on a song made famous (infamous?) by Britney Spears — "Baby One More Time" — in which the last two lines of the chorus are: "And give me a sign. Hit me baby one more time." Laurie Schick (2014: 39) notes that the language and performance "exemplifies not only how sexually charged media can contribute to the normalization of sexist, abusive, and thus also violent behavior toward women, but also how local caretaking adults can contribute to these socialization practices even within the context of official educational activities." Writing in the *Atlantic*, Elizabeth Sweet (2014) strikes a pessimistic note in terms of moving forward:

> When it comes to buying gifts for children, everything is color-coded: Rigid boundaries segregate brawny blue action figures from pretty pink princesses, and most assume that this is how it's always been. But in fact, the princess role that's ubiquitous in girls' toys today was exceedingly rare prior to the 1990s — and the marketing of toys is more gendered now than even 50 years ago, when gender discrimination and sexism were the norm.

PEERS

The importance of friends for boys, indeed for all of us, is well understood. Kimberly Maxwell (2002) documents both the negative and positive impact of peers on behaviours relating to smoking, the use of alcohol, chewing tobacco and sexual activity. Engles and ter Bogt (2001) found that the quality of peer relations as measured by group size, longevity of the networks and the intensity or quality of the relationships impacted behaviours with regard to alcohol and other drug use, although less with regard to criminal activity. Self-esteem is the critical factor in understanding the relative importance of peer and school networks, as Ross Wilkinson (2004: 491) demonstrates: "The evidence presented here is that adolescent attachment relationships with parents and peers are not in competition but play additive and complementary roles in psychological well-being during adolescence." We know that best friends with whom boys are able to share their deepest secrets are important for younger boys and that this begins to change as boys move into adolescence; however, this apparent diminished need can be overstated. In working with adolescent boys, Judy Chu has found that even as boys come to know and understand cultural messages regarding masculinity, they continue to need relationships. For many boys, as the pressure to man-up in sports and at school grows, their parents remain a bastion of support that they can always count on because they are "always gonna be there" (Jeffries 2004: 124). Low, Polanin and Espelage (2004) studied the role of peer groups in adolescent aggression. Given the importance of peers during adolescence their conclusion is not surprising:

> In a more novel contribution, our findings suggest greater within-group similarity for relational aggression, and that networks may be even more germane to the elaboration of relational aggression. This is not surprising given that social networks cultivate a level of intimacy that reinforces tactics that protect group identity and boundaries. In other words, many relationally aggressive acts mandate group participation. (2004: 1068)

And, while there doesn't seem to be any significant gender element to cyber bullying, peer rejection and having been a victim of cyber bullying seems to be a triggering mechanism that, as we shall see, can produce gendered responses (Wright and Li 2013: 671–72). Additionally, peers are important with regard to particular sorts of behaviours: "Evidence suggests that children's interactions with peers are tied to increases in aggression in early and middle childhood and amplification of problem behaviors such as drug use, delinquency, and violence in early to late adolescence" (Dishion and Tipsord 2011: 189).

MEDIA AND VIDEO GAMES

The omnipresence and role of the mass media in socialization has been discussed and debated since the advent of the radio, if not before. The daily advent of new technologies and modes of communication has rendered the phraseology of the "mass media" somewhat irrelevant; however, television, radio, newspapers, magazines and now, in its various guises, the Internet, remain an important part of the lives of boys. Television, for example, is not only holding its own as an important part of our lives, it is expanding. Writing in *Time* magazine in 2013, Lily Rothman reported that U.S. children born after 2005 were watching more than thirty-five hours of television each week or the equivalent of a full time job in some countries. Rothman notes that on average children were watching just over two hours a week more than they did in 2009. As for other forms of the media, a Harris Poll reported by Metrics 2.0 reports that 94 percent of American boys play video games. On average, boys between 8 and 12 years old played sixteen hours a week while teenaged boys played eighteen hours per week (Metrics 2.0 n.d.).

An examination of adolescent use of all the various modes of communication concluded that: "Today's teens spend more than 7.5 hours a day consuming media — watching TV, listening to music, surfing the Web, social networking, and playing video games, according to a 2010 study of 8- to 18-year-olds conducted by the Kaiser Family Foundation" (Ahuja 2013: n.p.). While it may tax the imagination, clearly boys will be exposed to hundreds of thousands, indeed, millions of images of men, pictures of masculinity and gender prescriptions and proscriptions of every sort over the period of their boyhood.

The important element in this is, of course, the actual content. Early work focused on the predominance of white male characters and roles in various early television shows, while noting the potential impact on children in terms of narrowing their definitions of sex roles (Busby 1975). Although the data is dated, at the time research indicated that in advertising women were overwhelming shown as involved in housework while housework was also denigrated, while other ads showed women as sex objects, submissive and dependent on men (Busby 1975: 108). In children's shows women were again typically portrayed as homebound, dependent and often over-emotional (111). Like many others who have studied the content of the media focusing on roles and role models, Erica Scharrer (2012) examined 210 characters in twenty-four top-rated police and detective shows that ran between the 1950s and the 1990s:

> Some aspects of the police and detective genre appear to be rather consistent over time, including the tendency for male characters to express anger and to carry a weapon. Across the sample, two-thirds of all characters engaged in physical aggression (with a peak in the 1960s).

This supports past research showing police dramas to be a relatively aggressive program type and is an important finding for its potential to socialize viewers into perceiving aggression to be a necessary element of masculinity. (103)

The potential negative implications, not just for gender representations and behaviour but also for modeling and encouraging various forms of risky behaviour involving dangerous if not impossible physical feats, has been extensively and intensively studied by various experts. In 1993 the official journal of the American Academy of Pediatrics warned of the relationships between media use and engaging in risky behaviours (Klein et al. 1993). In spite of all this, I must also add that the media sometimes, albeit too rarely, offers opportunities to explore alternate or disruptive representations of gender. Gournelos (2009: 143) summarizes his thesis on *South Park*'s disruptive approach and potential: "The episodes discussed demonstrate the possibility for a fluid conception of gender and a highly inter-textual approach to gender development."

Karen Dill and Kathryn Thill studied the visual content of top-selling video game magazines and surveyed college students with regard to their understanding of the representation of females and males in video games. Assuming that video game characters are in fact agents of socialization, their conclusion is troubling: "The vision of masculinity video game characters project is that men should be powerful, dominant, and aggressive. The story video game characters tell about femininity is that women should be extreme physical specimens, visions of beauty, objects of men's heterosexual fantasies, and less important than men" (2007: 861). Kristen Myers (2012: 125) argued that "the non-hegemonic males actually helped reinscribe the dominance of hegemonic masculinity, ultimately reinforcing the traditional gendered order. Although children do not passively accept messages from television, these messages do shape larger gendered scripts that inform interactions." She subsequently elaborated:

On these programs, characters co-constructed hegemonic masculinity at the expense of non-hegemonic characters. They constructed hierarchies, emphasized ideal masculine bodies, and celebrated hyperheterosexuality. Although few of the male characters actually achieved hegemonic status, they all were affected by it. (134)

Christo Sims (2014: 849) states: "It is well documented that many popular video games are gendered technologies that play a role in producing gender divisions among contemporary children and young people." Noting other scholarship in the field he goes on to observe, "many popular video games provide a context for Western boys to accommodate traditional ideas about masculinity." Tracy Dietz's

(1998: 425) study of violence in video games produced an alarming conclusion regarding the potential impact of video games on the behaviour of children:

> There were no female characters in 41% of the games with characters. In 28% of these, women were portrayed as sex objects. Nearly 80% of the games included aggression or violence as part of the strategy or object. While 27% of the games contained socially acceptable aggression, nearly half included violence directed specifically at others and 21% depicted violence directed at women. Most of the characters in the games were Anglo.

Commercials of all sorts are, of course, omnipresent in the lives of boys and girls. Scholars have documented the impact and content of commercials on children with expected and unexpected results. For example, Jennifer Pike and Nancy A. Jennings (2005: 88) found that boys tended to be more impacted by commercials depicting traditionally gendered toys and that fathers "gave less positive responses to sons who engaged in stereotypical girls' play than do mothers," leading them to conclude: "Boys are socialized, particularly by fathers, to be more sensitive to the gender appropriateness of the toys that they select." Lois Smith's (1994) extensive content analysis of sex roles in commercials indicated a very strong tendency to sex and gender stereotyping. A cross-nation content analysis of commercials found: "boys were depicted as being more knowledgeable, active, aggressive, and instrumental than girls. Nonverbal behaviors involving dominance and control were associated more with boys than girls" (Browne 1998: 83).

Children's literature, despite some change in recent years, is still dominated by male characters, often in heroic roles. In a recent analysis of over 5,600 children's books McCabe et al. (2011: 197) found that male characters predominate:

> Compared to females, males are represented nearly twice as often in titles and 1.6 times as often as central characters. By no measure in any book series (i.e., Caldecott Award winners, Little Golden Books, and books listed in the Children's Catalogue) are females represented more frequently than males ... these disparities are evidence of symbolic annihilation and have implications for children's understandings of gender.

BOYS TO TEENS: GAINING MASCULINITY

To understand some of the mechanisms that are at work and the processes that underlie the making of a boy and then a man, we need to reflect back on the theories of socialization and personality. Some of the learning that I noted above might well be understood with reference to rewards and punishments. Male children are rewarded and punished by parents, particularly fathers, for behaviours deemed appropriate or inappropriate. Such an approach is, however, unable to explain the more subtle and complex learning that a boy experiences and undertakes, because, as Chu noted above, we are not just talking about something that happens to boys, imposed by some purely external agent, because socialization is an active process involving a conscious subject agent.

A key dimension of social learning is the self-fulfilling prophecy, a concept linked to Cooley's "looking-glass self." In *Pygmalion in the Classroom* (1968) Robert Rosenthal and Lenore Jacobson describe how the expectations of teachers impact the performance of students. They state: "The central idea ... has been that one person's expectation for another's behavior could come to serve as a self-fulfilling prophecy" (174). That is, expectations can generate behaviour in line with those expectations, especially where expectations are set up by socially and personally significant others. One example is teachers' communications with students:

> Teachers demanded better performance from those children for whom they had higher expectations and were more likely to praise such perform-ance when it was elicited. In contrast, they were more likely to accept poor performance from students for whom they held low expectations and were less likely to praise good performance from these students when it occurred, even though it occurred less frequently. (Brophy and Good 1970: 365)

If we are to use this approach to understand the construction of masculinity and the gendering of boys, we need to understand the types of behavioural and temperamental expectations parents and teachers, among others, have of boys — behavioural, character and temperamental expectations that inform the subsequent self-fulfilling prophesies. We noted the impact of teacher expectations on academic performance above, and we have no reason not to believe that the same process would hold true for other aspects of the behaviour of boys. Judy Chu was standing with a teacher as children were coming into class, when the teacher "points out how nicely, calmly, and quietly the girls arrive at class, adding for emphasis 'especially compared to when *they [the boys]* come in'" (2014: 145, emphasis in original). Chu subsequently notes that regardless of the accuracy of the observation, it betrays expectations that "mainly serve to reinforce a narrow and stereotypical depiction of boys' capacities and to reify conventional notions of masculinity" (146). Susan Jones and Debra Myhill's (2004) British study found: "Underachieving boys may be different from underachieving girls principally because teachers perceive them to be so. Not only do teachers see boy underachievers as being different from girl underachievers, but much of what they describe as typical boy behaviour has also become the epitome of underachieving behaviour" (560; see also Brophy 1983).

Perhaps more important than teacher expectations are the expectations and attitudes of parents. Chu reports on the joy with which fathers commented on the energy, spunk, spirit, pizzazz and vibrancy of their young boys. Additionally, fathers were pleased with the fact that their boys were joyful, friendly, charming and imaginative. However Chu recognizes a predicament related to the fact that these same fathers understood that a time would come when their sons would lose or have to give up these characteristics and behaviours as they matured and entered the world of men. Many fathers recalled having to undergo a transformation themselves as they confronted the gendered world of men with the apparent requirement that softness and sensitivity be blunted and replaced with toughness and, when required, by bluffing your way through (Chu 2014: 174–75). As Chu puts it: "The fathers suggested that in being expected to accommodate to other peoples' expectations and subsequently learning to 'tone down' their emotions and 'regulate' their behaviors accordingly, there was a risk the boys would lose their vibrancy and versatility and get 'locked into' enacting unidimensional and stereotypical roles that leave little room for the full range of their feelings, qualities and capacities" (177–78). It was recognized, however, as the price of growing up.

Mothers, on the other hand, discussed "challenges of trying to understand their sons" (186). Some of the mothers in Chu's study spoke of boys being harder to understand than girls. Although they noted the emotionality and attentiveness of young boys (187), mothers also worried about what was coming as the boys grew up:

> For instance, the mothers described how in transitioning from pre-school and daycare to elementary school, their sons were feeling vulnerable, confused, and anxious as they tried to figure out how to engage with and relate to their peers in this new world of big kids and expectations for "big boys." (2014: 188)

It is clear that much of the gender instruction that passes from parents to children is quite direct, often involving either explicit or implicit rewards and punishments for certain behaviours and attitudes, while other learning experiences involve subtle communication of expectations. Hilary Aydt and William Corsaro studied how children learn about gender, and while they emphasized the active role of children in processing and interpreting gender messages they also note that "gender roles can be communicated in subtle ways by adult caregivers because children are very perceptive of what makes them valued in a culture" (2003: 1309). They further note that children "creatively interpret adult information to form their own peer cultures, which are different from what adults might expect" (1311).

THE DATING GAME

One of the essential transitions in the lives of boys comes with puberty and the emergence of dating and the associated potential shift in priorities from boy friends to girl friends. Roth and Parker (2001: 281) note that these patterns of friendship and intimacy among and between boys may be threatened when dating begins:

> As a result, existing friends, especially those who have not yet begun dating themselves, may regard themselves as neglected and feel lonely. Even where established levels of contact are maintained, existing friends may resent the perceived encroachment into previously sovereign aspects of their partner's life (e.g. serving in the role of confidant).

The result can be dilemmas that require careful emotional negotiation and diplomacy.

Other scholars offer an alternative to the largely incorrect stereotype of young males as hormone-driven hounds, illustrating how both males and females demonstrate the capacity to resist dominant narratives of sexuality (Allen 2003). In a similar vein, Andrew Smiler (2008: 22) found that more than half of the boys he studied endorsed the following as among the most important reason for dating: "I liked the person," "I was really attracted to the person," and "I wanted to get to know the person better," indicating an interest in their dating partner as a person and not simply as a sexual partner. Andrew Collins et al. (2008: 632) were among the many to study the importance of romance in adolescence, noting that "romantic relationships are a hallmark of adolescence," with the additional observation that such relationships are very important: "adolescent romantic relationships increasingly are regarded as potentially significant relational factors in individual development and well-being." They also observe: "Two recurring themes ... are that romantic relationships during adolescence are more multifaceted than is often assumed and that their significance for development is multidimensional rather than unidimensional" (645). In a study using national survey data from the U.S., Joseph Pleck et al. (2004: 260) recognized the importance of becoming sexually active in the lives of adolescent boys; however they did not find evidence to support the stereotypes of sexually obsessed 15- to 19-year-olds.

Using U.S. national data from a survey, Risman and Schwartz (2002: 16–17) found: "In this nationally representative study of over 10,000 students, the percentage of high school students, ages 15 to 17, who reported they had engaged in sexual intercourse dropped from 54.1 percent in 1991 to 48.4 percent by 1997, a dramatic decrease of some 5.7 percent in a short time." In discussing their finding they ask and answer an important question: "So what is going on? Boys' sexual behavior is becoming more like girls' behavior. Among whites, boys are less likely than girls to be sexually active by age 17" (18). Finally, Giordano et al. found that the stereotypical male bluster regarding sexual activity and conquests turns out to be just that, bluster and not the truth. They state: "In contrast, however, to the emphases within much of the existing adolescence literature, we argue that boys often develop positive emotional feelings toward partners and accord significance and positive meanings to their romantic relationships" (2006: 166). Their research paints a picture of boys as complex emotional beings who are changed in some fundamental ways by the experiences of caring, intimacy and emotionality that accompany learning how to date and be with girls:

> These relationships set up conditions favorable to new definitions, to the emergence of new emotions, and, at least within these relationship contexts, to glimpses of a different and more connected view of self, and further that much of the research amounts to "global assertions that do not take into account the adjustments that boys as well as girls continually make as they begin to forge this new type of intimate social relationship." (282)

To complicate the picture I note that there is also evidence that those whose gender practices are more aligned with hegemonic masculinity have different relationship patterns. Joseph Pleck et al. (1993: 11) studied the impact of relationships characterised as related to hegemonic masculinity, finding "that males who hold traditional attitudes toward masculinity indicate having more sexual partners in the last year, a less intimate relationship at last intercourse with the current partner, and greater belief that relationships between women and men are adversarial — characteristics suggesting less intimacy in their heterosexual relationships."

MANNING UP IS NOT EASY

We know quite a lot about the manner by which masculinity and the "boy code" are enforced and reinforced by peers, whether at school or on the street. Emma Renold (2001: 372–73) studied how boys learned about gender as involving "relational, multiple and diverse" identities involving a hierarchy of masculinities in a matrix of power relations in which boys had to position themselves. She documents the tensions, contradictions and conflicts that ensue as some boys unsuccessfully avoid being studious and academically successful in order to at least appear to be practising what in this school was understood as hegemonic masculinity associated with fighting and football. She also notes the "cost" of attempting to practise alternate modes of masculinity. Referring to suggestions that boys be encouraged to practise alternate masculinities she notes: "Such recommendations however, do not sit easily alongside the widely held knowledge that to 'do boy' in non-hegemonic ways often involves inhabiting a marginalized and often painful position within a system of gender relations that carries a host of derogatory labels for any boy who dares to deviate from a normative masculinity" (248).

Nigel Edley and Margaret Wetherell examined how boys in an English school attempted to construct alternate masculinities in the face of a dominant group of boys who were marked by their skills on the rugby pitch. They document how some boys, in order to differentiate themselves from the rugby group, had to disassociate themselves from their masculinity; however, this proved to be difficult, and the boys tended to substitute an alternate form of strength, such as intellectual prowess, for physical strength (1997: 211). A boy opting for what the authors refer to as a complacent masculinity also had to "construct himself as *capable* of physical aggression" meaning that the group had "not really portrayed themselves as departing from the traditional definition of masculinity at all" (212, emphasis in original).

In a West Australian school described by Wayne Martino (1999), the dominant notion of masculinity was enacted as involving an opposition to anything feminine or deemed to be associated with homosexuality. Sports, in particular football, was important as the basis of being cool, a form of practice that "involves rejecting school work and high achievement" because studying and reading were viewed as passive and hence feminine (250). There was, however, room in this environment for some boys to find alternate ways of fitting in, as in the case of Nathan, who is cool because "as a high [academic] achiever, [he] has been able to successfully negotiate a position of acceptance within the dominant group since he is an esteemed football player and he enjoys surfing" (252).

C.J. Pascoe offers one last interesting take on how boys engage in reflection, negotiation, conformity and resistance. In her interviews with teenage boys, while the "jocks" emerge as exemplars of dominant masculinity, Pascoe (2003: 1425) explores alternate routes to manhood:

> Boys' experiences with sports and the role of the Jock maps out some ways in which masculinities are understood, constructed, negotiated, resisted, and justified in the face of a changing gender regime. Instead of assigning each boy to a "type" of masculinity in which Jocks are hegemonic and all other boys are marginalized, I show how each boy works with the dominant tropes of masculinity as embodied in the Jock so that they too may claim this masculinity for themselves.

In her conclusion, Pascoe (2003: 1425) suggests that the "boys' narratives reveal some of the ways in which contemporary boys experience, construct, and negotiate masculinity in adolescence." She also reminds us that "being seen by others and by oneself as masculine is central to being a boy in high school." To this end she finds that boys attempt "to infuse their own identity with recognizably masculine characteristics."

AGENTS NOT CULTURAL DUPES

A lot of effort goes into making make infants into boys, efforts by parents, teachers, the media, peers and so on. We must not think about boys as passive or simple victims of this barrage of ideas, images, instructions, pressures and representations. We know that humans are active, intelligent, reflexive and reflective beings with a mind that processes, interprets, filters, reflects on and attaches meaning to incoming stimuli before determining and undertaking an appropriate response. Indeed, in a sense it is this mind, the existence of a distinct personality that, in part, makes us human. When it comes to gender learning and socialization, the mind, our responsive and reactive personality, of course make a difference, a point Michael Messner makes explicit in his micro-level analysis of boys' and girls' soccer teams with the highly gendered names the "Barbie Girls" and the "Sea Monsters" (2000). Messner examines how 4- and 5-year old boys and girls construct gender on the soccer field, aided and abetted by coaches and parents. Messner uses multiple levels of analysis from the micro-interactional through to the structural and symbolic, demonstrating the exercise of agency within structural boundaries. Niobe Way et al. (2014: 242) make a similar point, noting that "children and adolescents are actively engaged in the socialization process." Judy Chu's (2004: 79–80) use of a relational approach that places emphasis on the essential and foundational role that social relationships play in people's lives obviously recognizes the creative and active roles that boys play in relationships, including those involved in socialization.

Clues to the diversity of the human condition — in this case, masculinities — are found in this very fact of reflection, thoughtfulness, emotion and a degree of choice. At a certain point, as they are subject to various pressures and social dynamics, boys come to gain a sense of their masculinity and where it fits into the world they inhabit. While acknowledging the existence of possibilities, potentials, options and choices when it comes to how we understand and practise gender, we must never forget the structural conditions and constraints within which we move. We know that boys in contemporary Western society face the spectre of hegemonic masculinity on a daily basis. We also know that some come to embrace this way of practising gender in a wholehearted fashion, while other boys opt for other modes of relating to girls, women and other men. In principle many options are available, but they come at a cost.

Among the many volumes that present and represent the voices of boys in this process is William Pollack's *Real Boys' Voices* (2000), which offers many snippets of the joys, pleasures, angst and trials of American boys. The voices cover a very wide range of issues with a number of the dominant themes emerging. 17-year-old Ethan identifies one such theme: "I think guys are terrified of being called gay, because they don't really understand it, and are also terrified of being called feminine" (2000: 15). Pollack identifies the anti-feminine theme as significant, noting that appearing feminine "is the biggest taboo of the Boy Code" and that labels such as "wimp," "fag," "homo" and "wuss" are among the worst insults a boy can suffer (6). Many boys spoke of the need to stifle emotions as Brad, 14, indicated: "I think guys feel ashamed to show emotions in public. We're not supposed to show emotion" (17). This sentiment was echoed by Glenn, four years older, but equally determined, noting that when he heads to school: "I'm always thinking, *Don't let your feelings show*" (22, emphasis in original). A related fear is crying in public. Teddy is 16 and quite clear about this matter: "I don't cry in front of people, but I'll do it sometimes when I'm in my own room or talking to one of my good friends on the phone. But not in front of the guys. I feel really embarrassed when I cry in front of the guys. It comes off as physically weak" (42). Think about this in the context of what we discussed above with regard to the emotional needs of younger boys.

Among the emotional needs noted among younger boys is "Having Male Buddies." 16-year-old James is clear: "Friendships are important. When a friend gets in trouble with his mom, I try to help him out. Or if a friend is mad at someone, I'll try to calm him down" (269). Graham, aged 17, concurs with the support role of good friends: "If I'm ever really upset I talk to my best friend Colin. It's so important to have a best friend" (270).

MANHOOD DAWNING

The complexity of socialization, social learning and the development of one's personality defy summary. Theories of personality discussed in Chapter 1 do provide a framework for understanding some the processes and dynamics discussed above.

To repeat an important theme, even as young boys learn and are influenced by a myriad of agents of socialization they are always agents themselves, never just cultural dupes but rather reflective and emotional creatures, therefore capable of reaction not just absorption. As emergent, not essentialist, creatures, human boys are knowledgeable actors engaged with others and themselves as they make their way through the world. Way et al. (2014: 241) confirm this fact:

> Recent studies suggest that although boys do, in fact, live in a culture that poses numerous challenges to their healthy development, they are not simply passive recipients of culture or nature ... They also have the capacity to resist or reject particular beliefs, values, and expectations about

being a boy or a man and the biological qualities commonly associated with being male.

And, lastly, they note:

> The study of resistance grows out of the recognition that children and adolescents are actively engaged in the socialization process and respond to cultural beliefs, norms, and practices as well as to their biology. They do not simply accommodate to messages received from parents, teachers, and peers about what it means to be a girl, with its emphasis on feminine goodness and selflessness, or a boy, with its emphasis on stoicism, toughness, and independence. (242)

Much about boyhood has been missed and slighted. The issue of sport and males will be taken up in a subsequent chapter, while notions of sexuality, desire and related issues such as homophobia were broached in our discussion of hegemonic masculinity. Hollywood and television notwithstanding, the vast majority of boys, however, will never be involved in gangs, gang violence, the illicit drug trade and other violent pursuits; therefore, these have escaped our notice.

In 2008 Michael Kimmel presented the outcome of what he calls several years of conversations with young men and women all over America in a book entitled *Guyland: The Perilous World Where Boys Become Men*. The topic of these conversations was, although Kimmel does not explicitly state so, obviously about the transition from boyhood to manhood, a route that in North America, at least, runs through "Guyland."

Anthropologists have documented the rites and rituals that mark the transition from one life stage to the other in various cultures. Definitions of the basis for demarking different stages in life vary culturally and historically. Kimmel suggests that for Guyland (mostly white and middle class, often college students or college bound or recent grads in the U.S.) there are five traditional markers of adulthood: 1) leaving home; 2) completing education; 3) starting work; 4) marriage; and 5) children (2008: 30). Given the poor, precarious employment prospects in the current globalized stage of capitalist development, the social context into which the recent high school graduates find themselves is tenuous at best. Kimmel describes an economy marked by few good jobs, globalization, downward mobility and an ongoing fiscal crisis of the state (33–35). He notes that young men have adapted the post-war notion of teenagers as a life stage, making it a liminal time between adolescence and adulthood. Despite the fact that children are apparently growing up faster, these guys have become a demographic akin to an eternal boyhood whose major interests are girls not women.

Given their location in the context of North American capitalism, dominated by a mass culture of consumption and a patriarchal gender order that creates virtually unlimited ambitions, expectations and entitlements, it is not surprising that the guys in Guyland have high expectations. The problem is these guys are mired in Guyland with few opportunities and dim prospects. Additionally, coming as they do from boyhood in a patriarchal gender order and multiple gender regimes, the guys know all about practising hegemonic masculinity. Kimmel (45) developed a "Top Ten Guy List" to illustrate the extent to which Guyland practises some version of hegemonic masculinity:

1. "Boys Don't Cry"
2. "It's Better to Be Mad than Sad"
3. "Don't Get Mad—Get Even"
4. "Take It Like a Man"
5. "He Who Has the Most Toys When he Dies Wins"
6. "Just Do It" or "Ride or Die"
7. "Size Matters"
8. "I Don't Stop and Ask for Directions"
9. "Nice Guys Finish Last"
10. "It's All Good"

The gender practice unfolds in the presence of, or under the gaze of, other men, whose roles as the gender police ensure that the gender performance of men adheres to the proscriptions and prescriptions of hegemonic masculinity. Such hegemonic practices emphatically avoid violating "the single cardinal rule of manhood, the one from which all other characteristics — wealth, power, status, strength, physicality — are derived is to offer constant proof that you are not gay" (50).

Kimmel further describes the three dominant cultures of Guyland: 1) Entitlement, 2) Silence and 3) Protection (the need to belong) (57–64). High school in Guyland is the "boot camp" where guys begin to learn how to perfect their capacity to practise hegemonic masculinity. There are sets of core elements of the practices that characterize life in Guyland. Among these are the obligation to be sports crazy, to make sports a social fixation and allow meaningless conversations about the merits and demerits of various sports, teams and cities to override various potentially divisive issues related to class, race and the like. The bonding and brotherhood of sports also serves as a powerful mechanism for isolating females by maintaining segregation and "expertise."

Other activities in Guyland revolve around the value and use of various boy toys, including the full gamut of video and other electronic games, many involving anger and violence as the dominant motif. Such boy toys, in addition to offering vicarious escapism, provide an opportunity in the realm of fantasy of what the guys lack in the real world, a sense of power, control and competence. Increasingly related to video games is the world of pornography linked to relentless heterosexuality. One can only begin to describe the situation of girls and women in Guyland as, to risk an understatement, grim verging on forbidding, as the elements of pornography, hook-up culture and predatory sex situate girls and women. Revenge fantasies (women getting what they deserve), anger, contempt and relentlessly negative images and roles of women characterize the tsunami of contemporary pornography. Hook-up culture involves mating taking precedence over dating based on male bravado, reputation, spontaneous, often alcohol-induced encounters, but definitely not relationships. Hooking-up leads to predatory sex and party rape based on the myth that "no" actually means "yes," predicated on often-erroneous assumptions of female sexual desire but really about retaliation, anger and power.

Lest all this drive one to total despair, Kimmel's last chapter, "Just Guys," describes the guys slouching toward manhood. His account of fathers and daughters is a fascinating story of the positive impact of healthy masculinities on both daughters and sons. The need males have for friendship that we noted with regard to young boys is still present, but somehow its relationship emotion has been replaced by "false bravado and toughness, a mutual recitation of allegiance to the Guy Code" (278). Ironically, Kimmel notes that girls and male victims of Guyland make the best friends.

OTHER PATHS TO MANHOOD

Guyland describes the route to adulthood, manhood of a particular cohort or demographic, with a distinctive ethnic, historical, cultural and class location. In complex societies such as the U.S., one can easily imagine adolescent males having different transitional experiences if their roots are variously in an Appalachian mining community, a struggling farm family in Kansas, an Oregon logging family, a Texas ranch, the family of a Michigan auto worker or in Silicon Valley.

Working-class men and working-class culture in a small resource-based Canadian city, for example, practice masculinity in a different way. For the lives of the men — "The Boys" — of this city, work is central: "the experience of work is constitutive of working-class ideas about knowledge, and these in turn provide the substratum upon which notions of how leisure time should be spent and the kinds of cultural activities that are enjoyable are constructed" (Dunk 1991: 66). Dunk goes on to describe the kinds of leisure and non-work activities that The Boys undertake. A key element of Dunk's description of the lives and times of The Boys is their relationships with women. The process of "manning up" for a working-class boy in this world is radically different than those Kimmel describes; nonetheless, the essential elements of the spectre of hegemonic masculinity lurk.

On the question of sex and gender: "In their treatment of women, The Boys are reproducing the system of inequality based upon gender which crosses all social classes." After reaffirming the importance of class, he continues: "Working-class men certainly contribute to the maintenance of a [hegemonic masculinity] which subordinates women" (99).

Separating boys from their mothers is often the mechanism for transmitting hegemonic masculinity. Post-war Canada, for example, saw a yearning to return to the normalcy of the pre-war era regarding sex and gender relationships (Grieg 2014). The normalcy was the pre-war patriarchal gender order and gender regimes. Greig documents various social efforts to create the "right kind of boy." Among the deliberate efforts was the separation of boys from excessive control by their mothers in order to ensure Ontario boys were not sissies or mama's boys. There were, however, more fundamental issues at work:

> To some degree, the efforts to separate boys from their mothers served both directly and indirectly the interests of the state and postwar corporations, which needed men who were aggressive, capable of some violence, unemotional, patriotic, and distanced from family. (2014: 19)

Other efforts to create the right kind of boy involved building the skills necessary for teamwork using sports, again an agenda that served powerful interests. Greig observes: "At a time when postwar capitalism depended heavily on teamwork and fair play, some adults promoted sport as a good vehicle for teaching boys teamwork as well as other corporate virtues, such as loyalty, sacrifice, promptness, civic responsibility, and subordination to leadership" (31). The post-war era also generated more than one moral panic relating to deviance, juvenile delinquency or rebels without causes. As Greig explains, media campaigns and the encouragement of athletics and boys' clubs were all part of efforts to keep boys on the straight and narrow. Normalcy in this expanding capitalist era was predicated on "normalizing white, Anglo-Protestant, middle-class, patriarchal, heteronormative definitions of masculinity" (121). As a result, "boys and men should value teamwork, selflessness, and fair play. They must be rational, physically and emotionally self-controlled and disciplined, upright and moral, loyal, and obedient" (122).

We leave our consideration of boys becoming men with a word on transitions in the human life cycle. Among the distinguishing features of different cultures are the rites, markers, rituals and social representations that accompany important life events. Such life events may be reaching a certain age, accomplishing a certain feat, exhibiting certain manifestations of physical maturity and so on. There are several in *Guyland* (leaving home, finishing school, getting a full-time job, marriage and becoming a parent) but none of these can be seen as a widely accepted and clear marker or rite of passage to, say, manhood. Joseph Vandello and Jennifer Bosson (2013) suggest that in many contemporary societies (I read in the Western world) there is a sense that manhood is something that is achieved, but there is no clear marker of that achievement other than assuming the behaviours associated with manhood, presumably exercising the local manifestations of hegemonic masculinity. Since, they argue, achieving manhood is a social act, something that must be confirmed by others, one can fail, hence the notion of precarious manhood. As they starkly put it:

> It is quite common to characterize manhood as an uncertain, tenuous social status that must be earned and demonstrated. Our mind's eye readily conjures the poor sap who grows old yet never knows manhood. This man is one who fails to pass certain mile-stones or accomplish certain goals and thereby never proves (in the eyes of other men) that he deserves to be called a "real man." (102)

While other cultures and other times had clear rites of manhood, few formalized "rites of passage" into manhood exist in most Western industrialized cultures (at least outside of certain subcultures such as gangs, fraternities or the military) (Vandello et al. 2008: 1325). As a result: "lacking formal manhood rituals, men may prove themselves with informal — and sometimes harmful — demonstrations of masculinity" (1325). In their conclusion they make a comparison: "In short, whereas womanhood is viewed as a developmental certainty that is permanent once achieved, manhood is seen as more of a social accomplishment that can be lost and therefore must be defended with active demonstrations of manliness" (1335). In a sense the remainder of this book will address some of these demonstrations.

MOVING ON

It is clear that there exists a sensitivity and emotional nature in young boys. Although cultural representations will be dealt with later, at this point I draw your attention to several brilliant motion picture accounts of boys' lives that focus both on the external forces that, quite frankly, repress the sensitivities and emotions of the boys even as they struggle to prevail. British filmmaker Ken Loach's *Kes* is the story of 15-year-old Billy Casper, who is abused by his father and bullied by his big brother and schoolmates. He finds solace and companionship in a kestrel falcon (hence the name) that becomes his best companion. Although tragedy ensues, Billy's humanity, sense of justice and capacity to love somehow seem to survive the harshest possible environment. Mark Herman's 2000 *Purely Belter* is the story of two teenaged boys obsessed with securing two season tickets for their home team, Newcastle United. Set in the carnage of de-industrialized, globalized contemporary

England, the two mates clearly love each other in a non-sexual way as they plan and plot, reflect on fatherhood and girls and dream impossible dreams. Although they have no chance of success and little chance in life, the drug-addicted sister of one of them observes that they are "down deep, nothing but bloody angels." Lastly there is Richard Linklater's much-acclaimed *Boyhood*, the twelve-year story of Mason through the trials and tribulations of parental dysfunction, bullying, changing schools and family road trips, all the while retaining his bearing, dignity and discovering that photography provides an outlet for his sensitivity and creativity.

Each of these films illustrates the precarious road through boyhood toward manhood, and how, despite the best efforts of the world to blunt them, they tend to, in the words of the Big Lebowski, "abide."

CHAPTER 4

CAPITALISM AND WORK
Sex, Gender and Economy

WORK, LABOUR AND HOMO SAPIENS

Homo sapiens are active creatures that don't just exist within or live off nature, but rather that actively transform nature, thus producing satisfaction to our needs. The verb "labour" is commonly applied to the human activities through which we intervene and transform nature in order to produce satisfaction for our various needs and solve our various problems. The importance of human activity and interventions in nature has resulted in our species being referred to as *Homo laborans* (loosely referring to humans as an essentially labouring species) and *Homo faber* (focusing more on the creative side of human activity). However we understand the productive activities commonly referred to as "work," such activity is a central dimension of what it means to be human. How work and labour are organized and conducted is fundamentally important to our character and behaviour and tells us much about how we live.

The modes and nature of human labouring activities have varied and changed radically and repeatedly over the millennia, impacted by numerous factors, including levels of technological development, culture, political regimes, patterns of ownership and control over productive resources, religious traditions and so on. The importance, meaning, nature and character of human labour have occupied philosophers and scholars throughout recorded history (see Theocarakis 2010 for more detail). While not exactly the same, for the present purposes labour and work can be deemed to essentially refer to this central feature of humanity, although

78

Philip Hansen cautions that, as understood within the context of critical theory, care should be taken when conflating the two concepts (1993: 39–43).

Economic institutions and larger economic orders have been among the most significant factors impacting the lives and social actions of boys and men. To understand work and the relationships of both masculinity to work and work to masculinity within the context of a capitalist economic order, a basic understanding of the nature and dynamics of the capitalist economic order is required.

CAPITALISM AS AN ECONOMIC ORDER

Capitalism is an economic order based on the private ownership of society's productive and economic resources (typically referred to as "capital") in which commodities are produced for markets. Markets are the primary mechanisms determining the prices and volumes of goods and services. An essential feature of capitalism is the ceaseless and ever-expanding production, accumulation and expansion of wealth. Robert Heilbroner (1992: 32) uses the phrase "the rage for accumulation" to describe the inner logic of the system, noting that the ceaseless accumulation of wealth produces an economic system that undergoes continual changes as those with capital seek new and expanding ways of accumulating more capital. Meiksins Wood (2002: 78–79) notes that it is not the simple seeking of wealth that characterizes capitalism since some humans have sought after wealth for millennia. What characterizes capitalism is the existence of a class, a capitalist class whose primary objective in life, whose *raison d'être*, is the accumulation of wealth, typically through investment in some form of profit generating enterprises. E.K Hunt (1981: 21) explains:

> One of the defining features of the capitalist system is the existence of a class of capitalists who own the capital stock. It is by virtue of their owner-ship of this capital that they derive their profits. These profits are plowed back or used to augment the stock of capital. The further accumulation of capital leads to more profits, which leads to more accumulation, and the system continues in an upward spiral.

Those in possession and control of the society's productive resources (capital in the form of land, mines, mills, factories and so on) engage in the ceaseless pursuit of enhanced profit through every means possible, including expansion or contraction when necessary, investment, reinvestment or disinvestment when necessary, innovation and/or whatever other actions are deemed necessary to maintain and increase the generation of profits.

Most individuals, however, do not own any productive resources or property that generate income or profit and, as a result, "make a living" through engagement in the labour market. What this means is they secure the income necessary to survive by selling their labour power or ability to work (the working classes). In short, they go to work for someone with capital that needs their labour to operate their mines, mills, factories, stores and other enterprises. The precise capacities, skills and credentials that individuals bring to the market and the conditions under which they engage in the labour market will vary from time to time and place to place; however, the overall structural relationship between those with capital (the buyers) and those without capital (the sellers) remains an essential characteristic of capitalism. That relationship, while it appears to be a simple market transaction, involves relations of power with the ultimate control over production and the availability of work residing with the owners of capital.

While the relentless pursuit of profit marks the essential logic of the system, the core activities that provide the basis for the accumulation of capital have changed radically since the emergence of the capitalist system in the early sixteenth century. If we are to understand the impact of the dynamic nature of capitalism and the manner by which the logic of the system bears on the lives of boys and men, it is to understand the various stages through which Western capitalism has passed since it emerged. In order to simplify the task and convey the notion of a dynamic system, the history of capitalism can be divided into a series of stages or periods. The different periods or stages are identified on the basis of patterns of ownership and control of the major societal productive resources and changing patterns of state involvement in the economy. Quantitative differences characterize each stage, and qualitative differences characterize the patterns of ownership of productive resources and thus modes of profit generation, as well as concomitant changes of many major social institutions.

1500S–1770S:
MERCANTILISM (MERCHANT CAPITALISM)

The sixteenth and seventeenth centuries did not mark the era of full-blown capitalism, but feudalism and the institutions we associate with feudalism were being radically recast as social, economic and political power was passing from the feudal aristocracy to merchants and large landholders often working in alliance with the monarchs who controlled the newly established and emerging nation-states. Enormous wealth was accumulated in western Europe through global military conquest, plunder, colonization and trade, often conducted by large joint stock companies that employed wage labour in both Europe and abroad. In England a number of important institutional changes occurred, including the decline of the Roman Catholic Church; the centralization of state power; the restructuring of the countryside as the enclosure movements resulted in the loss of common land and pastures, driving many peasants and serfs off the land; the growth of urban centres; and the rise of science and new forms of education. Additionally, the emergence of the putting-out system began to radically alter craft production, with traditional craft producers losing control as merchants and small capitalists began to provide raw materials, and sometimes tools and manufacturing. In short, virtually every social institution from the family through education and the state was radically altered.

1770S–1860S: INDUSTRIAL CAPITALISM

The pace of social, political and economic change increased dramatically in the Industrial Revolution. In England, population growth continued, creating new demand for textiles, stimulating technological development and innovation. The use of water power declined with the advent of steam power. Science and technology revolutionized the iron and steel industry, giving rise to increased demand for coal and iron. Steam power meant that industry could be located anywhere, resulting in new industrial cities emerging near sources of iron and coal while the railroad boom transported the products to once-distant markets. Part of the increasing demand for food was met by expanded agriculture involving both tenant producers and large landholders who were revolutionizing country life, resulting in the dispossession of thousands upon thousands of families who joined the growing industrial labour force. Family-based craft and small producers were driven out of production by less expensive products produced in the large factories that now employed thousands and thousands of workers, mostly at subsistence wages. The power of the church (now churches) was in decline.

These changes were, of course, really changes to the class structure. In England, the absolute monarchs who had been central to the creation of centralized nation-states in the mercantile era were essentially deposed in 1688 with the so-called Glorious Revolution, meaning that, in essence, the ascending "new middle class" of industrial capitalists increasingly controlled the state. The strong, centralized, highly regulatory mercantilist state that had been essential in setting the conditions necessary for the functioning of the emerging markets now came under systematic attack with the 1776 publication of the new gospel of competitive capitalism, Adam Smith's *The Wealth of Nations*. The state remained important because market society could not have developed nor could it exist without the constant supervision and action of a nation-state (Polanyi 1944).

The benefits and implications of social, cultural, economic and political transformations were, of course, not uniformly distributed across society or among the various social classes:

The workers bore the social cost of industrialization. The new factory system reduced most of them to poor, unhealthy, dehumanized wretches. Classical liberalism was not only impervious to their plight, it even taught that the desire to improve the conditions of the poor was quixotic and doomed to failure. (Hunt 1981: 64)

As a result, the era produced many radical thinkers, such as Karl Marx (1818–1863), Robert Owen (1771–1858), Henri de Saint-Simon (1760–1825) and a host of other radicals.

Although competitive industrial capitalism did increase the overall amount of material wealth, it also had internal mechanisms and dynamics that led to its transformation. In a competitive market, sellers compete for buyers in order to sell their products and thus make profits. Inevitable and necessary outcomes of competition are winners and losers. In a capitalist market the losers tend to go out of business, are bought up by more successful enterprises or merge with other firms. As a result, over time the number of producers will go down while the size of the units or enterprises remaining will increase. John Bellamy Foster, Robert W. McChesney and R. Jamil Jonna (2011: 3–4) describe the process:

> Monopoly, in this sense, is the logical result of competition, and should be expected. It is in the DNA of capitalism. For Karl Marx, "the larger capitals," as a rule, "beat the smaller … Competition rages in direct pro-portion to the number, and in inverse proportion to the magnitude of the rival capitals. It always ends in the ruin of many small capitalists, whose capitals partly pass into the hands of their competitors, and partly vanish completely. Apart from this, an altogether new force comes into existence with the development of capitalist production: the credit system." Credit or finance, available more readily to large firms, becomes one of the two main levers, along with competition itself, in the centralization process. By means of mergers and acquisitions, the credit system can create huge, centralized agglomerations of capital in the "twinkling of an eye." The results of both concentration and centralization are commonly referred to as economic concentration.

Robert Heilbroner (1968: 109) adds: "A system originally characterized by large numbers of small enterprises was starting to give way to one in which production was increasingly concentrated in the hands of a relatively few, very big and very powerful business units." There was, then, an inherent dynamic or logic operative in the age of competitive capitalism that eventually transformed the core economic institutions, changing the nature of the economy, economic activity, the class structure and the modes of profit-seeking economic activity.

1860S-1929/30: CORPORATE CAPITALISM

While the joint stock company had been an important part of the economic landscape for several hundred years, it was during the era of corporate capitalism that large corporations became the dominant economic actor. Between the end of the U.S. Civil War (marking the triumph of the industrial North) and the Great Depression, capitalism underwent a major transformation, resulting in a remarkable shift. In the immediate post-Civil War period, the size and power of the emerging large corporate enterprises allowed them to enter into what is commonly called cutthroat market competition. This competitive phase resulted, as one would expect, in the growth of some enterprises and the elimination of others, further exacerbating the concentration and centralization of capital in the hands of fewer and larger operations.

As corporations got larger and fewer in number, many came to understand that at a certain point excessive price competition is risky and counterproductive in terms ensuring profit generation. As a result corporate cooperative agreements or trusts emerged along with multiple mergers and the formation of holding companies, all geared to reducing competition among corporations and thus enhancing profits (Heilbroner 1968: 111–13). As a result, the market was changing, moving away from competition to monopoly and/or oligopoly price setting, meaning that rather than competition in the market setting the price, a few large producers were able to influence if not set prices, either as a result of actual collusion or an informal understanding that one supplier was the price setter and when that producer raised prices others followed.

Larger and larger multinational corporations, typically supported in their search for raw materials and markets by nation-states, controlled major sectors of many capitalist economies. The early twentieth century was characterized by the establishment of trusts, as in the Standard Oil Trust, as well as mergers and the creation of giant holding companies. So significant was the growth of concentrated economic power that Robert Heilbroner refers to it as the threat of economic feudalism (1968: 113). A short recession followed the First World War, but the great car boom marked the emergence of the so-called Roaring Twenties. Mitchell (1967: 172) notes that by the end of the 1920s there were over twenty-six million cars registered in the U.S., "enough to permit every person in America to go riding at once." The decade of excess accurately described by Mark Twain's *The Gilded Age* and F. Scott Fitzgerald's *The Great Gatsby* came to an unhappy ending in 1929. The Great Depression, the impact of the near collapse of capitalism on everyone, men and boys included, cannot be overemphasized.

1930S–1970S: KEYNESIAN STATE/CORPORATE MONOPOLY CAPITALISM

On October 29, 1929 (Black Thursday), the New York Stock market began a precipitous and catastrophic collapse that would see over eighty-five thousand business failures in the next three years in the U.S. alone. Among the casualties were over five thousand banks (Hunt 1981: 154–55). In Canada overall spending on all goods and services by everyone (including governments and corporations) fell by 42 percent while unemployment rose to over 30 percent (Struthers and Foot 2013). As unemployment rose and farmers lost their land, as businesses failed and banks closed leaving depositors empty-handed, social discontent and unrest increased. Membership in socialist and communist parties increased across the Western world as governments fretted and worried about an impending revolution. In the absence of a substantial welfare or social assistance system, in Canada the federal government initially reacted by pushing the problem off on the provinces and increasing repression. Lorne Brown (1987) tells the story of state repression and intimidation in the establishment of work camps and virtual slave labour for many of the unemployed.

Perhaps the most important outcome of the Depression was the Keynesian revolution, named after British economist John Maynard Keynes. He suggested that if overall total or aggregate demand for goods and services declines significantly, resulting in massive business failures and unemployment, the state should spend money to create demand. State spending on education, health care and welfare, or investment in infrastructure, for example, could stimulate or kick-start the economy, creating demand and thus stimulating investment and employment. Once the economy was up and running again the state would withdraw its activities and use tax revenues to pay off any costs accrued as a result of the expenditures it had engaged in. While many Western states such as Canada and the U.S. did engage in moderate spending efforts, ironically it was the massive state spending in the preparation for and the actual conduct of the Second World War that stimulated economic growth, particularly in those nations not devastated by the war.

The intervention of the state to ensure a smooth functioning, corporate-dominated economy marked the beginning of a new form of capitalism — an era of mass production and mass consumption of both consumer and capital goods under the growing international leadership of the U.S. The era also saw the emergence of the welfare state as part of an overarching political and class compromise in most Western industrial nations. That compromise involved a set of social and political arrangements through which business/corporations, labour and the state regulated economic, social and political affairs more or less to everyone's agreement and benefit. In this post–war "social contract," unions focused on the improvement of pay and working conditions. The state provided a social safety net and used its resources to direct investment and economic activity (especially economic development aid for selected regions and industries) for the benefit of both capital and labour. Business was free to make the most of the nation's economic decisions within these broad constraints. This overall system came to be called the Fordist accumulation regime, perhaps even "Happy Days" (to borrow the name of the 1974–84 ABC sitcom that represented the comfortable life of middle-class America in the 1950s and 1960s during the post-war boom).

By the late 1960s and early 1970s, however, the Fordist accumulation regime began to face a number of interrelated crises. After the destruction of the Second World War, Japan and parts of Europe had been rebuilt with American aid and now possessed new and more efficient technologies and were able to produce better consumer and other products more efficiently. Consumers in North America bought these less expensive and sometimes superior goods. In addition, capitalists, especially big business, found themselves with large amounts of cash and increasingly fewer investment opportunities. Ongoing investment in profitable ventures is a necessary precondition for sustained economic activity in the capitalist system. Added to these problems were the advancing globalization of business and growing state fiscal debts and deficits, partly as a result of the U.S. spending billions of dollars financing the Cold War, the space race, and the actual war in Vietnam.

Structural economic problems were emerging. In addition to the growing fiscal crises of various states and increasing inflation, in many Western countries individual or consumer debt was growing as a result of the successful sales efforts of the major corporations and the spread of suburbia (Sweezy and Magdoff 1974). The post-war prosperity of the Western world was based on very inexpensive petroleum energy; however, a series of international political events resulted in the formation of an oil-producer cartel, the Organization of Arab Petroleum Exporting Countries (OAPEC) in 1968. By the early 1970s OAPEC began to control the supply of oil, significantly raising the international price. The beginning of a transitional era was marked by disruptions to the international financial system, growing public and private debts, declining investment, globalization and a sense of malaise among those with capital.

1970S–2008/9: NEO-LIBERAL GLOBAL CAPITALISM

What emerged after the early 1970s was a new system or mode of economic organization called "flexible accumulation." The world was becoming smaller in terms of the ability of capital to circulate because of advances in telecommunications and transportation (Harvey 1989). It now became possible to establish factories literally anywhere in the world, monitor production activities electronically and have components and finished products transported anywhere by fleets of super-sized container cargo ships. Various international trade agreements, overseen by international financial institutions, facilitate the mobility of capital manufacturing operations to move to cheap labour zones. In much of the Western world, "flexible" work patterns emerged, characterized by workers on short-term contracts frequently changing jobs and moving to different industries and different places over their lifetimes. In addition, consumption and cultural patterns shifted, becoming more diverse with international foods and other commodities becoming readily available, marking a shift away from traditional Western or Northern industrial domination. Flexible accumulation also brought new roles and dynamics to the functions and operation of the nation-state.

The 1970s marked the emergence of a series of crises for the Keynesian welfare state system. These crises included growing government deficits, international competition among capitalist economies, increasing regional disparities and the growing internationalization of capital. In response to these upheavals, many governments began to implement a series of neo-liberal, pro-market public policies, including widespread and deep cuts to a wide range of social programs, such as Medicare, school support, day-care programs and international aid, all designed to reduce government spending and regulation while allowing the market to become more dominant in every aspect of our lives.

An associated development with significant implications for gender relations was the concomitant rise of an ideological climate that is typically called neo-conservatism. Partly a backlash to the perceived liberalism of the late 1960s and early 1970s in terms of sexual mores, lifestyles, acceptance of gay and lesbian rights, the gains of the women's movement, changing family patterns and so on, neo-conservatism took several forms. In some cases it was attached to and bolstered by conservative religious movements, in other cases by a reaction to some of the regulation and support of the Keynesian state. Despite its various manifestations, neo-conservative ideology emphasized individual freedom and responsibility, traditional family values (support for traditional nuclear family), less state involvement in many fields (except the military) and individual responsibility. Neo-conservatism was, in essence, the ideological justification or arm of the new liberal revolution.

2008/09 TO PRESENT: AGE OF UNCERTAINTY

Although perhaps less dramatic than the crash of 1929, the by now largely unregulated market activities in the banking, insurance, finance and housing sectors produced a major financial crisis in 2008/09. This crisis brought with it a significant number of bankruptcies, a collapse in many housing markets, bank failures in some countries and, of course, rising unemployment and growing poverty. Although most Western governments had been committed to neo-liberal deregulation and cuts in state spending, the crisis demanded action. As a result, 2009/10 saw the return to active state interventions. As the crisis threatened the entire economic order, Western democratic states rushed in with a variety of bailout packages for a variety of sectors of the economy, from the banks and insurance industries to the automotive companies, plus some infrastructure spending to create construction jobs. In Canada, for example, the Conservative government, previously die-hard anti-Keynesians, announced a $47 billion stimulus-spending package in its 2009 budget (Curry and McKenna 2014). The complexity of the American response is difficult to estimate; however, a U.S. Treasury document estimates the cost at 8.8 million jobs lost, $19.2 trillion worth of household wealth lost, while the Troubled Asset Relief Program (only one part of the government's actions) cost $24 trillion USD. (Financial Crisis Response 2012). Although the full impact of these measures is still to be determined, they did result in significant increases to debts and deficits in virtually every Western nation, deficits and debts it seems that we will be addressing for the next decade or more. Unlike the shift to Keynesian economics in the 1930s it does not seem that the most recent efforts of the state to stabilize global capitalism have changed the dominant ideological stance of most governments. Indeed, it seems as if governments are prepared to accept high levels of unemployment, unstable labour markets and growing poverty. The prevalence of neo-liberal thinking means that these deficits and debts will be addressed through cuts in government spending and services and government revenue increases, giving rise to another decade or more of instability in terms of the provision of social services.

CAPITALISM: A SUMMARY

I have argued that the last five hundred years have seen radical changes in how capital engages in profit generation and capital accumulation, including, first, a shift from mercantile and trade activities to small- and then large-scale industrial production. As industrial capitalism emerged in the seventeenth century, enterprises were typically small and the forms of organization often family based. As the capitalist system evolved during the 1800s, technology became more advanced and important, and as the size of enterprises grew, we saw larger and larger joint stock companies and corporations. Individuals with money to invest increasingly became stockholders in larger and larger corporations as opposed to running a family or individually owned enterprise. The role of the state changed in each era, being important during the initial era as new forms of law and state regulation were required to make markets function. As industrialization developed, capitalists became more secure in their operations and with the infrastructure necessary for the operations of markets in place, new ideas about the role of the state emerged. Although the state remained essential in terms of guaranteeing the smooth operation of the system, during the 1800s many argued that the state's role should be minimized. As capitalism continued to develop with the emergence of large multi-national corporations, periodic crises resulted in yet another shift in the role of the state, most dramatically demonstrated by the major state interventions that were required during the Great Depression. The post-war boom, partly based on successful state regulation of a "social contract" between labour, capital and the state, provided a temporary respite to the crises of the 1930s and 1940s; however, by the early 1970s storm clouds were on the horizon. Declining levels of corporate investment, growing personal and private debts and a neo-conservative ideology ushered in an era of deregulation, cuts to social spending and the resurgence of market ideologies in every aspect of life. What followed was a booming stock market, wildly increasing housing prices, the so-called dot-com bubble and eventually the 2008/09 collapse. As we struggle to understand the significance of all this, we can be sure of two things, that the system remains fundamentally capitalist in nature and that all these changes have radically transformed virtually every other institutional order and sphere of human activity, and in so doing the character, activities and practice of gender.

CAPITALISM AND WORK

The emergence of mercantilism in England and parts of Western Europe circa 1500 was a revolutionary event. In the 150 years that followed, every major institution, including family structures, the polity, education, religion and the church, family and gender order, and of course the economic order in England, was radically transformed. Feudal society was characterized by a patriarchal gender order, bolstered and supported by major institutions such as the church. The nation-states that emerged in England and Europe, despite the occasional period of formal rule by a female monarch, were largely male-controlled (Hartman 1976: 146). While the teachings of the patriarchal church would have been supported by the traditional feudal code of chivalry, and to the extent that they were known, elements of misogamy from classical Western philosophy, the adjective "anxious" has been applied to the patriarchy of the day (Harvey and Shepard 2005: 306). The anxiousness would be on behalf of the males, whose control of family members was tenuous at best given the importance attached to all roles in a domestic production unit not marked by a rigorous division of labour. As feudalism unfolded, the domestic or family basis of craft and artisan production, and the division of labour and relationships, changed in response to changing production techniques, new market imperatives and opportunities. Initially, production was organized around largely self-sufficient families; however, as populations grew, technology improved, markets emerged and the character of family-based production changed as the division of labour became more rigid, with some members working outside the family for wages. A somewhat similar process occurred for those families involved in agricultural production. As the economy grew, populations increased, trade expanded and technology developed, new products that characterized the putting-out system emerged and producers received what amounted to a wage and production. The final outcome was, of course, the centralization of production in factories eventually separated from the home site.

As these developments occurred there were concomitant changes to the overall class structure. The aristocracy was ever present, but the emerging merchant and nascent industrial capitalists were eroding its position, status and power. Divisions were emerging among the craft and artisan producers, as some were more able to keep abreast of the times, while others fell behind and were eliminated by the emerging forces of market competition. Likewise among agricultural producers, some prospered while others joined the growing ranks of those seeking to earn a living on the wage-labour market or fell into poverty and destitution.

THE FAMILY WAGE: SEX SEGREGATING THE LABOUR FORCE

Prior to the emergence of full-scale industry, the guild system had begun to sanction sex segregation in craft and artisan production, with men performing more skilled work and tasks and girls getting less training than boys (Hartman 1976: 150). In the absence of a full-fledged market, guilds controlled the entry of people into a line of production or activity as well as the quality and amount of products, training regimes and so on. The fact that men came to control the guilds, more so as they gained importance in the transition to capitalism, resulted in men using them to control competition and limit entry, dynamics that led to a degree of sex segregation (Hartman 1976: 150–151). As family industry and production declined and factory production became dominant, these patterns of sex segregation in production increasingly operated to the advantage of men, such as when guilds were able to organize higher pay rates for the work of their members. Additionally, in many cases women were denied the opportunity to work in factories and ended up in the household engaged in domestic labour. This was partly due, again, to the fact that men, who previously controlled the guilds, were better organized and thus able to take control of many new professions on matters such as entry and required skills. Add to this the patriarchal power and ideology of the organized Christian religious institutions, important at a time when religion and the church still played a role in the daily lives of many people, and we see an emerging picture of a sex-segregated labour force.

The emergence of a sex-segregated labour force as part and parcel of the emergence of industrial capitalism was given further impetus by the actions of Victorian upper-class reformers. Many members of the aristocracy clung to a rather unique set of beliefs, ideologies and practices, with a variety of origins, including mythology, religion, politics and poetry that I will loosely call the "code of chivalry." Whatever this mythic code was, it was a prescription and proscription for gendering. The explicit articulation of women's roles was as agents civilizing men and keeping them in line, thus making progress possible. While women were deemed to have a civilizing effect, it came at a cost to their public presence: "The home now became the abode of love and affection," but "the language of love was not the language of equality, quite the reverse" (Cohen 2005: 329). Indeed, many cast women as delicate and requiring protection, positioning men not just as superior but as protectors and governors because of their physical and mental strengths. "The man, as a protector, is directed by nature to govern" while the woman "delicate and timid, requires protection" and "conscious of inferiority, is disposed to obedience" (Cohen 2005: 329). Cohen (2005: 329) explains:

> This ordering of gender relations, integral to the notion of progress, was precisely embodied in the chivalric code, and the delicacy and weakness of women upon which revived chivalric masculinity was predicated was paradoxically the index not just of the refinement of a nation but of its progress and modernity.

Alarmed by the visible consequences of rampant poverty and suffering, informed by patriarchal and chivalrous ideologies, middle-class reformers (often the wives and daughters of the emerging capitalist class), some with their Christian consciences twigged, became aware that flagrant levels of inequality and social injustice were dangerous to the social order. Although many of the leaders, such as Edwin Chadwick (1800–1890), were males, many middle-class and wealthy women were involved in efforts to regulate child labour, improve working conditions in factories, address issues such as health, sanitation and crime and improve education. While progress was actually made, there were definite consequences for the sex and gender composition of the labour force. Many working-class women welcomed legislation that improved working conditions, but often the legislation went further by actually preventing women from taking certain jobs — a move that some men endorsed: "That male workers viewed the employment of women as a threat to their jobs is not surprising, given an economic system where compensation among workers is characteristic. That women were paid lower wages exacerbated the threat" (Hartmann 1976: 155).

Following parliamentary reform in the 1830s further social regulation followed in the 1840s, including the popularization of the notion of the family wage. Working-class men themselves would not have been immune to the patriarchal and chivalrous notion that they, as men, should be the providers for their families even if it meant keeping their wives and daughters out of the factory:

> In order to secure their own income, male workers actively sought to exclude female competition in agricultural labour, especially the more remunerative harvest tasks of all types. Here, the class agency of male labourers, rather than capitalists, seems especially important in explaining the further subordination of women in the wage-dependent division of labour ... pre-existing patriarchal norms were utilized as a resource for securing reproduction under the conjunctural conditions of the capitalist economy. In the process patriarchy was instantiated but also transformed in its specific social content. (Blank 2011: 24)

The question of the family wage, how the notion was promoted, who benefited and how it was implemented remains an important debate among feminist scholars. If we think back to the notion of the patriarchal dividend discussed in Chapter 1, then for men working in the difficult circumstances that characterized industrial production, the prospect of having meals prepared, the house cleaned and the children cared for at day's end was without a doubt an attractive prospect. Additionally, I have noted that the overall ideological climate of Western society is distinctly patriarchal, and like all climates it would have been pervasive and omnipresent. It seems clear then that when it came to establishing domestic labour as one element of the patriarchal dividend, the family wage was important. In their discussion of the modern political dimensions of the issue, Michelle Barrett and Mary McIntosh (1982: 53) commented on the emergence of the notion and developments in the early 1880s:

> Hence it became imperative, both from the point of view of the capitalist class as a whole and from the point of view of the working class, to protect the life and health of the industrial [working class]. There has been dispute as to whether the measures subsequently taken to assure the adequate reproduction of the working class are to be understood as the fruit of successful class struggle on the part of the working class, or as successful collective control by capital of the instruments of production — the labourers themselves. Certainly it seems the case that there was a coincidence of interests, though not of course a formal alliance, between [capitalist] philanthropists and the [capitalist] state on the one hand and the emergent ... trade union movement on the other. The Factory Acts of

the 1840s, limiting the length of the working day, the protective legislation aimed at the reduction of female and child labour and, later in the century, the introduction of elementary education all formed part of this process.

This conjoining of interests indicates the partnership between capitalism and patriarchy (1981: 19–25).

TRADE UNIONS AND SEX SEGREGATING THE LABOUR FORCE

Unions played a role in the development of sex segregation in the labour market. After the 1820s, when trade unions were made legal in England, they undertook efforts to impose closed shops to protect the jobs of members and extract better wages from employers. Burnette (2008: 244) notes: "Gender ideology and economic incentives played a joint role in leading unions to demand the exclusion of women from their trades. Unions desired to limit access to their trades, in order to reduce labour supply and increase their wages. Gender ideology made women a natural target." Economic imperatives and male resistance to competition for wages were more important, particularly the case with professional occupations where body size and strength could not be hauled out as the basis of discrimination (290).

Labour force and occupational segregation in Canada shifted between 1900 and 1960: "In 1900 almost one-third of the female labour force was employed in manufacturing, while clerical work represented only 8 percent of female employment. The largest share of the female labour force, 56 percent, was employed in services, including professional and domestic services" (Fortin and Huberman2002: S13). Over the thirty years from 1900 to 1930, one of the fastest periods of economic growth in Canadian history, significant changes took place: "By 1930, blue and white collar workers had traded places. Manufacturing had reduced its share of female employment to 14 percent, and clerical tasks claimed 22 percent of the female workers" (S13). There was further female concentration in "clerical work, sales, health occupations (predominantly nursing) and teaching."

There is considerable evidence that, in the past at least, trade unions played a role in this sex segregation of the labour force. Christina Burr, for example, argues that in the nineteenth- and early twentieth-century printing trades, "gender interests prevailed over those of class in the attempts by male trades unionists to exclude women from the better-paying jobs" (1993: 51). Unions tried to protect members; nevertheless, "between 1850 and 1914 … male unionists implemented exclusionary strategies in defence of masculine craft status which contributed to the perpetuation of the gender division of labour within the printing trades and restricted women to the jobs of press feeding and forwarding in the bindery — all jobs which were socially designated as unskilled by men" (72). In the male-dominated telegraph industry, that males tried to protect their jobs during periods of technological change is understandable, but such efforts must be deemed efforts to protect an aspect of a patriarchal dividend in that excluding women was about the self-interest of males. There was some sharing of tasks, however:

> By itself, cooperative labour shared by these women and men had little effect on the meanings they made of gender. Masculinity retained its promise of higher wages and superior status. When the fulfillment of this promise was jeopardized by technological change, unionists distinguished themselves from the automatic operators, and forced employers both to reaffirm the entitlements of skill and to entrench gender hierarchy in the industry. In this new class rapprochement, Morse telegraphy became, more than ever, "men's" work. (Tillotson 1991: 124)

Bonnie Fox and John Fox (2008: 377) make a more general point with regard to the nature of the internal competition men faced and their efforts to protect their income:

> The organizational strength of the male proletariat, in the early years of industrialization, was partly the product of a collective perception that low-paid female labour represented a threat not only to wages and jobs but also to masculinity. And the collective response to the upheaval of work due to industrialization involved a defense of the traditional, patriarchal family and male definitions of masculinity (involving notions of skill and family headship). Thus, not surprisingly, male unions controlled entry to apprenticeship in ways that excluded women, procured the labeling of many jobs held by men as skilled, despite their deskilling, established male monopolies over "skilled" work done with certain machines; and fought for protective legislation for women, and more generally for a "family wage" that would entrench male headship and female economic dependence.

Radical union politics were not immune to the patriarchal nature of the times. In the One Big Union (OBU): "Conventions where working men met and discussed politics were a tradition in Canada, and while there were three female delegates to the Western Labor Conference, the overtly masculinist atmosphere of the gathering was evident both in terms of numbers and the concerns it addressed" (McCallum 1998: 15). A delegate to the organizing conference of the OBU called on other delegates to take power into their hands "to save not only yourself, your mothers, wives and sisters, and your children, but the whole human race." Commenting on the speech, McCallum (52) writes:

In passages such as these, the revolutionary movement was centred around working men, who alone possessed the "might" to realize a socialist society. "The Spectre of Industrial Unionism" was perhaps the closest the practices of radical manhood came to being a consciously articulated program of male dominance through union power and familial control.

Although there is little evidence of formal legislative or regulatory bases for a sex-segregated labour force in Canada, such a labour force did emerge as industrialization occurred. In some cases it was partly the result of male efforts to protect their jobs and wages, while in other cases traditional values and patriarchal ideologies seemed to have played a role. The emergence of routine office work as largely the domain of females is illustrative of a process that, while not necessarily deliberately guided by the hands of males, segregated the labour force by sex. The era from approximately the end of the American Civil War was marked by the emergence of the large and increasingly multinational corporation. The normal functioning of such large and increasingly diverse enterprises required a significant bureaucratic effort. The process has gender implications:

> The ascendancy of corporate capitalism in Canada precipitated a revolution in the means of administration. Buoyed by the wheat boom on the western frontier, a growing population, and expanding markets, industrialization accelerated after 1900. By the end of World War I, Canada's modern industrial structure was largely in place. In both manufacturing and services the predominant form of organization became the modern corporation, a vast bureaucratic structure that separated ownership and control, delegating operating authority to specialized managers. Large administrative staffs were hired to handle the mounting flow of paper work. This expansion of the office can be traced to the growing scale and complexity of economic activity, as well as to the extension of managerial control and coordination functions. The office became the managerial nerve centre through which voluminous information vital for controlling all aspects of business was compiled, processed, and stored. (Lowe 1982: 15)

As corporate and other bureaucracies expanded and multiplied and as technologies impacted the office and the required skill sets, a process of gendering emerged: "By 1930 the clerical labour market had been Balkanized into male and female compartments. As a result, women competed among themselves for the new, bottom tier of detailed administrative jobs, while men contended for the better positions" (Lowe 1987: 83). Once labeled on the basis of sex, labour market patterns tend to become fixed and difficult to change, and when combined with societal (and patriarchal) expectations concerning work, marriage and a woman's "proper role," the die was cast (198).

MEN, MASCULINITY AND WHITE SETTLER NATIONS

The major economic and other institutional changes and dynamics of the global capitalist system take on national and local variations and manifestations in different locales. If you take a nation-state such as Canada as an example, the early part of the century saw the establishment of a significant new class of independent agricultural commodity producers — family farms — with the settlement of the Prairies. The creation of the Western wheat economy stimulated a period of sustained industrial growth in southern Ontario and the St. Lawrence Basin, fostering the development of an industrial working class in those regions.

The settlement of Western Canada largely by European immigrants, between the 1890s and the 1920s and under the auspices of the famous "national policy" of the late nineteenth and early twentieth centuries, is a story much recounted in Canadian history. Driven by state policy in the interests of industrial and finance capitalists, the establishment of hundreds of thousands of family farms was a distinctly patriarchal process with male property titles and lineage despite the vital contributions of women and girls. The long hours and arduous labour required to acquire, operate and maintain a traditional family farm was exceedingly difficult, strenuous and tedious for both frontier men and women; however, there is no doubt as to the patriarchal patterns of ownership, control, decision-making and rewards. This form of masculinity is both hegemonic and imperial: "It ensures that men have superior control over goods and property, over the state and the military, and over women's bodies" (Erickson 2011: 26). In the settlement of the British Dominions, this particular manifestation of hegemonic masculinity had an imperial and unsentimental — if not racist — element when it came to the removal of Indigenous populations in order to facilitate European settlement (see Daschuk 2013).

With Western settlement a major national economic priority, the North American frontier man emerged as an iconic figure. The frontier man represented men whose daily practices and activities, gender related and otherwise, came close in actuality to certain aspects of the hegemonic ideal. Mark Sheftall (2015: 98) describes this particular manifestation of hegemonic masculinity:

> It did not matter a great deal whether that frontier was imagined as the Canadian wilderness or the Australian outback, the martially-useful qualities attributed to the white manhood ... were essentially the same: courage, fortitude, tenacity, stamina, physical fitness, pugnacity, initiative, optimism, and so on. These virtues were, not coincidentally, also typically

associated with long-standing stereotypes of the "pioneer" or "frontiers-man," one of the stock figures synonymous with New World settlement, including in the British Dominions.

The frontier man was a geographic and occupational version of the kind of man developing in the late 1800s and early 1900s generally in Canada: "Competitiveness, aggressiveness, and ambition all became values in themselves and were no longer attached primarily to the economic sphere ... Toughness, physical strength, athletic skill, and personal appearance became vaunted male qualities: tenderness, self-restraint, and self-denial were no longer considered masculine virtues" (Nelson 2010: 75).

So powerful was the mythology and reality of this notion of masculine practice that it remains important to this day. Rural masculine practices in a number of countries represent a range of different masculine practices, not all of them in the hegemonic mode (Campbell et al. 2006). Masculine practice and ideology impacts whether a farmer pursues a traditional agrarian, an industrial or a sustainable approach to farming and the land. Research has demonstrated that farmers who adopted traditional hegemonic masculine practices tend to adopt discourse and language associated with the notion of the "self-made man" and the associated importance of toughness, hard work, individualism and self reliance, along with the use of big machines to dominate and control nature. Those farmers more interested in sustainability are typically more open to working with nature than controlling it and seeing what works as opposed to making it work (Barlett 2006: 54–59). Masculinity in the context of local social interactions, including those in the pub, impacted the lifestyles and life chances of various members of the community, including the extent to which men understood themselves to be members of a community that support each other or rugged individuals in a competitive struggle (Campbell 2006). Notions of manliness were modified yet clearly expressed in ways understandable as local expressions of hegemonic masculinity. Importance was attributed to masculinist virtues, and how through "aggressive competition and individualism, by self-reliance and self-control" society's goals would be met in the frontier environment (Hogg 2012: 174).

THE FIRST "GREAT" WAR AND THE GREAT DEPRESSION

That there was an imperial element to the frontier masculinities in Canada and the other British settler dominions was illustrated all too well by the First World War, a tragedy that was to reshape gender relations in a significant way. The global crisis of the First World War resulted in the battlefield deaths of about sixty thousand Canadians, and the first major entry of women into heavy industry in order to replace men who were at war. The practices and ideologies of hegemonic frontier masculinity in Canada and Australia, for example, were well suited for the war effort: "In both countries the prevailing ... cultural image was of hardy, athletic, resourceful individuals gifted with a natural talent for warfare (if not the discipline and submission to authority necessary for soldiering), thanks in large part to the biological influences and formative experiences of a frontier lifestyle and/or pioneer heritage" (Sheftall 2015: 84). The commander of the Canadian Corps (as quoted in Sheftall 2015: 85) said:

> The rugged strength of the Canadian is depicted in his broad shoulders, deep chest and strong, clean-cut limbs. His eyes are keen and steady, while behind the calm gravity of his mien lies a tenacious and indomitable will. These are the invaluable gifts of our deep forests and lofty mountains, of our rolling plains and our great waterways, and of the clear light of our Northern skies, gifts which have enabled the Canadian to adapt himself readily and well to the new conditions he found confronting him as a soldier.

And fight they did — over sixty thousand died in the killing fields of Europe and many more were injured. While wars unfortunately typically do not teach us much, among the outcomes of the First World War was the realization that young men, no matter how apparently manly and tough, are vulnerable. Although not understood well at the time, the concept of shell shock emerged from the unimaginable horrors of daily death, hunger, cold and disease. Michael Rop (2005) points out that virtually an entire generation of men suffered life-long physical, spiritual and psychological trauma as a result of what they saw and did. Megan Brush (2014: n.p.) explains the enduring impact of the war:

> By the end of the First World War, the British army had dealt with approximately 80,000 cases of shell shock or war neurosis. In 1917, one-seventh of discharges from the British military for disabilities claimed war neurosis as the cause. Four out of five cases of shell shock were never able to return to service. At the time, symptoms of shell shock varied from spasms, paralysis, mutism, deafness, and nightmares to uncontrollable trembling.

While many men were paying the price for their adherence to the dominant motifs of masculinity, many women were themselves increasingly demanding basic human and civil rights. The history of modern Western thought includes, although often ignored, the legacy of thinkers such as Olympe de Gouges and her critique of the limits of the human rights envisioned by the leaders of the French Revolution, Mary Wollstonecraft, Harriet Taylor Mill, Helen Taylor, Charlotte Perkins Gilman, Jane Addams and many others. What these and others did was to inspire those women we typically refer to under the general banner of First Wave feminism. Having been recruited to replace men in factories and fields, many women began to understand the importance of what First Wave feminists were advocating. There was a relatively rapid extension of the right to vote province by province, and of course, the formal recognition in 1929 of women as persons and not someone's ward or property (Nelson 2010: 76).

The boom that followed the First World War, the so-called Roaring Twenties, with its expansion of virtually every sector of the economy brought further changes to class and gender relations. The continual introduction of new technologies changed the workforce with new occupations and jobs emerging while others were rendered obsolete. The growth of larger and more complex enterprises brought with it a proliferation of managerial, administrative and white-collar jobs. By the 1920s the Western frontier was largely settled and many of the strenuous tasks in economic sectors such as farming and forestry were becoming mechanized. Likewise, in industry many of the most physically demanding jobs were mechanized. As Jane Nicholas (2012: 45) says of masculinity during this period: "By the early decades of the twentieth century, Canada's patterns of settlement had changed along with the rapid expansion of urban industrialization, but the dominant discourse of rugged, natural masculine landscape remained and was caught in the representations of modern masculinity." She notes that, although artistic expressions of Canada such as the work of the Group of Seven expressed this vision, the real lives of many men was different, partly because of the impact of the war: "During the interwar period, sparked by the health crisis among military recruits during World War I, a renewed 'crisis of masculinity' seemed to require that both men and the nation take an active role in developing manhood" (45).

The post-war emergence of the radio plus the continued importance of newspapers and magazines offering various consumer goods provided an opportunity to use the emerging advertising industry to market images, resulting in some men adopting a more feminine masculinity. The advent of what Nicholas calls "consumer masculinity" was the result; however, it was soon to become apparent that a purely consumer-driven capitalism exhibits inherent instabilities.

The calamity of the Great Depression was, not surprisingly, felt differently across the class structure although few escaped unscathed. For those, regardless of their occupation, who relied on the sale of their labour power the impact was immediate and direct:

> In Canada the changes were dramatic. Between 1929 and 1933 the country's Gross National Expenditure [overall public and private spending] fell by 42 percent. By 1933, 30 percent of the labour force was out of work, and one in five Canadians had become dependent upon government relief

for survival. The unemployment rate would remain above 12% until the start of the Second World War in 1939. (Struthers and Foot 2015: n.p.)

It is clear that the Great Depression also had a major impact on gender practices. First off, there is the fact that many men viewed themselves as the breadwinner, a sense and fact reinforced by notions such as the family wage. Indeed, it is safe to say that for many men the breadwinner role was part and parcel of their identity and the way they practised gender at home, on the street and of course at work. Susan Ware (n.d.), on the basis of her study of women during the Great Depression, concludes: "Men were socialized to think of themselves as breadwinners; when they lost their jobs or saw their incomes reduced, they felt like failures because they couldn't take care of their families." The fact that most Western capitalist economies were increasingly sex segregated also played an important role in how the Depression impacted sex and gender relations:

> The Great Depression affected women and men in quite different ways. The economy of the period relied heavily on so-called "sex-typed" work, or work that employers typically assigned to one sex or the other. And the work most directly associated with males, especially manufacturing in heavy industries like steel production, faced the deepest levels of lay-offs during the Great Depression. Women primarily worked in service industries, and these jobs tended to continue during the 1930s. Clerical workers, teachers, nurses, telephone operators, and domestics largely found work. In many instances, employers lowered pay scales for women workers, or even, in the case of teachers, failed to pay their workers on time. But women's wages remained a necessary component in family survival. In many Great Depression families, women were the only breadwinners. (Boehm 2015: 1050)

Among the consequences of the Great Depression was political instability with the rise of social protest and an increase in support for left-wing political parties and causes; however, the era also saw increasing support for fascism, which had an impact on gender and the importance of social relations within the patriarchal family, focusing on the role of the father in the development of personality and learning to be submissive to authority, as the father was as a source and controller of money and income: "To yield to his father because the latter has the money is, in his eyes, the only reasonable thing to do, independently of any consideration of the father's human qualities" (Horkheimer 1972: 106–7). Dangerous circumstances unfold when the patriarchal father who has imbued his children with an acceptance of authority loses his position, perhaps due to unemployment: "The father is unable to justify his image in his child's eyes. In this situation the child retains a concept of the powerful but searches elsewhere for its fulfillment" (Held 1980: 132). As a result, "a general state of susceptibility is created to outside forces" (132). Such outside forces may be a political leader, a club or even another individual, the danger being that the authority-seeking child is adrift and looking for an anchor.

The relationship between the desire or need to exercise power, control and domination in gender practice and the inherent instabilities of life, particularly for those reliant on the sale of their labour in market society could be seen as a thread running through twentieth-century Western masculinity. Michael Kimmel (2005: 9) draws our attention to the question through a series of rhetorical questions:

> How could men feel secure in their manhood? How could men determine that they had made the grade and were successful as real men? If the marketplace, the very arena which they had established to demonstrate manhood was now fraught with peril and danger, where could they go?

As it turned out, the Second World War provided men a place to go, but unfortunately it too was fraught with life-threatening and life-taking danger.

THE SECOND GREAT WAR, "HAPPY DAYS" AND ANOTHER CRISIS

The system-threatening crisis of the Depression resulted in radical changes in economic theory in the form of the Keynesian revolution. Whether the anemic efforts of R.B. Bennett's Conservatives or Mackenzie King's Liberals to stimulate the economy would have eventually worked is a mute point because the onslaught of the Second World War ushered in an era of massive state spending in preparation for and then the conduct of the war. The importance of the war on men and gender relations is difficult to overestimate. Over 40 percent of men between the ages of 18 and 45 were in the Canadian military (Canada at War n.d.). In the wake of this massive exodus of men from their normal position in the labour force there was an influx of women into all sectors of the labour force (see Honey 2014). More than one million Canadians (both men and women but the majority were men) served in the Canadian Armed Forces, with more than 42,000 killed. As was the case with the First World War, many of those who survived were to bear the physiological and psychological scars of the traumas they endured for the rest of their lives. Needless to say, the absence of men and the increased labour force participation of many women resulted in significant changes to familial and gender relations. This was also the case when the soldiers returned.

Despite the absence of over one million individuals from their normal duties in various economic institutions, the Canadian economy prospered during the war in large part because of the increased labour-force participation of women and girls. While the war was costly and resulted in significant debt, the overall impact on the economy was positive. Indeed, Canadians were "buoyant if nervous" as they welcomed the returning soldiers because: "After sixteen years of war and depression, families now had money to spend" (Morton 1999: 226). Among the reasons for the optimism were the defeat of fascism internationally and the expansion of a range of social programs associated with the Keynesian welfare state. Donald Creighton (1976: 116), perhaps inadvertently, put it in more stark sex and gender terms: "The boys were coming home," noting that some had been away for as many as six years:

> All had accepted the long separation from family and friends, the cancellation of their plans, the interruption of their careers or the postponement of their education. They had sacrificed much for their country; and in return their country made a considerable effort to re-establish them, or to start them out in the best possible circumstances, in civilian life. They were given preferential treatment in finding jobs and financial assistance in setting themselves up again as householders and entrepreneurs. The great majority returned to their former employments, or settled on farms and smallholdings, or used their re-establishment credits to start new businesses or buy new equipment and tools.

Missing from this account are the women, some of whom came home with the "boys," but more of whom were displaced from their wartime jobs in mills, factories, stores, offices and farms by the retuning men.

Reintegrating men into the Canadian economy, actually, was not so much about reintegration into the economy as it was re-establishing patriarchy. Many women had taken paid employment to maintain their families during the Depression, while many more had joined virtually every branch of the economy during the war. Women had demonstrated once more that they were equally competent with men when it came to virtually every task, including running male-absent communities and families. Such a vivid demonstration of the competence, strength and capacity of women in patriarchal gender order and regimes produced turmoil: "This social, and gender turmoil was the backdrop to many Canadians' desire immediately after the war, that everything should return to normal" (Dummitt 2007: 4). What this meant was the hope "that Canadians' pent-up desires to marry and start families could now be realized and that the idealized type of family life, with male breadwinner and female homemaker, could now be reestablished" (4).

Resulting from the social and economic dynamics of the Depression and the Second World War there was a significant desire among many Canadians for stability and a return to order, the same pre-War ideological climate. The contradiction was, however, that the two main challenges to so-called normalcy, male unemployment and female paid employment, were outcomes of the Depression and the war (Dummitt 2007). There were a number of mechanisms in this "modernist project" that were engaged by various agents in an effort to restore patriarchal families and bolster hegemonic masculinity (Dummitt 2007). Among the measures taken to facilitate the return of veterans were a royal commission, officially titled the Royal Commission into the Complaints of Walter K Kirchner; the promotion of major infrastructure projects, many with attendant risks and stereotypical masculine job qualifications; the growth of masculine hobbies and leisure activities; when necessary, the use of the medical and judicial systems; and of course television and radio. In the end, the development of post-war Canada as a modern and more complex society was rife with contradictory tendencies and pressures; however, central among them were efforts by various social agencies to re-establish or perhaps establish in the new context, male authority and social power (Dummitt 2007).

Hard, gender-related work was necessary to re-establish some degree of commitment to patriarchal families when, "after World War II, Canadian men and women were expected to settle back into their former roles, despite the fact that women had moved beyond the domestic sphere for almost half the decades of the twentieth century" (Nelson 2010: 77). Further, "in changing and enlarging their behavioural repertories, women had demonstrated to themselves and men that they were capable of holding down jobs while managing family and home" (77). Nevertheless, there was relentless pressure from a variety of sources to re-establish the nuclear family as ideal, aided and abetted by the emerging social sciences, as in Talcott Parsons' pontification on the merits of the "normal American family."

Importantly, this was also the era of the post-war baby boom, with procreation rates that far outstripped any other era in the history of Canada, Australia, New Zealand and the U.S. During this time, a "procreation ethic" stressed marriage, parenthood and multiple children (Nelson 2010: 78). Baby experts such as Benjamin Spock, popular magazines and mainstream television promoted parenthood and the importance of the "breadwinner-homemaker conjugal model of nuclear family life" (Rutherdale 2012: 78).

The complex post-war economy was creating new opportunities, occupation-wise, for men even as workplaces were restructured by mechanization and technological innovation. Indeed, new occupations emerged in fields such as electronics, significantly stimulated by the Cold War, the space race and continued and growing U.S. military spending. The growing international presence of U.S.-based multinational corporations was changing; among other things, men's clothing styles, as the Western business suit became the costume of international business.

Globalization, although it was not necessarily called that yet, was the trend of the future. After the economic crisis that began in the early 1970s it was clear that the Happy Days were over in North America and that a new world was emerging.

NEO-LIBERALISM AND MASCULINITY

The post-war Happy Days were short lived, at least as the era of the patriarchal "normal American family." Second Wave feminists successfully analyzed and documented the negative impact of the nuclear family on women, even as some men began to assess the implications of having to practise gender with a narrow code of conduct expected of them. The legitimacy of the capitalist economic order was being questioned across the West and abroad; even though decolonization was occurring in many parts of the world, international corporations increased their investments across the global south in search of cheaper labour and raw materials. Neo-liberal political regimes in the U.S., Canada, England, Australia and New Zealand gleefully stripped away many social benefits and protections for the marginal, allowing previously supported and now deregulated enterprises to restructure by closing plant after plant, region after region, moving thousands of jobs to the global east and south.

The neo-liberal agenda had significant negative impacts on the lives of many women; however, men also faced a major challenge to the basis of their traditional manhood:

> Impacted by the global restructuring of capitalism, which has increased job insecurity and heightened competition within the labour force, in particular working class men, whose power and status depend primarily on their breadwinning ability, the loss of well-paying work and the attendant power that comes along with it represents a considerable threat to the authority of the Canadian male. (Greig and Holloway 2012: 127)

To the extent that such males attempted to engage in hegemonic gender practices, the restructuring of the labour force in Canada as a result of neo-liberalism and globalization has "worked to unsettle and undermine traditional white male entitlement, power and privilege" (128).

The destruction of major sectors of various Western industrial economies by neo-liberal deregulation and the flight of capital to low-wage regions in developing economies produced the economic context for the emergence of one of many "men in crisis" narratives. Among the many volumes examining the plight of post-industrial men in North America was Susan Faludi's *Stiffed: The Betrayal of the American Man* (1999). As a self-identified "feminist and journalist" (1999: 7), Faludi set out to investigate an apparent crisis that was manifested in the form of men's movements, domestic violence and expressions of political anger, believing at the onset that "the crisis of masculinity was caused by masculinity on the rampage" (7). Faludi contends, however, that what she found was not masculinity on a rampage, but men in a particular situation, that is, men who "had without exception lost their compass in the world." She elaborates: "They had lost or were losing jobs, homes, cars, families. They had been labeled outlaws but felt like castoffs. Their strongest desire was to be dutiful and to belong, to adhere with precision to the roles society had set out for them as men" (9). The roles of which she speaks are, of course, those of traditional males in patriarchal society practising their gender as being master of your universe; not in a superhero motif, but rather as the "common man" version of provider and not necessarily dominator.

Faludi (1999: 26) identifies four elements to the time-tested national male paradigm: 1) a frontier to claim; 2) an identifiable enemy to crush; 3) a group or brotherhood to which one might belong; and 4) a family to provide for and protect. The so-called crisis comes from the sense that in post-war America: "The frontier, the enemy, the institutions of brotherhood, the women in need of protection — all the elements of the old formula for attaining manhood vanished in short order" (30). Faludi tends to describe the impact of the changing global capitalist order without actually seeming critical of the necessary class dynamics of such processes, and as a result focuses excessive attention on men, fathers, brothers and sons while paying scant attention to the structural environment. As much as "fathers abandoned their sons" (36), in fact the neo-liberal restructuring of global capitalism resulted in fathers, sons, mothers, daughters, boys and girls in the U.S. being abandoned. She suggests that perhaps men could learn from the success of feminist women in promoting their interests. She does recognize the recession of the 1980s as pivotal in the destruction of the traditional industrial work arena and the entry of women into the dissolving labour market as catalysts for any male backlash. The irrational attachment of men to football clubs in an era of deindustrialization and other changes in men's social practices — from various men's movements to the various wars, the emergence of an ornamental male culture and pornography — speaks to the male paradigm and the lack of opportunity for men to engage in traditional hegemonic masculinity as enacted on a frontier, in engagement with enemies, alongside brothers and all while being providers. Overall, her study remains innocent of a serious critique of that supposed paradigm as an oppressive way of practising gender predicated as it is on the existence of a patriarchal dividend.

But, it is the plight of men and work in the era of neo-liberal global capitalism producing a sense of aggrieved entitlement that is the thread that ties the diverse issues together. For white males in the U.S., for example, it is the context of declining incomes, lack of hope generating anger, downward mobility and a general sense that the American dream is lost. Michael Kimmel (2013) points to the over 3500 right-wing talk shows spreading confusion, hatred and anger while reasserting a conservative patriarchal revival of masculinity. Even while some men resort to toughening their bodies in response to a sense of lost manhood, others seek escapism or some form of exclusion, ironically via inclusionary sexist, racist, anti-immigrant or nativist ideologies. The outcome of these coming avenues are not positive, often violent, not socially constructive, confusing and counter-productive to a more human world. The picture is not pretty as Kimmel (2013: 255, emphasis in original) explains:

> It is through a decidedly gendered and sexualized rhetoric of masculinity that this contradiction between loving America and hating its govern-ment, loving capitalism and hating its corporate iterations, is resolved. Racism, nativism, anti-Semitism, antifeminism — these discourses of hate provide an explanation for feelings of entitlement thwarted, fixing the blame squarely on "others" whom the state must now serve at the expense of white men. The underlying theme is *gender*.

Much more could be said about the ongoing right-wing backlash against femi-nism, immigration, social programs, minorities and all so-called entitlements other than those of supporters of global capital and patriarchy. But has the patriarchal dividend been eroded and how close are we to sex and gender equity in the labour force?

CANADA'S SEX-SEGREGATED LABOUR FORCE

In the past a number of mechanisms, factors and forces played roles in the develop-ment of the sex-segregated Canadian labour force. These included the impact of an English and European heritage; the overt actions of men; the overall patriarchal gender order with its modes of practising gender; state actions and policies; and the overall ideological environment. The focus is on women's work, however, it can be applied to the world of men's work, the other side of the coin.

One can examine labour force data in any number of ways; however, our prism will be the context of hegemonic masculinity and the patriarchal dividend, that is to say what jobs might typically pay more or less, have more or less power and social status. In 2006, for example, among the lowest paid jobs in Canada, women predominated, yet men in those same jobs earned more.

Table 4-1: Low Paid Occupations, Female/Male, Canada, 2006

Occupation	Number	% Female	Median Female Earning $	Median Male Earning $
Cook	47,565	48	20,385	23,490
Light duty cleaner	46,690	67	22,329	23,370
Cashier	41,460	88	18,706	22,585
Food counter & related	40,085	75	19,164	22430
Food/bev. server	34,285	75	16,576	20,755

Source: Armstrong and Armstrong, 2010: Introduction)

In the highest paid occupations, men mostly dominate, but still, where women are the highest proportion, men earn more.

Table 4-2: High Paid Occupations, Female/Male, Canada, 2006

Occupation	Number	% Male	Median Female $	Median Male $
Managers- computer, utilities	31,225	75	$75,863	$85,098
Sr. managers- utilities, transport	28175	87	$74,616	$92,803
Sr. managers- finance	24,755	88	$94,507	$112,047
Lawyers	24,670	50	$84,263	$96,688
School principals/sr. admin	17,160	46	$81,186	$84,752

Source: Armstrong and Armstrong, 2010

At the level of all jobs, even though there are almost as many women in paid work, occupational sex segregation is quite stark in most industries. In very few industries are there relatively equal proportions of men and women.

Even a cursory glance at this information reveals clear patterns. Women dominate those occupations that offer lower levels of income, while men tend to be overrepresented in those occupations with higher incomes. When some measure of social status or prestige is attached to various occupations, "the scores do support the claim that women are segregated in the least desirable jobs" (Armstrong and Armstrong 2010: 54).

Table 4-3: Labour Force 15 Years and Over by Occupation and Sex, Canada, 2006

Occupation	Males	Females
All occupations	8,884,810	7,976,375
Management	1,032,940	598,790
Business, finance & administrative	863,425	2,162,005
Natural, applied sciences	865,820	242,225
Health	188,845	761,515
Social science, education, government service& religion	451,145	963,175
Art, culture, recreation & sport	225,340	276,855
Sales & service	1,716,465	2,321,255
Trades, transport equipment operators	2,374,600	175,690
Primary industry	503,790	144,525
Processing, manufacturing & utilities	662,430	330,335

Source: Statistics Canada 2006a

We can use total income by sex for all earners in Canada to create a measure of the earnings elemental of the patriarchal dividend. A clear illustration is based on female income as the base and male income as a percentage of female income. For example, in 2011, total male income was about 150 percent of female income, making the extra 50 percent the patriarchal dividend or the reward one receives for being a male in Canada.

With regard to labour-force sex segregation and the associated inequalities in income, Canada is by no means unique:

Occupational segregation of males and females remains a prominent feature of most OECD countries and is the basis for concerns about equity of labour market outcomes. Employment equity, pay equity, and/or affirmative action programs and policies are in place in most countries to address segregation, based on a number of social and economic objectives. (Olfret and Moebis 2006: 58)

Table 4-4: Average Earnings Women/Men, Canada 2011 ($ constant 2011)

Year	Women $	Men $	Women's Income as Percentage of Men's	Patriarchal Dividend %
2002	29,300	46,700	62.8	59.4
2003	29,000	46,000	62.9	58.6
2004	29,400	46,200	63.5	57.1
2005	30,000	46,900	64	56.3
2006	30,500	47,100	64.7	54.5
2007	31,300	47,800	65.5	52.7
2008	31,700	49,300	64.3	55.5
2009	32,600	47,400	68.6	45.4
2010	32,600	47,800	68.1	46.6
2011	32,100	48,100	66.7	49.8

Source: Statistics Canada 2013

However, such measures may not be sufficient: "Segregation unexplained by human capital variables or preferences (to the extent that they can be inferred) may reflect systemic bias and discrimination" (58). The reference to "unexplained by human capital variables" refers to differing educational levels or length of service in a position that might impact compensation. The obvious question is why such segregation and inequality persist even in the face of the fact that Canada, like most Western democracies, has enacted a battery of legislative prohibitions and protections to ensure there is no overt discrimination on the basis of sex. As early as 1960, Canada had *The Canadian Bill of Rights* enshrine basic rights for women and men. Additionally, there is the Canadian Human Rights Act of 1977 and the Canadian Human Rights Employment Equity Act of 1995, each of which might be thought to generate a more egalitarian labour force.

MOVING ON

Labour and work are essential dimensions of the human condition, and the character of work and the social relationships involved are fundamental to the nature of our existence. In capitalist society, the structures and dynamics of class (ownership and control of society's productive resources) and the character of the gender order are inextricably bound together. As capitalism has developed and evolved, the means by which capital accumulation operates and expands changed, as did the social relationships between those in possession of capital and those without. Of equal magnitude have been the changes to sex and gender relationships and patterns of interaction. While the gender order remained patriarchal, the emergence of corporate domination of the economy, periodic crises, two major World Wars and shifting patterns of state involvement resulted in differing manifestations of gender practice in capitalist patriarchy/patriarchal capitalism.

As the patterns of work and family transitioned from feudalism to capitalism in Western Europe, focusing on the British experience, and the social dynamics that marked the emergence of a factory system, a central trend was apparent — a sex-segregated labour force. Some of the mechanisms that generated that particular labour-force configuration were cultural, some religious, some involving the deliberate actions of men to exclude women and some related to the actions of the state. As capitalism developed, matured, experienced crises and passed through different stages, the labour market changed as new jobs and occupations emerged while others were lost; however, the inequalities associated with a sex-segregated labour force persisted. The emergence of the multinational corporation as the dominant economic actor in an increasingly global marketplace has impacted employment patterns and opportunities in all regions of the world, bringing with it the typical Western patterns of male control and dominance.

From this emerges the politically difficult question: In whose interest do these institutional arrangements work? Certain aspects of the contemporary sex-segregated labour market reveal a patriarchal dividend. Thus, it seems clear that such a structure presents an advantage to men as a whole, albeit one that is not equally realized. From this point it might be said that capitalism is a masculine enterprise.

CHAPTER 5

FAMILY MEN?

While work and what we do for a living are among the most important aspects of our lives, equally important are family relations, particularly when we are considering the costs and benefits of the patriarchal dividend. It was within the context of the historical development of household or domestic relations that a key element of the patriarchal dividend emerged and took hold. Since we know that the forms of gender practice I identified as patriarchal hegemonic masculinity are historical creations, it behooves us to ask when the hegemonic patriarchal masculinity emerged as the idealized or dominant form of masculine social practice. If we can get a grip on this question two additional questions may well be answered: 1) Why did these particular practices emerge as the idealized or dominant form of social practice? 2) How did these practices take hold as the idealized or dominant form of social practice, that is, what mechanisms were involved? Before I plumb Western history for possible answers we need a bit more conceptual clarity.

Despite the fact that we use the phrase often and widely, the notion of "the family" is among the least understood and ideologically loaded phrases in the social sciences and everyday conversation. Often heralded as one of a few universal social institutions, the concept of family or "the family" is used frequently, loosely and emotionally to refer to a wide range of social phenomena and arrangements. Tamara Hareven (1991) states that there is no such thing as the history of "the" family because there is no such thing as "the" family. Even in a discipline such as sociology in which the study of family is an entire sub-field, we find numerous definitions. Yet, the family can be said to be the institutionalized arrangements among a group of people, often related by descent, lineage, ritual or custom, that facilitates biological reproduction and early childcare, while often providing various other types of support to members. Even at this high level of abstraction there are many types of families, such as nuclear, extended, matrilineal, patrilineal, polyandrous, monogamous, conjugal, consanguine and so on. The vagueness and qualifications in this "definition" are deliberate because, like any analytical concept, its purpose and function is to direct our attention to certain phenomena, organize our observations and make a point of departure for our analysis.

HISTORICAL CONTEXT

In the previous chapter I noted the significant changes that occurred in family arrangements in England and parts of Western Europe as feudalism declined and capitalism emerged. While there were major society-wide changes in institutional arrangements that facilitated biological reproduction and childcare, the particulars of these social arrangements and patterns of behaviours were radically different depending on whether one is looking at rural, land-based peasants, village craft producers and artisans, members of the military, the emerging merchant classes and the aristocracy and so on. In addition to class-based differences, there were local, ethnic, regional and religious differences that impacted the precise arrangements and how gender was practised in these families. I noted how the sex-based division of labour changed with the emergence of putting-out systems and then factory-based production. Within a generation or two entire villages were transformed as home-based production involving women, girls, boys and men were eliminated and replaced with arrangements in which all members of a unit might have worked for wages, or possibly just the males or possibly just the father. For those craft producers able to expand and take on the displaced as wage workers, the residence and family were deliberately located away from industrial sites and, in an effort to emulate the fading aristocracy, wealth and status in a community meant women and girls remained in the home. As the social status and economic basis of the remnants of the feudal aristocracy eroded, the pattern may have been reversed as members of the family entered the world of business, the professions or even wage labour. If there was a common element, it was patriarchy. Yet, given their particular form and content, gender practices in patriarchal society do not always operate so as to benefit males, ensuring their overall social, economic and political positions of power, control and dominance. So, we would expect to find various men engaging in various cultural, social, political and economic mechanisms to establish, maintain and reinforce their advantaged positions. Such mechanisms might have involved advocating for and supporting the legislative exclusion of women from certain jobs in order to reduce competition, membership in craft guilds, friendly societies and fraternal organizations to reinforce public and personal identities as men or even the cultivation of myths surrounding the complexities and inherent manly dangers of certain jobs. Additionally, given that the family as a social institution was developing and changing in concert with the capitalist economic order, we would expect to see the imprint of that economic order on family structures and processes.

There is much debate about whether or not the transition from feudalism to capitalism marked the transition from an era in which extended families were predominant to an era in which nuclear families were prevalent. That there were radical changes to family structures is not in question; however, the precise nature of those changes and their implications for gender practices are important. We know that the transitional era and the first period of capitalism were marked by the increasing importance of markets, in particular the labour market, and the increased size and complexity of all branches of material production. As capitalism emerged, the putting-out system and then industrial production outside the home necessarily involved a change in the nature of the household from being both a production and consumption unit to a consumption unit. The separation of home and workplace and the emergence of factory production were to have dramatic and radical consequences for gender relations and gender practices (Barrett 1985).

GENDER, CLASS AND FAMILY RELATIONS

When production — whether agricultural, artisan or craft — was largely organized around family and household units, the economic and productive functions of the patriarchal family straightforwardly involved a variety of different relations of production that were appropriate to the field of activity. When family-based production was reorganized, socially and spatially, and outside the household unit, many family members became dependent on the sale of their labour power, and the social and gender dynamics of the family and household became less clear.

A series of major changes in economic production radically changed the nature of the family as capitalism developed and took on definite class forms, among them one that was broadly called the working class. As wage labour became dominant and production shifted to factories, mines and mills, and as the work outside the home in the public sphere became men's paid work, the family became focused inward on the personal and the intimate. That is, "the family became the major sphere of society in which the individual could be foremost — it was the only space [working-class people] 'owned'" (Zaretsky 1986: 44). However, while the home, hearth and family may have given respite to the factory worker, the work in the home — domestic labour in the private sphere — also came to be devalued and identified as the realm of the feminine (48). The work that was performed by women in the family was, however, vital for capitalism and the capitalist class because it involved producing and reproducing the physical, emotional and biological capacity of those who provided present and future labour power. In order to keep workers rested, well fed and with sufficient creature comforts to allow them to go to work for capitalists day after day, week after week, month after month, year after year, family members must consume a wide range of goods and products — goods and products that the capitalists themselves produced and sold for a profit. Thus, the working-class family in capitalist society changes and becomes the site for the production and reproduction of labour power and of commodity consumption.

As capitalism developed, changes were occurring in the sex and gender dynamics of various classes. Among the remnants of feudal aristocracy and courts of European monarchs we find a high degree of male control, with relative leisure marking the lives of both females and males, even though there was the obligatory occasional attention to business and diplomacy. In such families, domestic labour mostly remained in hands of servants and maids. The role of the landed aristocracy and nobility as cultural icons that the new middle class often sought to emulate is noteworthy. The main focus and activity of the men of the new middle class of aspirant and successful capitalists was the world of business and commerce, which at this stage in capitalist development was very competitive and even cutthroat. For the entrepreneurs and the men of commerce and industry, success required a significant degree of competitiveness, aggressiveness, ruthlessness and callousness. What emerged in this class were dual spheres of activity, with males at work in trade/industry/business, while females oversaw the domestic sphere. While without doubt the powerful presence of patriarchal religious traditions, the remains of feudal codes of chivalry, and the remnants of the iconic status of the elegant ladies of the aristocratic tradition played a role in the emergence of these forms of gender practice, so too did the harsh realities of everyday life in the heyday of industrial capitalism.

By the turn of the nineteenth century the separation of work and home was essentially complete among the working classes. As the classical novels of Charles Dickens so aptly demonstrate, this was a period of time in the life of the working classes that went from bad to worse. During the eighteenth century it was not uncommon for men, women and children to all be working, sometimes as a family unit on a piecemeal basis with payment to the unit, and sometimes as individuals pooling their pay. It is generally understood to be a period characterized by quite ruthless exploitation and degradation of many workers, so much so that it posed a potential threat to the system in terms of generating working-class militancy and protest. This is the era of spontaneous food riots, the emergence of Chartism, the Luddites (1810–1816), Owenist utopian socialism and widespread strikes and political protests. The demands of workers for basic rights eventually resulted in the partial legalization of trade unions in England in 1824 (Clark 1997). Even prior to the emergence of Victorian reformers after the 1830s some restrictions on the employment of children and legislation governing hours of work for women and children had been passed.

The life of industrial workers, men, women and children was difficult in that the omnipresent mechanization and technological innovations that characterize capitalism often threatened jobs. As industrialization advanced, at least during boom periods, there was often the emergence of new occupations; however, on the other side of the coin was the tendency of mechanization and technology to deskill work and fragment tasks, leading to specialization as well as competition and the occasional bout of unemployment resulting from periodic cyclical crises. This was the environment that produced and encouraged campaigns to limit competition through the exclusion of women and children from certain jobs. Closely associated were demands for a family wage, that is, a wage on which a man could support his wife and family. An associated notion that was gaining traction was the breadwinner ideal for men.

What we can see during this period are a number of dynamics and processes that might generate a change in gender practices. In addition to male-dominated trade unions seeking to limit women's employment in some occupations, there were middle-class reformers seeking to protect women and children from often difficult if not nasty working conditions, some restrictive state policies and the ever present patriarchal ideological representation of females as weak, vulnerable and in need of protection. Add to this the disincentive of women to work that resulted from lower pay plus the unpleasantness of much of the work available to them, and the option of stay-at-home housework or domestic labour might well have made sense.

As industrial capitalism matured, the world of business and commerce increased in terms of its competitive character. The capacity to accumulate wealth, the only objective of the system, required a significant degree of aggressive competitiveness. An emphasis on expansion and unending accumulation, legitimized by the notion of "possessive individualism," drove the system (Macpherson 1962). The measure of a man becomes success in the competitive marketplace in the form of the individualistic, competitive, entrepreneurial self-made man. In the period of competitive capitalism, success required a punishing work ethic and the capacity to be as ruthless as was necessary in order to succeed. It was a world of "winner-take-all" yet the Victorian era brought a concern with maintaining an air of respectability, moral character, restraint and quiet strength befitting a gentleman. How was the new middle class of capitalism to integrate the necessities of success in the cutthroat commercial and industrial marketplace with aristocratic ideals and sensibilities? How to accommodate the necessity of work and the illusion of the dignity of self-sufficiency that is "above the daily din"?

Elements of the new middle class of capitalism had always looked to and sought to emulate the social conventions and behaviours of what I call the remnants of the fading aristocracy. The notion that women avoided being tainted by the concerns of the estate and monetary matters remained a cultural motif. For the successful Victorian capitalist, success as a man was demonstrated by the capacity to provide a fashionable home and clothes in the latest styles for all his dependents. In short, the Victorian middle-class or bourgeois family became characterized by a strict separation of domestic and business lives. The home and family became the refuge for the harried entrepreneur, a place to recharge his batteries and regain his humanity, a place where, of course, others performed domestic duties (Tosh 2005; Mangan and Walvin 1987; Roper and Tosh 1991).

Anna Clark's aptly named *The Struggle for the Breeches: Gender and the Making of the British Working Class* (1997) is brilliant exposition of the dynamics of working-class families and the emergence of a working-class masculinity in England in the 1800s. Clark describes how skilled artisans fought very hard to exclude women from their workplaces in order to protect wages and jobs. Further, she examined measures taken by men to solidify their notions of themselves as men and appropriate ways to practise masculinity in workplace networks, pubs, fraternal organizations, unions, friendly societies and cooperatives. As the application of technology and ongoing mechanization created new crafts and highly skilled trades such as machinists, carpenters, mechanics, line workers, metallurgists, welders, engineers and railroaders, these tended to exclude women while men fought hard to maintain the family wage. Clark also discusses the emergence of a labour aristocracy that embodied an emerging hegemonic notion or an "ideal" masculinity tied to supporting a family: man as breadwinner and provider.

This said, only focusing on economic dynamics is problematic, as it "is interesting in that it does recognize the importance of the social construction of personal life, but is ultimately frustrating in that it collapses the object of inquiry into the 'effect' of capitalism" (Barrett 1985: 191). Merely looking at capitalism alone will not allow a full understanding of the dynamics of gender relations in families. While the development of capitalism and changes to the class structure and the labour market had a direct impact on the family and gender relations, there was an additional dynamic at work. A critical understanding of the nature and dynamics of capitalism is part of the story but such an analysis must be integrated with a feminist analysis of sex and gender relations in the family (Barrett 1985). The obvious biological differences between females and males are not sufficient to explain the social and political dimensions of gender, hence the need to look at social structure and culture. More specifically, it is necessary to examine the wider institutional context, including the role of the educational system in transmitting gender and reproducing existing gender relations as well as the family. This leads us to an alternate language explaining why the notion of "the family" is so ideologically charged in gender terms: "'The family' provides the nexus for the various themes — romantic love, feminine nurturance, maternalism, self-sacrifice, masculine protection and financial support — that characterize our conception of gender and sexuality" (Barrett 1985: 205). In order to explicitly recognize this ideological element, an alternate concept, familialism, refers to the ideology and ideas about domesticity and maternity for women, and breadwinning and responsibility for men. We can then combine the two concepts into the "family household," which can be used to refer to the real concrete institution with the history, structures and social relations previously called family (Barrett 1985).

Seeing the family in this way gives rise to the key question: "If the family-household system of contemporary capitalism is oppressive for women and divisive for the working class, the question arises as to who benefits from it (if anyone) and how and why it is maintained?" (1985: 212). Dismissing claims that no one benefits, Michèle Barrett explores several possibilities, including women, men, the dominant class and the working class, concluding that benefits do not accrue to women as a general category or to the working class as a whole given its role as a site of commodity consumption. The dominant class, however, benefits in the sense that the system produces and reproduces the labour power required to operate the economy, plus facilitates the consumption of commodities, while stabilizing the system via ideological transmission and worker passivity because of the attention directed to providing for a home and hearth (216–22).

Men as a group also benefit; however, the breadwinner role in a capitalist labour market involves alienation and exploitation (217). Nevertheless, men do get a range of domestic and personal services provided for them. As for understanding why we have the sex-based division of labour that typifies patriarchal society, two key social processes must be considered: 1) the role of ideology; and 2) the role and actions of the state.

Ideology is an important element. It is not just a dominant ideology that justifies capitalism as the only possible and logical form of human social and economic organization, although this is important. There are also patriarchal ideologies that justify male domination, making unequal power relations between the sexes seem "natural" and inevitable. As for the state, rather than see it as a neutral institution working for the entire society, it is better understood as an integral part of a system of power and domination. The state, through various actions and policies, serves to establish and perpetuate patriarchy and male power and domination (Barrett 1985).

Regardless of the extent to which various pre-capitalist family arrangements involved smaller nuclear-type arrangements or broader, extended family arrangements, and regardless of the important contributions of women and children to family income, there was an underlying patriarchal element to the transformation of Western families over the past several hundred years. Males did organize and direct most economic activity, males did typically have high levels of skill and training, and men tended to control emerging political and union organizations (Rose 1988). Additionally, powerful ideological currents were afoot:

> Skilled men argued for the exclusion of women, especially married

women, from employment on the grounds that they were to be wives and mothers, not the competitors of working men. The male counterpart to this ideology of domesticity for working-class women was the ideal of male breadwinning, which increasingly meant being the sole provider within the family. (Rose 1988: 205)

The exclusion of women and the emergence of a sex-segregated labour force are historical facts. Why this happened is complex. On one hand, in order to protect their jobs and wages, men and their unions attempted to limit female employment. On the other hand, the efforts of males to exclude women from the labour force were really about attempts to drive up the family wage, thus in the end benefiting all members of the family by virtue of higher male incomes (Humphries 1977). In the end, the result was the same.

The core questions, if answered correctly, move us out of circular functionalist logic. That is, certain family forms serve some societal interests and, some potential mechanisms are and have been employed by those interests to maintain certain patterns of social interaction. Most Western nation-states have taken various measures to support and bolster the traditional nuclear family. These include gendered social assistance regimes, divorce laws, reproductive rights and labour legislation to name just a few (MacKinnon 1989; Jenson 1986; Brodie 1996). It is important to note that the so-called "Fathers of Confederation" were indeed all male, which partly explains why "the state is heavily implicated not only in the process of controlling production and capital accumulation, but also in shaping conditions in which women have and do not have children" (Hamilton 1996: 107). Since both class and gender interests are implicated in the operation and dynamics of various types of households in capitalist society, it is important to see if such interests exist.

THE PATRIARCHAL DIVIDEND WITHIN THE FAMILY

The basic operations of any family unit require a certain amount of domestic labour or housework. The precise nature of that work will vary with class position, the age of family members, occupation, geographic location and so on; however, one measure of the degree of equity in a family is the share of domestic labour performed by men and women.

At one end of the domestic labour time spectrum, 12.8 percent of males did no unpaid housework as compared to 7.4 percent of women. The interesting pattern is at the other end of the spectrum, 24 percent of women did fifteen to twenty-nine hours per week as compared to 15.7 percent for men. Nearly 14 percent of women were in the thirty- to fifty-hour group as compared to nearly 6 percent for men. Lastly, while only 1.8 percent of men did over sixty hours, 5.8 percent of women worked those long hours. That more men are in the labour force and more women are at home might explain the differences.

Table 5-1: Hours Spent Doing Unpaid Housework, 2006

Sex	No Hours	>5	5–14	15–29	30–59	60
Males	1,506,420	3,797,600	4,247,925	1,960,155	731,890	226,800
% Males	12.80	30.50	34.10	15.70	5.90	1.80
Females	979410	2416285	4030035	3159280	1839745	768680
% Females	7.40	18.30	30.50	24	13.90	5.80

Source: Statistics Canada, 2006b

While such an argument might have held more credence fifty years ago, labour-force participation rates for women have been increasing for a number of years. In 2014 there were 9,328,000 men employed, as compared to 8,474,200 women in Canada. (Statistics Canada 2016). The participation rate for men was 70.6 percent, and 61.6 percent for women. So, yes there are more men in the labour force and male participation rates are higher, but does this really explain the differences?

Table 5-2: Time Spent on Unpaid Care of a Child in the Household, 2010

Household Arrangement	Women Hours/Week	Men Hours/Week
All women and men	50.1	24.4
Dual earner couples; respondent working full-time	49.8	27.2
Dual earner couples; respondent working part-time	59.4	40.5
Single earner couples; respondent working	50.8	25.5
Lone parents; respondent working	26.9	12
Single earner couples; respondent not working	81.3	36.9
Couples; neither partner working	59.9	36.3
Lone parents; respondent not working	30	8.1
Age of youngest child in the household 0–4	67.5	30.2
Age of youngest child in the household 5–14	37.7	19.7

Source: Statistics Canada, 2010

The time spent on childcare, in the context of employment status, however, shows a familiar pattern. It does not seem to matter whether both members of a couple or one or none are working, women do significantly more childcare work than men, for example nearly fifty hours a week with both working compared to just over twenty-seven hours for men. The story is quite easy to summarize — in each and every situation women are doing more childcare work.

If we move from the childcare work to more the more general category of household domestic work — the routine work required to keep a household running (food on the table, toilets clean, laundry done and so on) — once again a clear pattern emerges regardless of employment status. When both partners in a couple work full-time, women do nearly fourteen hours a week, while men work less than nine.

As Pat and Hugh Armstrong (2010: 129) note: "As is the case with women's waged work, their domestic work has both changed significantly and remained the same in important ways." While technology and the nature of some of the products that this work produces have changed, fundamental sex and gender practices have not: "Work in the home continues to be primarily women's responsibility, whether or not they have labour force jobs, whether or not men help, and whatever women's personal characteristics or social location" (129).

It might be that younger cohorts of males were doing more domestic labour. A study of the domestic labour practices of men in Generation X, born between 1965 and 1979, notes some optimism in terms of equal commitments to domestic labour, partly because: "These men have sat in university classes surrounded by women; their mothers were among the second-wave feminists; their partners have clear career paths. These same men are also subject to a barrage of popular, media-produced images of 'New Men' and 'New Fathers'" (Singleton and Maher 2004: 239). Yet:

> Despite the prevalence and appeal of positive rhetoric that "things will be different for young people" — even among Gen Xers themselves — we found a picture of continuity rather than change with respect to young men's domestic roles, identities, and obligations. Men remain largely peripheral to work in the domestic sphere while the responsibility for managing the household falls to their partner. The males … did not see the need or express the desire to do more housework. It is only in the area of childcare where any change is taking place, and this is largely the product of the way in which paid work is organized in late modernity. (239)

Additionally they found "men's comfort with prevailing patterns of domestic labor, where women continue to take greater responsibility, appears to be the major impediment to achieving equality" (239). We need to consider the basis of the comfort referred to above or the overall benefits bestowed by the segregated work patterns described above.

When we consider domestic labour it becomes clear that, like many aspects of life, it is a double-edged sword. Those with experience as parents will know the unspeakable joy of holding your baby and the less pleasurable but necessary task of disposing of or cleaning diapers. Cooking for your family can be an act of love, creativity and satisfaction, but not so much the baked-on stickiness of the pots and pans. A refreshing bath or shower may get the day rolling, but not a dirty toilet in need of cleaning. One might even say that it is a sign of the "good life" to eat, but never cook or do dishes, to enjoy a baby but not change a diaper, to bathe but never scrub a toilet and to sleep but never launder the sheets. Domestic labour may be undertaken in order to ensure that the family performs its essential functions for society as a whole, or in order to facilitate the production and reproduction of labour power for a dominant class; however, clearly there is a direct benefit for those who are the immediate recipients of the products and services, be these meals, a clean house, clean clothes or cared-for children. If we were to consider such benefits to be part of the patriarchal dividend, in the case of traditional sex-segregated domestic labour in patriarchal families, the answer to our "in whose interest" question is simple — those men for whom the products and services are provided benefit.

MAINTAINING THE DIVIDEND

A logical follow-up question is: "How is the arrangement, institution or situation maintained?" In the case of the subject at hand, the question of how it is maintained relates to the sex-segregation of domestic labour. How do men keep their benefits rolling in?

Men do resist changing patterns of domestic labour. There are a number of strategies, including passive resistance, which includes simply ignoring requests or suggestions from a partner, or simply appearing to be oblivious to what is happening around them. One woman said of her male partner:

> He plants himself on the couch. As soon as he's home from work sometimes … If there's something going on with the kids, the kids could be screaming and yelling. He's totally oblivious to it. I'm listening to it (while preparing dinner) and I have to come out here and say something to them. (Deutsch 2010: 413)

Other forms of resistance include grouchiness, as when a man does agree to do something he does not want to. Such forms of resistance can be effective because they require so much energy from the woman that she gives up. One woman put it this way: "I have to direct him and it's easier for me to just do it" (Deutsch 2010: 413). Men are known to employ two other seemingly opposite tactics: seeming incompetent and offering praise. Men may not undertake domestic work or be excused because they are, or appear to be, incompetent at tasks such as laundry or dressing the kids. We can dismiss the justification that men have not been socialized into the necessary skills by noting that most of the tasks are routine and easily learned by any adult. After all, any adult of average intelligence can learn to run a washing machine. The praise side of the coin involves heaping elaborate praise on the woman and her skills, making it seem obvious that she is best suited for the task (Deutsch 2010). Other resistance tactics are articulating different male standards for cleanness, as in "that looks good enough for me." Some men will resort to unfair comparisons with previous generations (their grandfather or father never went in the kitchen except to eat) or the examples of other men who are even less prone to any domestic tasks.

An often-used strategy is simply the denial of substantial inequality: "A husband's resistance or receptivity can also effectively foster or prevent any changes from taking place. Although women may try to bargain successfully for a change in the division of labor, their attempts may be thwarted by men who refuse to relinquish power or to change their beliefs and attitudes" (Deutsch 2010: 322). One woman commented: "I said he should clean the bathroom more and he just laughed." This particular response by a husband amounted to "essentially stating his opposition to her request, an act that quite probably will thwart any other desires to pursue a different division of household labor" (Mannino and Deutsch 2007: 322).

Barbara Arrighi and David Maume (2000) adopted a different approach. Using survey data they examined the relationship between men's paid workplace experiences and their willingness to undertake domestic labour. Given what we know about masculinity in patriarchal society, particularly hegemonic masculinity, their findings are interesting. They set their argument out as follows:

> Control and autonomy in paid work are important for maintaining a masculine identity, as is the avoidance of housework. Men who experience challenges to their masculinity on the job are doubly resistant to engage in tasks that traditionally have been associated with feminine, namely women, hearth and home. (2000: 465)

Their conclusion is definitive: "When men face challenges to their masculinity at work, they resist engaging in housework, which for them is a female-typed activity" (481).

An Australian study examined power relations between men and women and the extent to which men were able to use their greater power resources to maintain an unequal division of housework. A survey found that the ideological power of "the breadwinner" was significant in that women tended to see themselves as co-providers and not providers, and thus were somewhat deferential to men in their lives (Dempsey 2000). As a result, women tended to ask their husbands to help out more than to actually expect them to take responsibility and "women exercised unstable influence or were effectively powerless because their partners either repeatedly fobbed them off, or helped only grudgingly and only intermittently" (2000: 23).

In a similar study conducted in England, Jenny van Hooff (2011) interviewed young couples. She found a pattern of traditional domestic labour, although it was a pattern of which the couples themselves were critical. Speaking of housework the women said:

> I do everything, then I have a raging fit and start shouting at Ian, then he'll do something, but it's because he doesn't realise something needs doing. (Jane)

> It's kind of ended up that I do the cleaning and shit, and I don't know how it happened, but it's like two years later I'm a 1950s housewife or something. (Ali)

> I do it. It's not something that we've ever discussed, I just sort of have done it, and neither of us is sort of bold enough to bring it up now, so instead I just do it. (Anna)

> I don't think it was really a decision, but I am the cleaner in the relationship, just because I'm better at it. (Chloe)

> I do all of it. He is just so useless at cleaning, I mean he lived on his own for ten years before we got together, and you think he'd be independent, but even then he was taking his washing round to his mum's, and she came round to clean. (Sara)

As for the males this is what they told her:

> Well (pause) I suppose Jane would do most of it, really. But I do cook. She'd say she did it all, but I do some stuff. I hoover now, because we've got this really cool Dyson, so I do that sometimes. (Ian)

> Ali would do most of it. We argue about it quite a lot. It's not fair, really, I should do more. (Ben)

Well, I would clean, but by the time I get there Chloe's already done it. (Paul)

Sara does do most of it, I've got to admit, but it's not because I think she should do it because she's a woman, it's just because she's got higher standards of cleanliness than me (laughs). (Steven)

I would never expect Teresa to do it because she's female, I think it's more down to personality, she's a clean freak and I'm not bothered by mess as much. (Alex)

Some of the women and men expressed guilt, anger and frustration and even provided justifications. Among the justifications were the apparent longer hours worked by men, male incompetence, higher female standards and females getting a sense of satisfaction. There was some indication that men did some cooking but few did any cleaning (van Hooff 2011). What these young modern couples say "revealed a gulf between the ideology of late modern relationships and the lived experiences of couples, as well as the interplay between the two" (2011: 27). It was not just men who provided rationales and resistance to change:

Both the male and female partners ... deployed strategies to justify the continuing inequalities ... rather than challenging them. Traditional gender roles resurface when couples move in together, undermining any attempts at equality. However, gender roles are rarely explicitly named as an explanation for the division of domestic labour; instead the [couples] couch their justifications in terms of the demands of the workplace, pragmatism, or female respondents' higher standards. All of the younger women ... were educated to at least degree level, and worked full-time in professional occupations. (2011: 28–29)

THE STATE AND THE FAMILY

Given the view of the family as a very private, inward-looking institution, it might seem, at first blush, that the state would not be involved in producing such private relationships. Yet, the state and some state agencies have directly and indirectly supported and bolstered patriarchy. Over its history, the state is involved with marriage and divorce legislation and related court actions involving important issues such as alimony, child support, relations of marital authority and criminal assault and domestic violence. Among other things there is a clear difference between the rhetoric of official myths and the reality of women's lives. On the matter of domestic violence, during the nineteenth century in Canada, "judicial adherence to the patriarchal model of marriage contributed to an environment in which women were often denied basic protection against savage mistreatment" (Backhouse 1986: 303). On the issue of marriage and the role that the law and its agencies played in maintaining traditional patriarchal structures, "the Canadian judiciary played a pivotal role in expunging the newly-emerging model of companionate marriage and in shoring up the patriarchal family in nineteenth-century Canada" (1989: 312). The expunging in question occurred as a result of the courts refusing to even consider the possibility that men and women entered or participated in marriage as equals, while defining marriage in very narrow terms thus eliminating the possibility of any property or other support claims from those in common law or cohabitation relationships.

In a more recent review of some legislative regimes and court decisions relating to the maintenance of patriarchy, Shelley Gavigan (2012: 273) comments, with humour, on the health of patriarchy:

> The relationship between law — as opposed to state and social policy — and patriarchy is arguably an uneven one, and this unevenness has led both critics and defenders of patriarchy to suggest its demise. However, to borrow from Mark Twain, reports of the death of patriarchy have been greatly exaggerated.

The entrenched power and the "enduring appeal" of patriarchal ideologies pose barriers and constraints to restructuring family law so as to promote gender equality (Gavigan 2012: 275). Gavigan (2012: 275) explains: "Without an appreciation of the power and enduring appeal of patriarchal ideologies, of their complexities and contradictions, and of the barriers and constraints they impose, the development of alternative perspectives regarding gender and familial relations, and of real gender equality within and without the family, will remain an illusory ideal in Canadian society." The types of ideology she is referring to informed family law in the early decades of the last century; however, they were eroded somewhat with the advent of the post-war Keynesian welfare state. Innovations in public policy such as mother's allowances and the expansion of universal programs such as social assistance did not really provide security nor economic equity for women. Thus, they "never supplanted nor replaced the patriarchal nuclear family as the primary site of obligation and responsibility for family members" but rather ultimately bolstered it (282).

The negative impact of neo-liberal deregulation and the elimination and restructuring of state supports for women has been extensively documented across Western societies. In Canada, for instance, there are gendered implications of changes to macro-economic policies, free trade, pay equity policy and legislation, as well as health care, marriage and other issues such as the regulation of pornography. In the field of health care, the deinstitutionalization of care for those with mental illness and the elderly tends to increase the domestic workload of women while traditional female occupations such as nursing bear the brunt of neo-liberal inspired cuts to public expenditure (Armstrong 1996). International trade deals such as NAFTA have been demonstrated to erode the power of nation-states in important areas, such as imposing the necessary legislative and regulatory regimes to enshrining pay and employment equity (Cameron 1996).

MOVING ON

As a concept in the social sciences, family is omnipresent. George P. Murdock's 1949 announcements on the universality of the family set the stage for decades of debate on defining family. It is a concept heavily loaded with cultural and political meanings:

> The family is viewed both as the bulwark of western civilization and as so imperilled as to threaten that very civilization. This central significance of the family reflects both its importance in maintaining the current socio-economic and political system and its importance in the ideological framework of society. (Havas 1995: 1)

The family is a site of gender relations and gendered social practices. In historical context, while at a very high level of abstraction, some form or type of family is common to most societies, but when examined in the context of locale, history and culture the arrangements we call the family are dynamic, changing and evolving. When placed in the context of a particular gender order (patriarchy) and a particular economic order (capitalism) the family takes on a particular hue. The arrangements in a patriarchal nuclear family provide some necessary survival-related "comforts" for its members; however, someone must in fact provide the necessary products and services. To the extent that products such as food and services such as childcare, laundry and cleaning are provided individuals can be understood as being lovingly cared for. However, for the individual excused from this rather mundane but vitally necessary labour, the provision of these goods and services might be seen as a benefit, a dividend.

It is clear that familial relations are among the most complex in human affairs. The power of the familial ideology is strong and abiding. The myths and realities of enduring romantic love and the great many emotions surrounding such love, fidelity, jealousy, hate and so on are the stock and trade of Hollywood and Bollywood. The fact that an act of love and caring can also be an act of exploitation through which benefits accrue more to some than others far removed and closely associated with the provider adds a level of complexity. We know that reality is complex and what we think is happening or going on is not what is really going on. The acts of love I referred to (cooking, cleaning, childcare and the other hard work it takes to maintain a household) that women might perform daily, like the hard work some men might perform in order to earn what they might have hoped is a family wage, tend to obscure the mechanisms that are really in play. The vast majority of paid labour, whether it is apparent or not, is related in some manner to the global circuits of wealth creation and accumulation with the major benefits increasingly appropriated by a smaller and smaller segment of the population. This fact fuels the recent interest in social inequality among the media, academics and the public as a whole. It would seem that the hard work of many, even when it is not understood as oppressive, inordinately benefits those who do not perform it. In a similar fashion, we need to think systematically about the possibility that real benefits accrue to those who are excused from performing routine household and domestic labour because it is performed by others. Just as financial benefits or, using the term loosely, dividends accrue to those with capital, so too do personal benefits accrue to those who don't perform domestic labour and household duties in the form of one element of the patriarchal dividend. Hope may be drawn from the fact that history provides glimpses of options in terms of the potential for more egalitarian arrangements, since the last three hundred years clearly demonstrate the possibility of alternatives to regimes in which unearned dividends are accrued. For now our immediate task becomes examining a less hopeful element of familial life.

CHAPTER 6

VIOLENT MEN
OR MEN
AND VIOLENCE?

Are men violent? That is a common but perplexing and very complicated question. There are at least two possible answers. One possibility, quite frankly present in so-called common sense narratives and discourse, is that men are violent, just plain violent, likely as a result of their biology or genes. The other possible answer draws attention to the fact that, while men practise violent behaviour more than women, explaining this fact is much more complicated than the genetic answer provides.

DEFINING VIOLENCE

The question of how to define violence and different types of violence is contested. While defining violence may seem like a relatively easy task, it is in fact not so when one attempts to provide some degree of specificity in terms of perpetrators, victims, modus operandi and the objectives of perpetrators. While a dictionary definition may be fine for some purposes, when it comes to violence in the context of gender analysis, a more refined approach is required. When trying to understand male violence it is important to understand that there are different forms of violence based on the purpose or objective of the violence. As we shall see, sometimes violence is directed at other males, the purpose of which is often about establishing and/or maintaining one's status as a hegemonic male and thus enhancing one's status and power among and over other men. On the other hand, many of the actions men engage in that are violent are directed to women and might be understood in the context of maintaining power and control over women, perhaps to establish or maintain one's claim to a share of the patriarchal dividend. I will begin by establishing some degree of clarity regarding the issue of what constitutes violence toward women.

Using the definition of violence against women provided in the 1993 United Nations Declaration on the Elimination of Violence, it can be defined as: "any act of gender-based violence that results in, or is likely to result in, physical, sexual or psychological harm or suffering to women, including threats of such acts, coercion or arbitrary deprivation of liberty, whether occurring in public or in private life" (Sinha 2013: 4). The issue is, however, not clear cut. Definitions, particularly when developed by academics and other "experts," must be broad enough to encompass the subjective experiences of "those who are battered, psychologically abused, or sexually assaulted" (DeKeseredy 2000: 742). Such a widening of the definition of violence against women should include "physical violence, sexual violence, and threats to commit physical or sexual violence," as well "as stalking and psychological abuse ... Using this definition of violence and abuse against women permits us to disaggregate violent acts from abusive ones but to also capture the full spectrum of acts that are harmful to women" (Kilpatrick 2004: 1225). Furthermore, "we should broaden the definition of violence against women to include not just violent acts, such as physical assault, sexual assault, and threats of physical and sexual assault, but also nonviolent acts, such as stalking and psychological and emotional abuse" (Tjaden 2004: 1246). These definitions resist the tendency in much public discourse to de-gender the issue of violence resulting in misleading and incorrect understandings of what is really going on by constructing much of the violence against women as human violence as opposed to domestic abuse linked to the relations of domination that might be seen to typify patriarchal society, or by occasionally construing women as the actual cause, as in "she had it coming" (Berns 2001: 265–268)).

It is difficult to define the complexities, extent and essence of violence involving individuals in intimate circumstances. As Nelson (2010: 311–12, emphasis in original) observes: "Gender-neutral terms (e.g. *family violence, domestic violence, marital violence, conjugal assault, spousal abuse*) and gender-specific terms (e.g. *violence against women, women abuse, wife abuse, wife battering, husband battering, husband abuse*) all reflect the theoretical, empirical and ideological orientations of their creators and/or users." The debate is ongoing; some criticisms have been directed to gender-neutral language while others defend the approach. The strength of a broad definition from the United Nations General Assembly is its breadth and ability to encompass a broad range of acts that constitute gender-based violence. Those would include, to name just a few, rape as a war tactic through sexual slavery, forced pregnancy or abortion, female infanticide, trafficking for the purposes of forced labour, prostitution or marriage and genital cutting, all of which would be considered gender related (Johnson and Dawson 2011).

None of this, of course, is to say that all or even most men engage in overt acts of violence either against each other or against females; however, the data we have regarding the extent of violence reveals patterns.

QUANTIFYING VIOLENCE

In the simplest terms, there is no doubt that men are more violent than women. In 2013 a total of four hundred men were accused of homicide, as compared to fifty-two women. The largest cohort was male, ages 18–25 with 123 charges. During that same year the victims were also predominantly male, with 358 male deaths and 146 female (Statistics Canada 2015b).

Table 6-1: Victims of Police-Reported Violent Crime, by Relationship of Accused to Victim and Sex of Victim, Rates per 100,000, Canada, 2010

Accused-Victim Relationship	Female Victim #	Female Rate[1]	Male Victim #	Male Rate[1]	Total Victims	Total Rate[1]
Intimate partner	82,168	574	20,545	147	102,713	363
Spouse[2]	39,297	422	9,359	104	48,656	265
Dating partner[3]	42,871	672	11,186	186	54,057	436
Non-intimate partner	121,609	719	170,151	1,017	291,760	867
Other family member[4]	29,518	175	20,783	124	50,301	150
Friend/acquaintance	59,526	352	78,725	471	138,251	411
Causal acquaintance	41,935	248	54,349	325	96,284	286
Business relationship	6,654	39	10,755	64	17,409	52
Close friend	7,998	47	8,250	49	16,248	48
Criminal relationship	414	2	1,991	12	2,405	7
Authority figure	2,525	15	3,380	20	5,905	18
Stranger	32,565	193	70,643	422	103,208	307
Total	203,777		190,696		394,473	

1. For intimate partner violence, rates are calculated on the basis of 100,000 population aged 15–89 years. For non-intimate partner violence, rates are calculated on the basis of population aged 0–89 years. Populations based upon July 1 estimates from Statistics Canada, Demography Division.

2. Spousal violence refers to violence committed by legally married, separated, divorced, and common-law partners (current and previous). The spousal category is based upon victims aged 15–89.

3. Dating partner violence refers to violence committed by boyfriends/girlfriends (current and previous) and other intimate partners. The dating partner category is based upon victims aged 15–89.

4. Other family member includes parents, children, siblings, and extended family.

Source: Statistics Canada 2015c

A few simple calculations show that 80 percent of the victims of intimate partner violence were women, as were 81 percent of spousal violence victims. As for
dating partner violence, 79 percent were female, while the number drops to 59
percent in the case of other family member assaults. Males, on the other hand, are
victims more often than women in the categories non-intimate partner, friends,
casual acquaintances, close friends and criminal associates, authority figures and
strangers. In the latter category males represent 68 percent of all victims.

Other information about the types of violent crime and the sex of the victims
is equally telling.

**Table 6-2: Victims of Police-Reported Violent Crime, by Intimate[1] Partners,
Type of Offence and Sex of Victim, Canada, 2010**

	Female Victims #	Female Victims %	Male Victims #	Male Victims %	Total #	Total %
Homicide/attempts	146	0.20	53	0.30	199	0.20
Sexual assault[2]	2,309	3	60	0	2,369	2
Physical assault	57,989	71	16,304	79	74,293	72
Criminal harassment	7,075	9	1,057	5	8,132	8
Indecent/harassing phone calls	4,022	5	1,316	6	5,338	5
Uttering threats	7,820	10	1,580	8	9,400	9
Robbery	257	0	49	0	306	0
Other violent offences[3]	2,550	3	126	1	2,676	3
Total offences	82,168	100	20,545	100	102,713	100%

1. Intimate partner violence refers to violence committed by legally married, separated, divorced, common-law partners,
dating partners (current and previous) and other intimate partners. The intimate partner category is based on victims
aged 15–89.
2. Includes sexual assault, classified as one of three levels according to the seriousness of the incidents. Level 1 sexual
assault is the category of least physical injury to the victim; level 2 includes sexual assault with a weapon, threats to use
a weapon, or causing bodily harm; and level 3 includes aggravated sexual assault, which wounds, maims, disfigures, or
endangers the life of the victim. Also includes other sexual crimes such as sexual interference, invitation to sexual touch-
ing, sexual exploitation, incest, corrupting children, luring a child via a computer, and voyeurism.
3. Includes abduction, kidnapping, hostage-taking, arson and other violent violations.
Source: Statistics Canada 2015d

In addition, Statistics Canada also breaks down the category of physical assault,
reporting that of the 57,989 physical assaults against women, 8,506 were major
assaults, 46,685 common assault and 2,798 other forms of assault. The general
pattern was the same for assaults against men.

A cursory look at this data illustrates that, for both males and females, the greatest number of incidents involved physical assault, with men as victims 8 percent more frequently. Since this is police-reported data, it shows a relatively low number of sexual assaults on women and a negligible number for men primarily because most sexual assaults go unreported and, while men are also victims of sexual assault such events are rarely reported.

Commenting on homicide statistics Roxan Vaillancourt (2011: 11) noted:

> From 2004 to 2008, homicides accounted for less than 1 percent of all violent crimes reported to police in Canada. Adult males were more likely than adult females to be a homicide victim, accounting for 74 percent of victims of homicide during this five-year period.

Nevertheless, compared to men, women were more often killed by a current or former spouse (38 percent of female homicides versus 4 percent of male homicides) and were at greater risk of being the victim of a spousal homicide. From 2004 to 2008, females accounted for more than three-quarters of spousal homicide victims, more specifically, of the total of 315 homicides, 275 of the victims were women (Vaillancourt 2010: 11). One of the clear patterns on violent behaviour is, when directed at women, men who had been intimately involved or knew the female victim were the ones to inflict it. For example, "in 2004 at least 200,000 Canadian women were physically assaulted and 160,000 were sexually assaulted by intimate partners; 460,000 sexual assaults were committed by other men" (Johnson and Dawson 2011: 1). Although sexual assault is sometimes perpetrated by strangers, the apparently large number of 460,000 sexual assaults committed by "other men" does not represent strangers because that same year the General Social Survey data indicated that "55 percent of reported sexual assaults were committed by friends or acquaintances of the victim" (Johnson and Dawson 2011: 97). The discrepancy with the data in the tables above results from different data sources, in that police-reported crime rates are often lower than actual individual experienced rates.

SOCIALLY SANCTIONED VIOLENCE?

The use of various forms of violence is subject to a variety of laws, social conventions and circumstances. Sociologist Max Weber (1946: 78, emphasis in original), for example, defined the state as "a human community that (successfully) claims the *monopoly of the legitimate use of physical force* within a given territory." The notion of legitimate violence is typically understood to refer to the legitimacy given by the state on behalf of its members to the use of force by the police and army and other state-sanctioned agents. While questions very often arise as to the extent of the powers granted such public agents, there are also other arenas of social activity in which considerable latitude is given to acts of violence such as sports and athletic competition. The emergence of professional spectator sports, a multi-billion-dollar arena of the spectacle in which men (there are of course women's sports but as we have seen the scale and economic importance are less significant) are allowed to enrobe themselves in increasingly sophisticated armour and pound away. I will comment on the spectacle aspect of this in the next chapter; however, for now I want to focus on the violent actions of some athletes off the playing field.

On April 15, 2015, a former New England Patriots football star player, Aaron Hernandez, was convicted of first-degree murder. The Hernandez case was only one of a number of high-profile cases of former NFL players involved in off-field violence. Other instances of high-profile football players who have committed acts of violence include Adrian Peterson (Minnesota Vikings), who pleaded guilty to reckless assault in connection to a child abuse allegation; Ray McDonald (formerly with the San Francisco 49ers), who was charged on suspicion of felony domestic violence in 2014 and in August 2015 charged with rape by intoxication; Greg Hardy (traded by Carolina Panthers to the Dallas Cowboys), who was found guilty of assaulting his girlfriend, but later the conviction expunged on appeal when she failed to attend a hearing. The infamous and much-publicized elevator assault by Ray Rice (Baltimore Ravens) on his girlfriend did not produce criminal charges as a result of Rice's agreement to enter an intervention program (Wilson 2015). *Newsday* (2014) published a longer list of star athletes who have become embroiled in legal matters as a result of alleged off-field violence involving women that they know.

The matter of player violence against women became such a public issue that the NFL was forced to run an anti-violence public service ad during the 2014 Super Bowl. While the mechanisms that connect domestic violence to the ideologies and practices of professional football may not seem that direct, one cannot but wonder about the impact of a life spent in violent contact with others predicated on a "winning is the only option" philosophy. Having said that, one set of causal mechanisms is clear and direct — the relationship between sports like football and hockey to brain health and injury.

Tragically, on February 15, 2015, 35-year-old former NHL player Steve Montador was found dead in his Toronto-area home. Montador's career in the NHL was ended by concussions, but he was far from being alone. "For the past 15 months, amid the quiet consolidation of subsequent suits and obscure legal wrangling, the case against the NHL has been a faint echo of the similarly constructed class-action suit against the NFL. It involved thousands of former players and was settled in 2013 for $765 million." (Branch 2015: n.p.). On February 21, 2015, the front page of *Toronto Star* sports section featured two pictures, one of two boxers getting ready to deliberately and legally try to damage the brain of the other under the byline in red, "Ready to Rumble," the other of NHL star and former concussion patient

Sidney Crosby in a hockey fight. One week later the front page of the *Star*'s sports section featured a large, tough-looking facial picture of former football player and professional wrestler Angelo Mosca who has Alzheimer's disease. Mosca is quoted as saying: "The MRI showed a lot of brain damage. I couldn't believe it. I wasn't bitter; I was hurting" (Rush 2015: n.p.). On April 23, 2015, a United States federal judge approved a settlement to resolve thousands of lawsuits by retired players suffering from brain damage that will see the NFL pay over a billion dollars over the next sixty-five years to support brain-injured retired players (Dale 2015).

VIOLENT MEN

Notions that humans, particularly men, are somehow by nature violent have been a part of human thought for centuries. Often the bases of such "explanations" of human behaviours are found in genetic/chromosomal, hormonal and brain structures of humans. As we saw in Chapter 1, while such explanations constantly reappear, it is not because there is supporting evidence, but rather it is their simplicity and apparent congruence with what appears on the surface to be patterns of human action and interaction. Substantial evidence counters these reductionist arguments (see Chapter 2; Knuttila and Magnan 2012: Chapter 6), yet, highly reputable scholars and sources continue to support the thesis that complex human behaviours can be reduced to simple biological determinates. Recently the *Philosophical Transactions of the Royal Society* published an article titled "Evolution and the Psychology of Intergroup Conflict: The Male Warrior Hypothesis," in which Melissa McDonald et al. (2012: 676), ignoring decades of cultural and social anthropological cross-cultural evidence, claim:

> Conflict between human groups is a pervasive social problem, to which a solution remains elusive. One potential reason for this difficulty may be that our evolutionary history has shaped the human mind in ways that tend to perpetuate intergroup conflict. The male warrior hypothesis argues that, for men, intergroup conflict represents an opportunity to gain access to mates, territory and increased status, and this may have created selection pressures for psychological mechanisms to initiate and display acts of intergroup aggression.

Approaching the same problem leads others to quite different conclusions:

> Violence is a complex problem, which no simple biological approach can diagnose or remedy. Factors such as political instability, population density, and income inequality are associated with massive differences in violence across cultures, and these differences are observed while gender

ratios remain constant. Of course, men still hold most of the power in the world, and it is no surprise, then, that they perpetrate most of the violence. But that too is a historical fact, not a biological given. If we focus on biology instead of economic and historical variables, we will miss out on opportunities for progress. (Prinz 2012: n.p.)

The supposed evolutionary role played by violence, again particularly men's violence, remains an important part of the trope of evolutionary psychology/socio-biology. The entire approach is predicated on the assumption that somehow one of the most significant purposes in life, driven apparently by our genes, is ensuring our genetic present in posterity. As Daly and Wilson (1988: 519) put it:

Cognitive structures of all creatures, including Homo sapiens, have been shaped by selection to produce social action that is effectively "nepotistic": action that promotes the proliferation of the actor's genetic elements in future generations, by contributing to the survival and reproductive suc-cess of the actor's genetic relatives.

This promulgation notion has many critics (see Lewontin and Rose 1984; Rose and Rose 2000; Lewontin 1991) asking if there is a link between this supposed species-wide desire to promulgate one's genes and violence. If the only issue was random violence directed to strangers and non-family members, the answer might be easier to accept — folks are aggressive, even to the point of homicide, towards those who might be rivals for the necessary resources to maintain one's gene pool. But a significant level of violence occurs between people who know each other well, to the point of intimacy. In answering this, the argument shifts to consider the role of emotions: "Male sexual proprietariness is the dominant issue in marital violence. In studies of 'motives' of spousal homicide, the leading identified substantive issue is invariably 'jealousy'" (Daly and Wilson 1988: 512). The issue here is apparently control of the woman's reproductive functions in the interests of facilitating the reproduction of the male's genes. However, I think we can do better by way of explaining this behaviour.

SOCIAL MEN

If we are to understand these patterns of violence, it is now time to begin to connect some of the dots that I have been playing out in preceding chapters, particularly regarding acquiring gender material.

A behaviouralist would look for patterns or instances in which a male child was rewarded for engaging in certain behaviours and punished for others that the child's caregivers wished to discourage. In the case of male aggressive and violent behaviour, most accounts of the lives of boys are replete with stories of being either overtly, or through expectations and subtle clues, encouraged to be active, to get out there, be involved, win at all costs, to be sturdy oaks, to give 'em hell, no sissy stuff and always make a difference, that is, be the "big wheel." Similarly, many males can tell stories of being made fun of by family, friends and others if they showed emotion, failed to fight when they were expected to, cried, retreated, failed to aggressively defend their honour and the like. So on the surface it would seem that a behaviouralist approach is capable of explaining how a male might come to learn to be violent and aggressive as a result of the messages (rewards and punishments) dished out by those with authority to do so (trainers).

The problem with this approach is its simplicity and tendency to only confront surface appearances. An obvious issue relates to the origins or basis of the apparent violent behaviour of the "teacher," that is, why would some men encourage and discourage certain behaviours? When we probe a bit deeper it becomes apparent that not only does the approach not recognize any significant degree of agency or free will, it ignores the role the mind and our personality play in our actions, and is ultimately reductionist.

According to behaviouralism, animal actions, including those of humans, are typically understood as reactions to a stimulus. Even while acknowledging that the stimulus can be a conditioned stimulus and the response a conditioned or learned response, the process is still essentially like this: Stimulus ==> Response.

We know, however, that humans have minds and personalities that play a role in our behaviours and social actions. Since the mind or personality symbolically interprets stimuli, the messages or stimuli we receive from the environment are subject to interpretation and reflection. As a result, the human mind first interprets the meaning of a stimulus and then decides on an appropriate response. In the case of humans, the process looks more like this: Stimulus ==> Mind/Personality ==> Response.

Psychologists and many others have argued the human mind is the key to understanding behaviour. It is not so much the stimulus but what we make of it, how we interpret it and what we take it to mean that is important in explaining how we react.

Several lines of argument are available if one is to explain male violence and aggression by utilizing Freud. Freud understood the development of human personality to involve the ceaseless process of addressing and reducing instinctually based tensions. As humans pass through the various stages of development (anal, oral, phallic and genital) the id, ego and superego work out, in the context of the ever-present life and death instincts, a distribution of psychic energy among and between them, while developing a range of defence mechanisms. The relentless pressure of the id to address ever-emerging tensions and the rather flagrant desires of the ego require that the superego be constantly active in whatever environment.

Perhaps Freud's description of the basis of the human personality has significant implications for understanding male violence. He wrote: "We approach the id with analogies: we call it chaos, a cauldron full of seething excitations" (1933: 65). As the ego acts to take the organism beyond the ultimate frustrations of the pleasure principle into the real world of real satisfaction and pleasure, it encounters frustration at the hands of the superego, or as Freud refers to it, a "tyrannical master" (69). The rule of the tyrannical master makes possible civilization, but at a cost, since it requires the deployment of many defensive mechanisms (Freud 1961). Instincts, including both the death and life instincts, are constantly invoking action. The desire for pleasure and the need to address sources of tension based in sexual energy and other sources of excitation/tension are constant, as are frustrations when there is a need to delay gratification, repress desires and sublimate instincts. Humans constantly face the inevitable trade-off — civilization for a degree of discontent.

Mead and Cooley provide an understanding of the social dynamics and processes regarding the development of the personality. Mead moved the human agent, the Self, to the centre of his analysis, recognizing the fundamental importance of the symbolic world, and stressing the importance of the mind as a social outcome. His concepts of the Self comprises both physiological/biological and social/cultural components (the "I" and "Me"), and the notion that each changes as we mature socially and physically. Mead's Self is not just a bundle of roles; it is a complex composite, an embodied Self with a sense of itself and of others. When we add Cooley's insights regarding the importance of the constant gaze of others for our self-concept and social action, we have the potential to understand how males begin to see themselves as masculine and how important that masculine self-image might be. However, there are essential lacuna — power and the sources of the values, practices and beliefs that become the core of the Self.

Many factors correlate with societal and domestic violence; however, correlation and causation are not the same. Alcohol consumption, for instance, is sometimes presented as causal when at best it is contributory, in the sense that it can lower inhibitions resulting in aberrant behaviours with their roots in deeper causes. Rather than discussing mere "triggers," we need to probe deeper for underlying mechanisms generating the behaviours and explore the possibility that hegemonic masculinity and the patriarchal dividend might help explain male violence. Much behaviour associated with practising hegemonic masculinity is geared to domination, power and control, or at least seeming to be in control. It is also about expressing one's status as a man in the sense of being the "big wheel" and being in control.

Patriarchy is a gender order predicated on relations of domination, on inequalities in power and control and economic, cultural, institutional and other social resources. History teaches us that all regimes that are based on and characterized by domination, and patterns of unequal resource distribution (including power and status), require mechanisms of social control ranging from ideological persuasion to various types and levels of force and coercion. Such actions are required because systems of oppression and domination inevitably generate opposition and resistance. Humans, it seems, have an enduring desire or even need to have a measure of autonomy, to do it themselves, as it were. If you watch an adult trying to get a typical 2-year-old to do something, at some point you will hear the child say something akin to "I want to do it myself." Noam Chomsky argues "that humans have an instinct for freedom, that they really want to control their own affairs ... They don't want to be pushed around, ordered, oppressed, etc., and they want a chance to do things that make sense" (1988: 756). Chomsky's hope that humans have a so-called instinct for freedom may not be the case; however, humans do tend to resist systems of oppression and domination, and those in positions of power in such systems typically need to use various forms of manipulation and force in order to maintain their positions of superiority.

To complicate the process even further, successfully practising hegemonic masculinity is also a precarious process, requiring displays to enforce one's status with peers (other males), subordinates and even oneself. Social and domestic violence and other forms of belligerence surely represent efforts to establish, enforce and maintain some men's apparent position of authority, power, control and dominance as hegemonic males in a patriarchal gender order. As Connell (1995: 83) puts it:

> Many members of the privileged group use violence to sustain their dominance. Intimidation of women ranges across a spectrum from wolf-whistling in the street, to office harassment, to rape and domestic assault, to murder by a woman's patriarchal "owner," such as a separated husband.

If this analysis — that males engage in overt acts of violence as part of the repertoire of social behaviours required to establish, maintain, enforce and reinforce one's masculine status in the face of omnipresent hegemonic masculinity — has traction, might it explain one of the most brazen examples of seeming "mindless" violence?

SCHOOL SHOOTINGS AND MEN: WHAT'S GOING ON?

Among the most public and notorious acts of male violence in recent decades are school shootings, more specifically targeted school shootings as opposed to rampage shooting, mass murders, terrorist attacks and government shootings (Muschert 2007: 62). Excluded from mass targeted school shootings are murders and acts of violence directed at particular individuals for specific reasons related, for example, to drug deals, gang violence or interpersonal conflict. Such acts are typically spontaneous, as opposed to being systematically planned, and do not target institutions, specific groups of peers or authority figures. We could include killings and shootings at universities such as the December 6, 1989, mass murder of fourteen female students at the L'école Polytechnique de Montreal by Mark Lepine, or the April 16, 2007, Virginia Tech shootings in which thirty-two were killed and seventeen wounded. Not included as well are other mass shootings, such as the July 20, 2012, killing of twelve and wounding of thirty-eight at the midnight screening of the film *The Dark Knight Rises* in Aurora, Colorado, the fourteen teachers and students that died in San Bernardino in December 2015 and the fifty killed and fifty-three injured in Orlando in June 2016.

School shootings are a particular manifestation of violence that, when they happen, draw immediate media and public attention but seem to quickly be forgotten. Although not strictly a North American phenomenon, more happen here than elsewhere. Various Internet sites keep lists of school shootings; however, I will draw your attention to a few of the more widely known and reported instances.

On October 1, 1997, Luke Woodham, age 16, entered Pearl High School in Pearl, Mississippi, with a gun and killed two girls and wounded seven others. He had been bullied and rejected by one girl he targeted. Two months later, on December 1, 1997, 14-year-old Michael Carneal shot and killed three girls and wounded five more in Heath High School, West Paducah, Kentucky. Reports indicate he had felt alienated from school and his friends since kindergarten. About four months later (March 24, 1998) Mitchell Johnson, age 13, and Andrew Golden, age 11, shot and killed four girls and one teacher and wounded other students and a teacher at Westside Middle School, Craighead County, Arkansas. Of the fifteen victims killed and wounded, fourteen were female. The boys, who were reported to have a history of macho swaggering, targeted girls who had turned them down. Jumping ahead three years, on March 5, 2001, Charles "Andy" Williams, age 15, killed two students and wounded thirteen others in Santana High School, California. The evidence shows he had been bullied and called names like "bitch" and "faggot." He singled out many of those he thought had been involved.

Shortly after, on March 22, 2001, Jason Hoffman, age 18, shot and injured three students and three teachers at a high school in El Cajon, California. He is reported to have said: "No matter what I do, I can never manage to succeed at anything. No matter how much I work and study, I will never be able to attain the position in life I want to." Reports of being disciplined at school, breakups with girlfriends and being bullied and ostracized accompany the cases of James Sheets, age 14, who killed the principal at his school in April 2003; John Jason McLaughlin, age 14, who killed two students in September 2003; and Jeffrey Wise, age 16, who killed five students, his grandfather, his grandfather's girlfriend, a teacher and security guard in Cold Spring, Minnesota. In November 2005 Kenneth Bartley, Jr., age 14, shot and killed the assistant principal and wounded the principal at his school in

Wisconsin. Thomas "T.J." Lane III, age 17, killed three male students and wounded two others on February 27, 2012, in Chardon, Ohio.

The following year, on October 21, 2013, 12-year-old Jose Reyes shot and killed his math teacher and then killed himself in front of his class. He left two suicide notes indicating that he had been bullied. His parents reported that their son was tormented and mistreated. Just months later, in New Mexico on January 14, 2014, Mason Campbell, age 12, critically wounded an 11-year-old boy and 13-year-old girl. In court his defence claimed had been chronically bullied. In Marysville, Washington, Jaylen Fryberg, age 15, took a gun to school on October 24, 2014, and proceeded to kill four students (one of them his ex-girlfriend) and wound one other before taking his own life. There are reports that he was bullied.

I could go on noting a variety of other such murderous events in colleges and universities, nevermind those at workplaces, churches, temples and shopping malls. The killing of two young boys and two teachers in La Loche, Saskatchewan in January 2016, for example, shocked many Canadians. The event caused the typical media frenzy and a flurry of visits and lamentations by politicians of every ilk with much speculation as to the cause or motive. Hidden in the press coverage of the difficult economic circumstances of the area was a report that the 17-year-old arrested by police had been bullied and teased about the size of his ears. One report notes he was selective in his victims, choosing to not shoot some students who had been kind to him saying, "Oh no not you bro" as he passed them (Warwick 2016).

These tragic events and others have generated an extensive array of studies, books, articles and reports as experts, law enforcement agencies, academics and the public at large attempt to come to grips with them. In 2000, under the leadership of the FBI, the Critical Incident Response Group and National Centre for the Analysis of Violent Crime undertook a major study. The result was *The School Shooter: A Threat Assessment Perspective*. The report presented a model and not a profile or checklist of danger signs because "those things do not exist" (O'Toole 1999: 1). Rather, it focused on threats, suggesting a four-pronged assessment approach related to the personality of the student, family dynamics, school dynamics and social dynamics. It offers a long list of personality traits and behaviours (forty-six in all) covering the four areas, but is far too sweeping and general to even offer any hints as to what is causing these events. The assessment model lists a series of behaviours and personality traits that include, to name a few: low frustration level; poor coping skills; failed love relationship; signs of depression; narcissism; alienation; exaggerated sense of entitlement; blaming externalization; inappropriate humour; manipulation; rigidity and opinionated. Importantly, however, the words "male," "masculinity" or "masculine" do not appear in the document.

A second government study, entitled *The Final Report and Findings of the Safe School Initiative: Implications for the Prevention of School Attacks in the United States*

(2004), was prepared for the United States Secret Service and United States Department of Education. The report is based on the study and analysis of thirty-seven incidents of targeted school violence that occurred between 1974 and 2000. The report examines what it calls the "attackers"; however, it concludes, "there is no accurate or useful 'profile' of students who engaged in targeted school violence" (2004: 19). Curiously, it does go on to note, "all the attackers in this study were boys." Rather than noting that being male might be a characteristic, they discuss demographic data such as family background. They note one commonality: "Many attackers felt bullied, persecuted, or injured by others prior to the attack" (21). The ten key findings really are a summary of some of the characteristics of school shootings, including that they are typically planned, often others knew something was being planned, most felt bullied and often had a sense of failure and most had access to guns.

There are many other attempts to understand school shootings and possible causes. One is a model that focuses on sequences of events and the accumulation of strain factors such as "anger, frustration, disappointment, depression, fear and ultimately crime" (Levin and Madfis 2009: 1230), as well as strain caused by "failure to achieve positively valued goals and the disjuncture of expectations and achievements" (1231). This model suggests that, in a period of vulnerability, such as adolescence, an event or catalyst can result in drastic action such as a school shooting. Planning such violence is a "power-asserting moment" (1237), thus "the massacre serves to solve their most pressing problems of damaged personal identity and tarnished self-worth" (1238). Such actions and reactions might be related to regaining masculinity because "much Western culture equates violence with masculinity" (1238). However, having introduced the notion of masculinity as a potential cause, prevention focuses on deterrence and reducing strain, life skills, internal discipline and conflict resolution in curriculum, but disappointingly virtually nothing about gender and masculinity.

Another similar approach is to search for risk factors. Some identify a variety of commonalities among the cases: "Individual Factors" (with fifteen subheadings); "Family Factors" (four subheadings); "School and Peer Factors" (seven subheadings); "Social and Environmental Factors" (three subheadings); "Situational" (two subheadings); and "Attach-related Behaviours" (six subheadings) (Verlinden, Hersen and Thomas 2000: 43). The large number of subheadings tends to reduce the list of factors to a catalogue of common adolescent behaviour. As a result, such long lists do not really offer any substantive reasons for the behaviour, as illustrated by remarks such as: "The attacks do not appear to be motivated by pursuit of secondary gain, and appear to be acts of angry young men seeking to kill and injure multiple victims" (41). Others reduce the number of factors. Katherine Newman and Cybelle Fox (2009: 1286), for example, identify five: social marginalization;

individual disposing factors; cultural scripts; failure of surveillance systems; and the availability of guns. But identifying these patterns does not mean we can predict violence, as the approach is limited: "Common conditions help us understand patterns" (1294). These factors make only passing reference to masculinity; indeed a complex table that lists the conditions mentions masculinity as an issue or challenge in only two of nine cases cited (1295).

Even though school shootings are very rare events, focusing in on particular cases can help isolate the dynamics involved. There are potential difficulties with looking at specific cases as "there are only a handful of cases of rampage school shootings and almost a dozen variables that have been proposed as likely causes, including firearm availability, violent media, family breakdown, southern culture of violence, bullying, and so forth" (Harding et al. 2002: 179–80). With so many possible causes and so few cases, it is difficult to isolate the effect of any one variable or impute causality. For example, in the cases of the shootings at Westside Middle School and Jonesboro and Heath High School: "The media and scholarly press have advanced almost a dozen hypotheses to account for school shootings such as those at Heath and Westside. These include media violence, bullying, gun culture, family problems, mental illness, biological predispositions, peer relations, demographic change, culture of violence, and copycatting, almost all of which offer some element of truth" (188–89). Beyond this, scholars suggest another five "necessary but not sufficient factors for school shootings: 1) gun availability; 2) cultural script that supports a school shooting ... 3) marginal social position of shooter; 4) individual problems for shooter; [and] 5) failure of social support system" (189–190).

It is necessary to understand such violence within the context of several aspects of male power. Particularly in "the convergences of (1) white entitlement, (2) middle-class instability and downward mobility in the postindustrial economy, and (3) heterosexual masculinity" (Madfis 2014: 67). This understanding places many of the factors pointed out by others in a broader social context of oppression and inequality that

> instead look[s] at the benefactors of patriarchy, racism, and heterosexism (though crucially not post-industrial capitalism) in order to stress how white heterosexual male entitlement fuses with downward mobility, subordinated masculinity, and other disappointing life course events in a way that drives some anguished individuals to retaliate in true hegemonic masculine form through large-scale acts of retaliatory violence and murder. (Madfis 2014: 68)

In other words, hegemonic masculinity contains an important element of entitlement in the male American dream, creating the tendency of privileged males to see themselves as victims when entitlement fails because of downward mobility. "Thus, masculine gender identity is paramount to the explanation of violence as a solution to the predicament of status loss to the entitled" (78). The result, in the U.S., is that violence becomes the solution to restoring lost masculinity. That is, masculinity plays a central role. Thus, there is a possible role of the patriarchal dividend and power, and "manhood acts" may be important.

Manhood acts are significant elements of gender inequality, of patriarchy as a system of inequality that is maintained by "human males behaving like men" (Schwalbe 2005: 75). Hence, hegemonic masculinity is "the standard against which men are judged as more or less worthy of full manhood status." Put another way:

> To live up to the hegemonic ideal is to show one's self worthy of all the privileges that normally accrue to men in a particular culture. To fall short is to take a lower place in the hierarchy of men and, if the failure is sufficiently egregious, to risk losing manhood status entirely. (Schwalbe 2005: 76)

In patriarchy, in order to be fully "deserving of full manhood status, a male must signify a masculine self." Further:

> He must, in other words, act in ways that can be interpreted as signifying an essential character that includes the qualities of strength, rationality, courage, resolve, and heterosexual potency. What matters is the virtual self, the imputed self, created by acts of signification. Manhood, it can thus be said, is a status achieved through skilful impression management. (76)

Manhood acts, then, are those acts through which men demonstrate the themes of hegemonic masculinity: "strength, rationality, courage, resolve, and sexual potency," thereby making things happen.

Thus, school shootings are in part male displays that exhibit a man in control. There is a link between masculinity, adolescent culture and school shootings:

> Masculinity is central to what makes a popular boy the king of the mountain. To be a man is to be physically dominant, competitive, and powerful in the eyes of others. Real men exert control and never admit weakness. They act more and talk less. If this sounds like the Marlboro Man, it is because adolescent ideals of manliness are unoriginal. They derive from cultural projections found in film, video, magazines, and the back of comic books. In-your-face basketball players, ruthless Wall Street robber barons, and presidents who revel in being "doers" and not "talkers" all partake of and then reinforce this stereotype. (Newman et al. 2013: 67–68)

Gender and masculinity are the significant missing elements in a much of the writing about school shootings and shooters:

> [The studies] use such broad terminology as "teen violence," "youth violence," "gang violence," "suburban violence," and "violence in the schools" as though girls are equal participants in this violence. Conspicuously absent is any mention of just who these youth or teens are who have committed the violence. They pay little or no attention to the obvious fact that boys committed all the school shootings — masculinity is the single greatest risk factor in school violence. (Kimmel and Mahler 2003: 1442)

To understand school shootings, we need to look at local and school cultures, peer and authority figure relationships as well as gender identities. Trying to make sense of why a particular boy on a particular day engaged in a shooting is complex, but that has to be put into the context of homophobia and bullying and the relationship of masculinity to violence.

Writing in *Ms. Magazine* in 1999, Gloria Steinem labeled school shootings and mass murders committed by men as "Supremacy Crimes." She argued that these crimes were committed by white middle-class males hooked on the "drug of superiority": "national self-examination is ignoring something fundamental, precisely because it is like the air we breathe; the white male factor, the middle-class and the heterosexual one, and the promise of superiority it carries" (n.p.). An additional dimension is sexual identity and the prevalence of homophobia in male youth culture. Heterosexuality is important for boys in their efforts to maintain their sense of masculinity. Derogatory language such as "fag," "pussy" and being called gay are used not so much to indicate a serious statement about sexual orientation as to indicate failure to practise hegemonic masculinity: "Boys reject femininity in order to establish their dominance, and they must continually degrade girls and feminize other boys so as to maintain their status — even as they pursue girls sexually" (Myers 2012: 128). Further: "Hegemonic masculinity is not easily attainable — indeed, most males will never accomplish it. But it serves as a ready-made tool that can be used by anyone to police a male's masculinity" (135). The portrayal of non-hegemonic males (adolescent and teen boys) in several popular television shows that ran (and are in continual rerun) on the Disney and Nickelodeon channels document how such masculinity is typically portrayed as nerdy, feminized, inept, with more than subtle hints of homosexuality. Myers discusses an episode of *Hannah Montana*, for example, in which the dancing style of a male character, Rico, is ridiculed as being feminine, while the exploits of heterosexual Zack are made to appear cool. In the highly charged environment of peer pressure it seems as if failure to live up the hegemonic ideas can be potentially catastrophic.

CONNECTING VIOLENCE AND MASCULINITY

When examining complex generative events and phenomena such as school shootings it may not be possible to establish strict causality; however, we can look for underlying mechanisms. When addressing a complex issue such as the school shooting data I presented, strict cause and effect is impossible particularly if one is offering a generative as opposed to a reductionist account. In the case of school shootings we know that there is a dominant or hegemonic mode of doing masculinity in patriarchal society. It is a spectre that haunts males on a daily basis. We know that there are benefits or entitlements associated with various masculinities and male dominance. Further, it is clear that masculinity in our society is rigorously policed and deviations from dominant practices have repercussions and sanctions (for both males and females). Given the vulnerability of adolescence and the adolescent identity, self- and peer-perceived inability or incompetence in performing masculinity are potentially extremely problematic. It follows that performing compensatory and overcompensating "manhood acts" to establish or recovers one's sense of power, lost entitlement and ability to dominate and control might follow. The nature of one's manhood act is clearly contextual, for example in the U.S. violence is an acceptable way of settling scores, securing what is passed off as justice and restoring patriarchal equilibrium (this is featured in just about every TV show and Hollywood movie).

In the light of what we know, we have to ask ourselves this: Is it possible that some boys (and men) find that the fear or reality of humiliation, the yearning for respect, the loss of entitlement, the need for power, the disinclination for affection and intimacy and the will to dominate overwhelms all else? Further, if this happens, what might follow? And lastly, how does this relate to school shooters?

Among Luke Woodham's victims was Christina Menefee, a girl who had rejected him. Fourteen of the fifteen victims of Mitchell Johnson and Andrew Golden were female. Mitchell wanted to shoot all the girls who had broken up with him. Luke Woodham said of the day of the shooting: "One second I was some kind of heartbroken idiot, and the next second I had power over many things." Further, he said:

> I am not insane! I am angry. This world has shit on me for the final time. I am not spoiled or lazy, for murder is not weak and slow-witted, murder is gutsy and daring. I killed because people like me are mistreated every day. I did this to show society "push us and we will push back!" I suffered all my life. No one ever truly loved me. No one ever truly cared about me. I only loved one thing in my whole life and that was Christina Menefee. But she was torn away from me. I tried to save myself with [student's name], but she never cared for me. As it turns out, she made fun of me behind my back while we were together. And all throughout my life I was

ridiculed. Always beaten, always hated. Can you, society, truly blame me for what I do? Yes, you will, the ratings wouldn't be high enough if you didn't, and it would not make good gossip for all the old ladies. But I shall tell you one thing, I am malicious because I am miserable. The world has beaten me. Wednesday 1, 1997, shall go down in history as the day I fought back. <https://schoolshooters.info/sites/default/files/Luke%20 Woodham%20 Writings.pdf>

Jose Reyes left a note about being bullied and called gay, and anger at the students who claimed that he wet his pants. Mason Campbell said he was tired of being bullied — the victims just happened to be in his line of fire. There is evidence that Michael Carneal had been bullied. The Associated Press reported Robert Butler Jr.'s last Facebook post as:

> Everybody that used to know me I'm [sorry] but Omaha changed me and [expletive] me up. and the school I attend is even worse ur gonna here about the evil [expletive] I did but that [expletive] school drove me to this. I wont u guys to remember me for who I was b4 this ok. I greatly affected the lives of the families ruined but I'm sorry. (Caufield 2011: n.p.)

In a disposition related to litigation launched by the family of a victim, Andy Williams later referred to feeling rejected because a lot of people were against him, particularly stuck-up people and a teacher who had disciplined him. In prison he wrote "Andy's Poem":

> March fifth two thousand one
> There was a kid who had a gun
> He finally decide he had nothing to Lose
> People all over saw him on the News...
> He thought nobody liked him he got messed with everyday
> He didn't like Santee and he didn't want to stay
> He would hurt emotionally bruised to the touch...
> One locked up wish someone said
> They loved him instead of making him feel dumb
> Santana High still and numb. (Perry 2002: n.p.)

Testimony at the Minnesota Supreme Court appeal case dealing with John Jason McLaughlin, 14, reads in part:

> McLaughlin told McDonald that his trouble with Bartell began in sixth grade, and that he was teased "basically about [his] zits and stuff." ...

> The conflicts these witnesses described involved pushing, yelling ...
> Two students testified that C.E. called McLaughlin names such as "fag"
> and "asshole" ... A third witness remembered one instance in which C.E.
> pushed McLaughlin out of the way by McLaughlin's locker. (Anderson
> 2007: n.p.)

Let's assume that a boy spends his life with the spectre of hegemonic masculinity ever present, and has been socialized to accept this mode of practising gender as appropriate. Let's further assume that there are a number of benefits that are seen to accrue to those who are seen to practise this form of masculinity as well as costs for not doing so. While few males actually fully practise hegemonic masculinity to the level of the "ideal," what happens to those systematically denied or unable to practise hegemonic masculinity, or whose efforts are unsuccessful, repudiated and ridiculed? We know that practising hegemonic masculinity in a manner that is appropriate for a particular male's historical, political and cultural setting can be tenuous and precarious at the best of times. The spectre haunts us, the gender police are omnipresent, the need to assert and reassert are constant and our insecurities manifest. When the threats mount, peer pressure grows and alternatives are lacking, so individuals may seek to engage the cultural mechanisms at hand. In a society in which violence and guns have played and continue to play a central role, what might we expect? If violence, vengeance and dramatic individual action (perhaps typified by the stereotypical gunfight scenario that highlights the solutions in many movies) are deemed the appropriate way to address those identified as the enemy or cause of one's failures, are school shootings then totally unexpected aberrations or the bitter fruit of a system of gender relations predicated on domination and power?

In considering this difficult issue it is important to consider that in order to understand a particular gender-related event and the behaviour of a particular individual in a particular circumstance, the insights of both the sociologist and the psychotherapist are required:

> Gender is an ongoing emotional creation and intrapsychic interpretation,
> of cultural meanings and of bodily, emotional, and self-other experience,
> all mediated by conscious and unconscious fantasy. We cannot capture
> this emotional, unconscious fantasy meaning either in terms of cultural
> gender meanings, as feminists have tended to do, or in terms of monolithic
> claims about genital structure or function or pre-Oedipal and Oedipal
> developmental patterns, which has been the characteristic psychoanalytic
> pattern. (I myself have done both.) The focus of the psychoanalyst or
> psychologist on intrapsychic or psychological elements, as if these can

be contrasted with or considered apart from the external world and culture, and the feminist theorist's focus on discursive or cultural processes and patterns both miss a large part of what goes to constitute gender. (Chodorow 1989: 540–41)

MOVING ON

How does one "move on" from these stories? I suppose perhaps with a sense of analytical detachment, but one informed by a commitment to changing what we can. The point is not to paint men and boys as necessarily violent, predominantly violent or prone to violence. Instead, social systems and institutions that are inherently predicated on relationships of domination, power, control and inequities typically have an underbelly of violence. Violence has long been understood to be an important element of social control, as are ideology, manipulation and the use of state power. While making connections between violence and the maintenance of power at a system level is difficult, interpersonal violence is a mechanism of control at the individual level. Ian Brown recently interviewed domestic abusers, social workers, therapists and others who work with violent men. He reports one clinical supervisor as stating that the men he deals with are angry, their anger rooted in the fact that they have difficulty living up to the message they have been getting since their playground days: "Be in control, show no weakness, and never admit to your fallible humanness" (2015: F6). Brown cites four reasons men hit their partners: patriarchy; witnessing domestic violence as a child; neurochemical imbalances; and because some women hit men. It is entirely logical to also assume that, as in the case of school shooters, violence can be understood as part of the process of either establishing, maintaining, re-establishing or reaffirming one's power, domination, control and authority; put otherwise, one's hegemonic masculinity.

In Chapter 3 we examined some of the ways that boys become men, partly through the dynamics of socialization. An important element of these processes is the images and representations of boys, men and masculinities that populate the various elements of popular culture.

CHAPTER 7

REPRESENTING BOYS AND MEN

This chapter considers some of the ways boys and men are represented in a limited range of media and various forms of entertainment and communication that typically are included under the rubric of popular culture. You will note that I have slipped in a new word — representation. As Stuart Hall (1997a; 1997b) has observed, representation is a complex process. A straightforward definition of "represent" is to present or depict something. Another meaning is to claim to represent or stand for it, as in my Member of Parliament claims to represent me. Moreover, it can mean re-present boys and men, that is, to allow us to have a second look, a deeper examination of what is really going on in their lives. I will, however, seek to use the notion of representation in yet another way in order to understand how cultural meanings, language, symbols and concepts become the basis and core of representations. Representations do not just happen, they are not out there waiting to be discovered, nor are they merely fantasies. Representations are created by human actors in the context of systems of social interaction and power. The capacity to create, promulgate, resist, reproduce, transform and reject representations is an important part of the political and ideological struggles in many systems of inequality. In what follows I will focus on how images of boys and men are both presented and re-presented as illustrations in regard to the content of what I will call the spectre of hegemonic masculinity.

There has never been an historical period in which visual imagery of all sorts is so omnipresent in our lives. On average, American children between ages 2 and 11 watch over twenty-four hours of television per week, while adults ages 35 to 49 watch more than thirty-three hours per week (Hinckley 2014). The comparable figure for Canadian adults is about fourteen hours for the 18 to 24 age group and over thirty hours per week on average for the entire population (Oliveira 2013a; 2013b). Add to this hours spent online (in many cases this includes imagery)

— twenty-three hours a week for Americans and more than thirty-one hours weekly for Canadians aged 18 to 24 — and the extent of imagery saturation becomes clearer (Mielach 2014; Oliveira 2014b). While it is more difficult to estimate the number of hours we spend at the movies, in 2015 Americans bought 1,340,884,120 tickets that cost $11,303,656,536 (USD) (Nash Information 2015). In Canada 61 percent of the population attended at lease one movie in 2014 (ERMResearch 2015). At the risk of saturating the reader with data about saturation, I will add one last element — video games. In 2013 American gamers over the age of 13 spent on average over six hours a week playing various video games (Aamoth 2014). A Canadian survey indicated 36 percent of those surveyed played video games with the average daily time spent playing among these users over two hours (Vanier Institute 2013). I could go on but I believe the point is made — we live in an image-saturated environment.

MOVIES

The movie industry predates electronic media such as television, and is significant because of the importance of the international movie industry, centred in Hollywood. Men dominate the industry, and there are consequences of this in terms of the portrayal of women. A New York Film Academy report (n.d.) of Hollywood films produced between 2007 and 2012 found that only 30.8 percent of characters with speaking roles were women. In terms of dress and costuming, 28.8 percent of women characters wore revealing clothes as compared to 7 percent of male characters. Just over 25 percent of women actors get partially naked at some point in the movie, again compared to just 9.4 percent of men. Only 10.7 percent of movies had a balanced cast, that is, half of the characters were female while the overall ratio of male to female actors was 2.25 to 1. For the industry as a whole, that is all jobs and occupations, the ratio of men to women was 5:1 (New York Film Academy n.d.).

The actual content of mainstream Hollywood movies, the ones that most folks watch, also has a sex and gender pattern. For example, of the top sixty-seven films from 2012, "55 of the lead characters were male, and only 12 of the characters were female" (Beighley and Smith 2013: n.p.). There is a simple test to determine if a movie is just about men or if women have a presence, which is composed of three short questions: 1) Are there are at least two women in the movie with names?; 2) Do these women talk to each other in the movie?; and 3) Is the conversation the women have about something other than men? (Bechdel 2009). In applying the test to number of 2014 movies, Walt Hickey (2014: n.p.) found that many of the major movies of that year failed: "Of 1,794 movies released from 1970 to 2013 ... only half had at least one scene in which women talked to each other about something other than a man." The message for boys and men watching films is simple — they tend to be the centre of attention and count as what is important.

In 2014 Hollywood released over 550 movies (Lang 2015). Given this fact, in order to examine the representation of boys and men in these movies I obviously need to be selective. Although, as we have seen, Hollywood seems to be a scene in which men play a dominant role, in some categories or genres men are totally dominant. In those genres — action, war, historical/epic, western, crime, science fiction and drama — men are typically the major and often the only main characters. For this reason and also because of what I will argue is the broader ideological messaging in some of these genres, I will draw you attention to certain aspects of the representation of men in westerns and war movies.

By focusing on these genres I am certainly not diminishing the significance of the action movie and the many so-called heroes that emerged in popular culture during the last decade of the twentieth century. The super-human feats and literal invincibility of Bruce Willis' character John McClane in the *Die Hard* franchise (five movies from 1988 to 2013) or Martin Riggs played by Mel Gibson in the *Lethal Weapon* series or many of Harrison Ford's characters, including in various iterations of *Indiana Jones* (*Raiders of the Lost Ark* in 1981, *Indiana Jones and the Temple of Doom* in 1984, *Indiana Jones and the Last Crusade* in 1989 and *Indiana Jones and the Kingdom of the Crystal Skull* in 2008), are important. Add to these the various characters portrayed by actors such as Arnold Schwarzenegger, Sylvester Stallone, Steven Seagal, Steve Austin, Vin Diesel and Chuck Norris, just to name a few, and you have a consistent message of aggression, vengeance, violence, inhuman strength and unimaginable ability to endure pain and physical suffering. Setting aside the interesting relationship to the emergence of these movies and characters with the role of the declining power, authority and domination of the U.S. in the arena of global politics, the individual representation of men and masculinity in these characters is succinct and blunt. Men are fearless, immune to physical pain and, when emotionally damaged (there is often a theme of revenge after a loved one is killed or one's country shamed), capable of truly fantastic levels of violence and mayhem.

The most recent financial crisis that emerged out of the recklessness and malfeasance that characterized the banking and financial sectors in the early 2000s produced alternate but, in their own way, just as brutal representations of aggressive, domineering and ruthless masculinity. Michael Douglas's Gordon Gekko in *Wall Street* (1987), Leonardo DiCaprio's Jordan Belfort in *The Wolf of Wall Street* (2013) and Kevin Spacey's and Jeremy Irons' characters in *Margin Call* (2011), not to mention the theft and fraud brilliantly depicted by the hustlers in *Glengarry Glen Ross* (1992), all exhibit and portray men prepared to do whatever it takes succeed. The masculinity they practise may not involve guns and bombs but their thoughtless disregard for others and their drive and determination to win at all costs represents hegemonic masculinity in another field of play.

FRONTIERS AND COWBOYS

For many men, the Western was a staple as we grew up, both in movie theaters and on television. The archetypal man in Westerns during the Depression, the Second World War and the post-war era systematically represented what we would now know as the hegemonic ideal: "steadfast, independent, resourceful, self-reliant, aggressive, rational, and controlling" (McGillis 2009: 1). Such movies had a "cowboy code," similar to the code of the mythical knights of feudal times and later the Boy Scout movement. In addition to those characteristics noted above, such a code placed emphasis on loyalty, honour and the duty to help women, children and the ill (McGillis 2009). Additional elements of cowboy culture stressed stoic individualism, control — often with the help of a gun — and power and status with the help of one's horse (McGillis 2009). The cowboy was inevitably white, as was his horse and hat, with those in the way of his geographical expansion west often depicted as less white and even as savages. The notion of the conquest of virgin territory speaks for itself, as does the need to do whatever one has to do to enforce justice. The consumer aspect of cowboy culture (I owned holsters, pistols and a Red Ryder BB gun as a child) was rampant and was ideologically related to private ownership, self-reliance and individualism as the unquestionable ideal.

Michael Kimmel (2012: 109) notes that the "cowboy occupies an important place in [U.S.] cultural history: He is [U.S.'s] contribution to the world's stock of mythic heroes." The rugged outdoor tamer of the frontier, the figure of the cowboy emerged in American literature at the same historical moment that wage workers were becoming the most common form of employment in the cattle industry. That the actual era of the cowboy had passed, to the extent that the myth ever matched the reality of working in the cattle industry, was irrelevant to the social and cultural role that the myth played in providing "men the possibility of imagining manhood in the traditional setting, consuming their manhood in idealized versions of those set-tings — even as the real men who were its consumers had to find new ways to adjust to the changing circumstances that transformed their lives" (Kimmel 2012: 114).

Various U.S. presidents, particularly Ronald Regan, used the cowboy image and mythology. This particular myth became so important because it is connected the utopian dream aspect of American capitalist expansion and the power of the American media to spread images (Hobsbawm 2013). Ideologically, the myth had appeal because it offered a dream, an impossible dream, but still a dream that in America anybody can have it all: "the cowboy, just because he was a myth of an ultra-individualist society, the only society of the bourgeois era without real pre-bourgeois roots, was an unusually effective vehicle for dreaming — which is all that most of us get in the way of unlimited opportunities" (2013: n.p.).

There is, however, a seeming contradiction between the notion of a dominant hegemonic representation of masculinity and the reality of multiple masculinities as illustrated in several film genres. In this regard, Ang Lee's 2005 film *Brokeback Mountain* is important. Set in period between the early 1960s and the early 1980s, the story focuses on two main characters, a cowboy who frequents the rodeo circuit while periodically working on ranches (Jack Twist) and a ranch worker (Ennis Del Mar). While working together, Jack and Ennis fall in love, but end up unhappily married in conventional heterosexual relationships. While the portrayal of two male cowboys in love offers a view into alternate masculinities that was much appreciated by film critics, the inability of the men to organize a permanent loving relationship and the movie's violent culmination speak to the social power of the heterosexuality of hegemonic masculinity, even in the movies.

MEN AT WAR

An equally important genre of films when it comes to representing men, and sometimes boys, consists of war films. That the website of the American Movie Classics Company uses five different sections or parts to document the history of war films speaks to the quantity and complexity of this genre. The site notes that the first war film was made in 1898 during the Spanish-American war. It depicted American troops tearing down the Spanish flag from a government installation in Havana and replacing it with an American flag. Since then films about war have been used to promote war, support war, as overt propaganda, to educate, to revise history and sometimes to criticize a particular war or war in general.

War movies typically fall under one of ten different genres, or typologies: 1. Last Stand; 2. Disillusioned Young Soldier; 3. Dumb Action Film; 4. The Comedy; 5. The War Romance; 6. Sweeping Historical Epic; 7. The Mission Gone Wrong; 8. The Documentary; 9. The Biopic; and 10. The Returning Veteran (Rico n.d.). Although the themes and storylines of the movies in these categories vary radically, they have one point in common — the central characters are male. Moreover, there is a common backdrop — hegemonic masculinity. For example, there are "key stereotypes of manliness in war films" (Donald and MacDonald 2011: 42):

> *The Mama's Boy.* Seemingly a sissy, but often maturity and manhood are achieved after combat but sometimes death to prove the savagery of the enemy.
> *The Wolf.* Competence, success and even valour in battle, while concerned with women and sexual conquests.

The Lothario. Variation on the Wolf, but in exaggerated form where sexual conquests are the central focus, sometimes making the character one of comic relief.

The Father Figure. Older experienced soldier, often the hero who takes the safety and well being of his troop as his sole responsibility.

The Rebellious Son. Immature, rebels against authority, but who generally comes through in a crisis or battle then matures and conforms.

The Gay Soldier. Rarely integrated into military apparatus. Homophobia and hint of being gay is treated as a matter of comedy or in extravagant mocking of homosexual activities among straight soldiers.

The Mate. The friend for whom a soldier will do anything up to and including dying. The death of a mate will result in acts of brazen courage and revenge.

Battling Brothers. Actual blood relatives in war. Blood will turn out to be thicker than anything else.

The Virgin. Rites of passage sexually and in terms of violence in battle will mark the emergence of the true soldier and man.

The Rapist. Although rape as a weapon of war has a long history, in Hollywood movies it is typically a morally questionable character that provides the threat or danger, but rarely the act unless it is an anti-war film. Death is the usual fate.

Woman Hater and Psychopath. As above except psychopathology runs deeper but there is often an element of hypermasculinity present as well.

The FNG (Fucking New Guy). The replacement might be a Virgin whose rite of passage will be dramatic but full induction is the norm.

The Courageous Boy. Not just a young version of the Virgin, often literally a boy, an orphan perhaps but with the heart of a man.

The Coward. Sometimes comical, often dangerous to the rest because his actions sometimes cost lives, sometimes recuperates in time to die.

Out of Control. Loss of manly control under fire or stress, panicky men who either die or pull it together.

The Sissy. Sometimes immature or a dandy, the Sissy is out of place in a man's army and war. Sometimes mans it up and joins the troops, sometimes a marginal character.

The REMF (Rear Echelon Motherfucker). The bureaucrats and office staff who run the war far away from the actual battles, typically lacking the first-hand skills, practical knowledge and even the courage to get it done.

The Hero. Cuts across all types because under certain circumstances almost anyone can be the hero, sometimes by obeying orders, sometimes by accident or circumstances.

David Ayer's 2014 film, *Fury*, illustrates that variations of these characters and their storylines are alive and well. Brad Pitt plays the commander of a U.S. tank (Don "Wardaddy" Collier as The Father Figure) in the dying days of the Second World War. The Virgin is a clerk-typist without front-line service, Norman, who joins the crew and is initially bullied by the other three members of the crew (The Woman Hater/Psychopath, and a few Mates). However, he learns to hate, kill, have sex and do all the things that are not just demanded of him but that prove his manhood. War movies such as *Fury* demonstrate how masculinity is sometimes practised in war and how, often when it falls short or violates core norms, recuperative moments are possible.

War movies and the masculinity they represent are an important part of Western popular culture, as illustrated by Hollywood's affection for war movies: seventeen war-themed movies in total won the Best Picture Academy Award between 1928 and 2009 (Dirks n.d.).

What is important in the type or representations noted above are the relations among the men. A discernible pattern in the movies is the desire to win. While the basis is likely not an inherent, primal urge to hunt and fight, the overall message (win at all costs) in these movies "is the most serious and potentially dangerous of all the absurd notions that American war films and sports fixations inflict upon the psyches of our young boys" (Donald and MacDonald 2011: 185). While it is understandable to worry about the socialization aspect with regard to children, the images and practices portrayed are representations that we all notice.

THE WORLD OF SPORTS

Perhaps there is no better illustration of the patriarchal dividend at play than in the world of sports, particularly professional sports. A BBC study in 2014 indicated that the German soccer team received more that £21 million more for winning the men's World Cup than did the Japanese women's team for winning the last women's World Cup. Moreover, the winners of the men's Football Association Challenge Cup, commonly called the FA Cup, got £1.8 million while the Women's Cup winners got £5,000 (Thompson and Lewis 2014). In 2015 the Ladies Professional Golf Association total prize money was $61.6 million USD, while in 2012 the male PGA total purse was $270 million USD (Burke 2011: n.p.). The point is clear: pro sports pay much more to male athletes than to female athletes.

As I noted in the previous chapter, sports, particularly high-impact contact sports, are among the iconic representations of hegemonic masculinity in one of its rawest forms. Sports such as ice hockey, rugby, soccer and football employ men, often at high salaries, to literally risk life and limb in the name of entertainment. Leaving aside the important issues of political economy that surround the big business of professional sport (corporate involvement in team ownership, taxpayer subsidies of virtually every aspect, stadium construction scandals, corporate involvement in ticket sales and concessions and so on), the issue here is how men and sports are represented in the media (Nauright and Schimmel 2005; Burstyn 1999).

For most of us, whether or not we watch sports on TV or online, read the sports pages of newspapers, watch sportscasts, pay attention to any of the dozens of specialty sports TV channels and websites or listen to sports radio, trying it once and paying attention to the narrative, imagery and representation of males involved in sports is instructive. One thing that is immediately obvious is the use of military jargon and analogies to describe, for example, football. Newspaper columnist Mike Royko (as quoted in Nadelhaft 1993: 27) writes:

> Many football coaches consider themselves military scholars and use military jargon: the blitz, the long bomb, etc. And many generals, even presidents, talk in football jargon. As President Bush said, this war was his "Super Bowl." In football, the coaches say careful preparation, planning, discipline and execution are everything. That's what the generals say too. In football, the coaches say it's essential to establish the air game and the ground game. That's exactly what the generals said we did in the desert. And most coaches loathe the press. So do the generals. They have so many qualities in common.

The view that sports is a battle, and like good soldiers the players go to battle when called (by the regular schedule) on behalf of their school, neighbourhood, town, city, province or country. The object of sport is to "beat 'em" (Bishop and Jaworski 2003). The words famously attributed to Coach Vince Lombardi — "Winning isn't everything. It's the only thing" — is repeated *ad nauseum* in the context of virtually any sport. Much of the public discourse regarding professional sports is based not just on a hegemonic notion of masculinity, but a hypermasculinity in which men are viewed as warriors (Burstyn 1999: 4).

As is their wont, the physical battles involved in contact sports have increased in intensity as equipment makers became better at armoring the players. The problem with the human body, particularly the head and brain, is it has limits, no matter how well encased in metal and plastic — a fact the growing injury toll in professional sports makes clear. The implications of a warrior's life are difficult to assess, but the reality of concussions is not, as tragically illustrated by the ongoing struggle of one of the Canadian Football League's former top receivers (Rush 2015; *Toronto Star* 2015). It is very likely that professional football and hockey players have always suffered concussions of some degree; however, in recent years the long-term impact has become apparent. Head injuries to superstar-status players like hockey player Sidney Crosby always make the news, but the early deaths of numerous former players have raised the profile of the issue. The emphasis on male physicality, invulnerability, strength and will to dominate is the underlying ideological and social message here, a message the tends to support and promulgate the social practices we know as hegemonic masculinity.

The relationship between on-field (or on-ice) behaviour and behaviour away from the sport is complex. However, there may be a quite direct connection: "Interpersonal aggression is common in the lives of these hockey players, both on and off the ice. For these hockey professionals, aggressive behaviors were seen as manifestations of existent tendencies as well as products of sport socialization" (Pappas, et al. 2004: 307). Further, gender is implicated: "A culture of masculinity can be seen to characterize the teams the players described. The athletes tended to share a set of ideological beliefs related to traditional forms of masculine expression, for example, preoccupation with achievement and maintaining status through fighting or risk taking, acquiring an identity of toughness" (308).

There are some in the media itself that now question the high physical and other costs of being a public and media warrior. On September 5, 2014, the *Guardian* published a critical assessment of professional football based on the record of misogyny and racism of some of those involved. Two days later, on September 7, 2014, Chuck Klosterman expressed concern about supporting a sport that seems so connected to concussions, even if the players are adults aware of the danger (*New York Times Sunday Magazine* 2014: 24). The front page of the November 9, 2014, edition of the *New York Times Sunday Magazine* wondered if football was going to be the new tobacco because of the many lawsuits from damaged players. In Canada, a confessed conflicted fan worried about the violence of the game (Di Novi 2014).

RESISTING HEGEMONIC MASCULINITY: LITERATURE IN CANADA

While the representations of men and masculinity in many professional sports (particularly full-body contact sports) are characteristically rough and tough, full-bodied hegemonic masculinity, in literature and art the picture is quite different. For example, based on a study of short stories, Neta Gordon (2014: 179) notes:

> What emerges from even this most cursory of critical perusals is a hegemonic masculine figure associated with dynamic physical labor, who — despite a rugged individualism in terms of activity — commits to a team or community-oriented pursuit; and whose moral authority rests in claiming a social position that is not quite at the top of the food

chain. Somehow the "real" Canadian man is not the Old World aristocrat or shadowy (American) corporate figure, but rather one whose claim to social privilege paradoxically derives from a civil rejection of the concept of elitism.

She says further that the key characters, white men contending with the negative impact of globalization by reaffirming their attachment to the colonial settlement myth, were "depicted as wounded either physically or psychologically (or both)" and did not exhibit warrior performances but rather "modest, anti-elitist, and socially progressive attitudes toward the work of belonging" (191). These characters were able to ignore the historical fact of the destructive impact of the Canadian colonial enterprise on Indigenous peoples and some immigrants and focus their attention on their own communities.

Other forms of popular culture do not show a particularly dominant representation: "English Canadian masculinities are constructed — sometimes explicitly and sometimes silently — in a dialogue between presumptions of what men are or should be primarily in terms of race, ethnicity, sex, class, and sexuality, and presumptions of what Canadians are or should be primarily in terms of distinguishing them from Americans" (Greenhill 2012: 128). Exploring the overall portrayal of masculinity in television, film, commercials, history and sculpture, she returns to the intersectional theme, noting that: "The intersectional need to consider race, ethnicity, ability, language (among many other social groupings), and the difficulty of pinning down sex/gender as much as nationality, makes representations of Canadian masculinities in traditional and popular culture particularly compelling — if not entirely satisfying." All this "renders Canadian men and their masculinities a truly fascinating if ever-changing, conundrum" (143).

Although, there may be "no single or stable literary definition of Canadian masculinity" (Tolmie and Shearer 2012: 109), studying something as complex as Canadian masculinity is a difficult but potentially rewarding process:

> Masculinities are historically and culturally specific, and yet one of the most interesting things about masculinity is that it is so powerfully conceptualized as an unproblematic universal, often through the didactic invocation of the ideas of "being a man" … It is this mystique that makes the concept so powerfully flexible; while masquerading as universal, the very lack of specificity of the phrase "being a man" enables it to express a wide range of meanings. (Tolmie and Shearer 2012: 106)

Two iconic figures in Canadian history and culture, historical figures and professional hockey players, help to separate myth from reality on matters related to social power. While "physicality and ruggedness" are important ideological expressions of masculine mythology for both types of males, a key social function of such myths is to support and bolster class domination (Robidoux 2012: 120):

> The romanticized corporal construction of masculinity is endorsed and enacted by most men, which provides them with social rewards. But as we see actual manifestations of the myth, we see these rewards quickly dissipate as they cater to and perpetuate the imbalance of power in male gender relations.

Furthermore, the individual costs and benefits of the types of rugged physical masculine practice imposed on professional hockey players do not weigh on the side of the players, making them "merely actors in the larger mythology of high capitalist patriarchy" (124).

No systematic motif of Canadian masculinity emerges. From film and literature of all sorts, to music, dance, theatre and more, a "truly diverse 'pattern of practice'" that speak to masculinities as a process, changing and developing with a portrait that "crosses multiple and converging lines of sex, gender, history, psychology, class, work, leisure, religion, subcultures, sport, race, ethnicity, regions, and nations in our contemporary globalized world" (Ramsay 2011: xxvii).

But surely one might argue that over the past decades movies and television have become more liberal given that many shows have male characters that do not practise traditional hegemonic masculinity or are openly gay. Yes this is indeed the case. However the situation may not be as radically different as it seems. Since the 1980s more diverse images of men are to be found. In particular, two different new types of masculinity that are represented as "man the nurturer" and "man the narcissist" (Milestone and Meyer 2011: 119). As the names imply, one image is of men that are more caring, emotional and supportive and committed to gender equity while the other man is a more self-interested, fashion-conscious consumer of men's styles.

In a provocatively titled article, "Nothing Queer about Queer Television: Televized Construction of Gay Masculinities," Guillermo Avila-Saavedra (2009) argues that the representation of gay men on conventional television, while it seemed like a potentially progressive development in terms of presenting alternate masculinities, in reality was less so. He points out that "the overwhelming majority of queer characters on television remain gay white males" (2009: 18). Furthermore, these men were affluent and held traditional family values. After studying a number of representations of gay men in movies and television, Shugart (2003: 67) concluded:

> In these texts, homosexuality is not only recoded and normalized in these representations as consistent with privileged male heterosexuality but is

articulated as extending heterosexual male privilege. In so doing, blatant sexism is reinvented and legitimized, and gay male identity simultaneously is defined by and renormalizes heteronormativity.

In recent years much critical attention has been directed to films that represent more diverse and realistic masculinities; however, while there is more diversity in the presentation of masculinity in films, the "development of a non-misogynist, non-racist, non-homophobic, non-hegemonic for of masculinity still seems to be an elusive goal" (Greven 2016: 4).

MOVING ON

There are important representations in many cultural practices such as those in video games, popular music and music videos, most genres of television, magazines, novels and fiction of all sorts, advertising of all sorts and on and on. While much attention has been devoted to sexist images of women in, for example, advertising, in recent decades the portrayal of masculinity has come under serious scrutiny.

We need to think seriously about all forms of representation and the important questions relate to the issue of cause, effect and reinforcement. Advertising, for example, is all about consumption, getting you to spend money on a commodity you might not need or otherwise would not buy. The fact that advertisers play off our emotions and stereotypes, and that advertisements can and often are just plain silly, stupid, flippant and nonsensical, does not mean that they are innocent in the gender representation process.

Hall (1997) documents the various ways that representation and representations can be understood, noting that, for some, representations are cultural constructions used in creating codes thorough which we understand the world, while for others they are the essential elements of the social discourse that, among other things, is important in situating the subject. Whether the representations of masculinities, particularly hegemonic masculinity are, to use Hall's terms, reflective, intentional or constructed, they are important to boys and men, providing images, models, behaviours and so on that might create, reinforce, stabilize or even question and destabilize patterns of behaviour. Addressing the precise impact of representations becomes, as was noted in the previous chapter, a matter of empirical investigation at a lower level of abstraction, that is, the actual lived lives of boys and men understood through the theoretical prism developed here.

Having the typology precisely correct is not important, because over the years and across many genres of movies, novels, television shows and now video games we find, at the level of individual characters, a range of different concrete ways of practising masculinity. We know that within a given gender order there are different types of masculinities. We have been focusing on one — hegemonic masculinity

— but many scholars have maintained that there are others. Indeed, in a given gender order, actual hegemonic practice may not be the most common form of day-to-day practice, but this does not alter its hegemonic status (Connell 2000b). The question as to what other masculinities exist and co-exist in a given gender order at a given time is an important theoretical and empirical question that can only be answered by theoretical and empirical labour. One thing is clear, though: "To recognize diversity in masculinities is not enough. We must also recognize the *relations* between different kinds of masculinity, relations of alliance, domination and subordination" (Connell 1991: 37, emphasis in original).

CHAPTER 8

DEFENDING, RESISTING AND COSTING THE PATRIARCHAL DIVIDEND

For the past five hundred years or more, Western masculinities have emerged in the context of the development of the capitalist economic order enmeshed in a particular version of a patriarchal gender order, or alternately, a particular version of a patriarchal gender order enmeshed in the developing Western capitalist economic order. Patriarchy, as a gender order, is predicated on the control and domination of some men over women, children and some other men. Patriarchy existed, of course, long before the emergence of full-blown capitalism; however, the emergence of capitalism over the past five hundred years provided opportunities for certain types of masculinity to emerge and become dominant.

The dominant or hegemonic mode of practising masculinity across the Western capitalist patriarchal world emphasizes control, power, authority, competition and domination; however, at the same time we know that there are also multiple alternate masculinities. Not all, or even most, males endorse or attempt to practise hegemonic masculinity. Many men, for example, may find themselves in economically subservient positions under the control of other men and without opportunities to express power, control or domination; likewise many men may choose alternate forms such as complacency or resistance. Questions as to the details of what masculinities are present, quantitatively important, dominant, emerging or receding and so forth can only be addressed at the level of a concrete historically existing social structure; however, a few general comments are possible.

We know that a patriarchal dividend exists. Although the precise forms it takes vary across history, locale and cultural context, in patriarchal society there are typically a range of benefits that accrue to males. These benefits are the patriarchal dividend and may include material benefits, the provision of range of personal and domestic services, social prestige, exclusion from certain tasks, security, access to positions of power and so on. Depending on how a gender order is nestled into other institutional orders, the patriarchal dividend may be unevenly distributed across classes, regions and ethnic and other groups.

Despite the importance of power, control and dominance for those practising hegemonic masculinity, such practices can be precarious. As I have noted, the consolidation of Western patriarchal masculinity over the past several hundred years has not been effortless nor has it been without resistance. Needless to say, given their position in patriarchal gender orders, the core of the resistance to the practice of Western patriarchal masculinity has typically come from women. Academics often use the analogy of waves (First, Second and Third) to analyze, typically in retrospect, the efforts of women to secure all the basic rights and privileges accorded to men. Staying with the theme of "waves," the Second Wave of feminism that emerged in the 1960s and beyond, because it was building on the gains of centuries of women's struggles, sought to make changes that were more profound and radical in terms of the core social relationships in our patriarchal gender order. The right to vote might have threatened a small element of the patriarchal dividend — male control of the polity — but it left untouched the core elements of the patriarchal dividend, particularly at the personal level, of many men. The call for a more radical understanding of equity hit closer to home because it raised fundamental questions like equal pay, shared domestic responsibility, female control over reproductive rights and increased power sharing across major institutions. Given what we know about the patriarchal dividend, such changes would involve serious erosion and very likely generate a reaction by some men and even women. In order to better understand the entrenched nature of the patriarchal gender order I want to consider the efforts of some men to defend the patriarchal order, albeit sometimes by appearing to change and other times through more virulent reactions.

DEFENDING THE PATRIARCHAL DIVIDEND

While the ostensive focus of some of the activities and arguments that emerged might just seem like a reaction and/or a critique of feminism, in reality they were about protecting and defending certain forms of practising masculinity and male privilege. I want to examine three such reactions using Kenneth Clatterbaugh's (1990) analysis of some reactions to feminism.

Among the responses Clatterbaugh notes was one rooted in what he calls the conservative legacy. Such a reaction, as the name implies, upholds the traditional notion that men are protectors, providers and fathers. The traditional nuclear family is understood as representing the natural order. He notes there are two different streams, represented by: 1) moral conservatives; and 2) biological determinists and sociobiological thought. The common tendency was to see "male nature" as needing taming, controlling, civilizing and domestication. Conventional masculine behaviour is seen as part of a moral universe and/or the nature of males that, however nasty men can be at times, is essentially natural, appropriate and necessary. Such arguments are typically supported by and predicated on "conventional wisdom," including the idea that masculine behaviours are the result of evolutionary natural selection. In short, feminism is seen as a risk to the natural order summarized as such: "You can't legislate natural behaviours."

The second reaction Clatterbaugh discusses relates to what is often called the men's rights perspective. Largely focused on protecting men's rights with regard to divorce and child custody issues, the Men's Rights Association was formed in 1973. By 1980s more than two hundred formal father's rights groups were active in in the U.S. (Clatterbaugh 1990: 62). One of these organizations, the National Coalition for Men, was founded in 1977 with a clear statement of purpose on their website: "The National Coalition for Men (NCFM) is a nonprofit educational organization that raises awareness about the ways sex discrimination affects men and boys." Further: "Since 1977 NCFM has been dedicated to the removal of harmful gender based stereotypes especially as they impact boys, men, their families and the women who love them." They spell out their core issue:

> Men have been systematically discriminated against in parenting rights, child custody, criminal sentencing, military conscription, education, domestic and sexual violence laws that neglect male victims and support false accusations, reproductive rights, genital integrity laws, international forced labor laws, public benefits and more, while men and boys face societal misandry and male bashing. Men make 80–99 percent of homeless adults, job deaths and injuries, incarcerated persons, combat deaths, dropouts and suicide deaths ("attempted" suicide rates are unreliable because it is unlikely men report failed suicides as often as women do). Men also die younger than women and have higher mortality rates for 13 of the 15 leading causes of death.

Among their other concerns are too many female teachers that they connect to boys apparently being poorly served by educational system. They speak of the "housework myth" that ignores all the work men supposedly do around the home. They complain about the "power feminists" who mislead the public on the so-called pay gap, and then there are the male rape victims who they claim are ignored. They claim that fathers are systematically disadvantaged in divorce and child custody, while male health issues and domestic violence against men are apparently ignored. Their site information includes various books and material promoting men's rights including a book by R.K. Hendrick, *How to Avoid "Getting Screwed" When Getting Laid, Volume 1*, one of dozens of books with similarly provocative titles.

In addition to this purely conservative reactionary stance there were efforts to revitalize what was seen as the loss of some supposed male spiritual centre. One side of this reaction was secular, emerging from the work of Robert Bly (1990). Bly's work spawned what is commonly referred to as the mythopoetic men's movement. Bly's book *Iron John* plays off a Grimm Brothers fairy tale, "Iron Hans." Bly's work is based in Jungian psychology with its notion of the existence of a deep innate collective unconscious within the psyche and shared by all humans. Among the elements of this unconscious trove for men are elements of masculinity rooted in the male ancestral and evolutionary history. Such elements are the basis of deep psychic archetypes that motivate common human behaviours and dispositions. While the complex story and myth are an interesting yarn, I will cut to the chase by noting that, according to Bly, industrial society has robbed men of opportunities to connect and realize their inner deep masculinity, while simultaneously eliminating most if not all rites of passage as boys pass to manhood. A part of our human heritage is the maleness of a mythical wild man embedded deep in the male subconscious that has been repressed and blunted, thus producing soft men, without zest and self esteem. The lost connection to the "wild man" is the basis of much male pain and discontent, resulting in anti-social behaviours and a loss of direction and centredness to life. In order to recover this loss and restore our innermost sense of our maleness and masculinity, males need to shed or flee from protection, safety and security and find their inner self in the world of trials and tribulations. The route to such a recovery typically involved activities with groups of men performing various rites and rituals from poetry readings to wilderness experiences or retreats into nature to listen to music, while eschewing the typical creature comforts of modern middle-class life in the suburbs. Getting back to nature in a homosocial setting was seen as one path back to one's true manhood. As an aside, because they are not men, women cannot be the source of men reconnecting and rediscovering their manhood — men have to do it themselves. This new way of being is not just always being nicer and kinder, but rather it is to live according to the male inner manliness, not as some sort of "savage man," but rather a restored masculinity that also embraces the internal feminine side of all men.

An alternate and also spiritually focused attempt by men to understand and restore their true manhood and masculinity amid the changing world of the late twentieth century was the Promise Keepers. Founded in 1990 by Bill McCartney, an ex-college football coach at the University of Colorado, the movement grew rapidly throughout 1990s, so much so that hundreds of thousands of men attended a rally in October 1997 at the National Mall in Washington. The Promise Keepers became known for their large rallies in football stadiums across the U.S. and Canada that attracted audiences of largely white and middle-class men. Members were to commit themselves to keep seven promises that were based on traditional Christian scripture and associated values. The core message was a combination of elements based on a particular form of evangelical Christianity (service, healing, reconciliation and brotherhood) alongside the diagnosis of an apparent male crisis men were facing. The call was for men to reclaim their leadership roles in a manner that respected for women and non-violence.

While these and other men's groups fought to restore the so-called lost rights, hearts and souls of men, a "fifth column" was forming in the academy, developing a narrative that constitutes men as victims of some nefarious feminist plot and claims about a growing misandry. In Canada, for example, some argue there is misandry in virtually every element of popular culture, from television, through to t-shirts and greeting cards (Nathanson and Young 2001). Sociologist Anthony Synnott (2009) wholeheartedly agrees, while arguing that masculinity has a strong biological basis. Suzanne Venker's *The War on Men* (2013: 18, 23) sees men as having been demoted from "respected providers and protectors of the family" to "superfluous buffoons." Blaming the feminist war on men and using evidence from depictions of men in situation comedies and commercials, she laments the decline of the nuclear family, a particular problem because, according to her, deep down girls and women want to be wives and mothers.

An alternate focus of the defenders of patriarchy was to focus on the supposed negative impact on boys of efforts to achieve gender equality. In February 2016 entering "boys in crisis" in a popular search engine produced nearly 99,000,000 results. This is because over the past two decades or more, an entire new genre of books exploded on the scene claiming that boys were in some kind of crisis. Writers such as Christina Hoff Summers (2000) have been at the forefront of a narrative that placed boys as victims of feminism. The tenor of her arguments is summarized in declarations such as: "It's a bad time to be a boy in America" (2000: 13). She both praises traditional masculinity and lambastes feminism for hijacking and corrupting the U.S. school curriculum. The core of her argument draws on a biological determinist position with regard to the natural propensities of boys. She notes that the war on boys is partly based on "forgetting a simple truth: that the energy, competitiveness, and corporal daring of normal, decent males is responsible for much that is right in the world" (14). The theme of boys in crisis at school identified by Summers has continued to resonate among many. In Canada the *Globe and Mail* published a series of articles beginning with one entitled "Failing Boys and the Powder Keg of Sexual Politics" by Carolyn Abraham. In 2006, *Newsweek* published an article entitled "Education: Boys Falling Behind

Girls in Many Areas." The common elements are claims that boys were failing in school, engaged in crime, missing out on jobs, drifting aimlessly and generally in crisis all because feminists have apparently seized control of major institutions and are pushing some undefined pro-girl agenda.

The supposed boy crisis narrative led former First Lady Laura Bush to announce that she was going to take up the cause of boys (Rivers and Barnett 2006). While the supposed causes vary, the usual suspects were frequently dragged out: biological brain structure; hormonal differences; innate characteristics making it impossible for boys to sit and learn from women teachers; weak fathers; and strong women. It turns out, however, that the so-called crisis was a myth, fostered by the simple fact that girls were doing better in a number of areas. The fact that girls were performing better in some subjects such as reading and staying in school longer with higher completion rates is not at the expense of boys (Rivers and Barnett 2006). This has not stopped organizations such as *Fox News* and the North American far right from continuing the narrative, as Soraya Chemaly (2014: n.p.) points out:

> It is a truth universally acknowledged, that a Fox commentator in pursuit of a good rating, must be in want of a boy crisis, a bad feminist and a single mother. That anyone serious is still having these conversations, using these words to describe issues that we know are born of gender stereotypes, implicit biases and stereotype threat is gobsmacking.

Social scientists seem to like the word "post," as in claims that capitalism and modernity have passed leaving us in a post-capitalist or post-modern or post-something circumstance. Rachel O'Neill (2015) observes that the claim that feminism is over, passé and that we are now in a post-feminist era is really a new form of sexism that is not just reactionary in the true sense of the word as harkening back, but it is also a form of neo-liberal individualism. She suggests that the argument implicit in the notion of post-feminism is that feminism is no longer required or useful, its goals having been reached and accomplished. Women, as individuals in the neo-liberal world of individualism and individual responsibility are in a position to benefit from the struggles of those who went before them. Put another way: "Heavily imbricated with neo-liberalism, postfeminist discourses rely upon a language of individualism, transposed by an ethic of personal responsibility" (O'Neill 2015: 102). Patriarchy, this argument holds, has been reformed and transformed and now it is possible for girls and women to have it all.

Perhaps a song first made popular by the duo of Sonny and Cher a half-century ago titled "The Beat Goes On" is an appropriate way to draw this discussion to a close. The Internet crawls with hundred of thousands of sites, diatribes, observations and interjections on the so-called crisis of men and boys and the inherent evils and dangers of feminism that run the gamut from humorous to hateful, serious to ludicrous, thoughtful to thoughtless and encouraging to terrifying. We can be sure that the defence of patriarchy and the patriarchal dividend will go on; however, there are also signs that men are changing, at least somewhat. While the evidence that real and radical change is underway is mixed, some are arguing it is real. It is to these arguments that I now turn.

MASCULINITIES GALORE

I noted some of the criticisms of the notion of hegemonic masculinity in Chapter 1, but I did not mention the work of scholars such as Michael Atkinson (2011) who have raised some important questions with regard to the possibility that the complexities of contemporary society may render traditional concepts used to understand masculinity irrelevant. According to Atkinson (2011: 9), we are in a era of "late modern industrialism" in which identities are less stable and more fragmented and fluid, meaning that men tend to live lives characterized by multiple masculinities, or "a pastiche involving the mixing and matching of masculinities with no one particularly dominant or hegemonic" (32). As he rather dramatically puts it: "*Masculine* hegemony has been fractured into a million pieces but not dislodged entirely, nor exposed to its deepest roots" (33, emphasis in original.) Atkinson does, however, identify the continued importance of power, albeit at the micro level. He also discusses the problems associated with violence and bullying but without a firm sociological foundation on which to explain the felt need for such displays of masculinity. Despite having assured the reader that the traditional notion of hegemonic masculinity passed on with the demise of traditional industrial society, he uses the term hegemonic masculinities (plural) to refer to the amalgam of apparently disparate performance options available to men, yet in which males retain major elements of social power. Apparently, not one but multiple masculinities are the continuing basis of male domination, the basis of which is not really explained.

To the extent to which Atkinson might be seen to be arguing that the concept of hegemonic masculinity as conventionally used in the critical men's studies literature is no longer relevant, Eric Anderson is even more direct in his rejection of the concept. Anderson argues that the gender world, across the West at least, has changed markedly since Connell first articulated the notion of hegemonic masculinity. As a result of much greater acceptance of same-sex relationships and a decline in homophobia, the traditional concept of hegemonic masculinity has lost its relevance. Anderson (2011: 253) proposes a new concept to replace hegemonic masculinity, what he calls "inclusive masculinity theory."

Based on data drawn from his research that focuses on university and senior school sports teams, he concludes that there is a significant decline in homophobia and an associated increased acceptance of gay men among members of the sporting teams. He sees sports an important signifier of masculinity, and rugby in particular, as a "leading definer of masculinity among youth and university-aged English men" (Anderson and McGuire 2010: 249). Anderson and McGuire argue that a new archetype of masculinity has emerged: inclusive masculinity. Further, he suggests that the multiple forms of masculinities he finds exist on a horizontal plane as opposed to a stratified hierarchy in which one form is dominant. Because boys and men are able to make personal individual choices, we live in a new era of free choice that yields multiple personalized inclusive masculinities.

As optimistic as this sounds, the limited database on which Anderson draws his conclusions is concerning. Without in any way questioning his actual research and data, it is indeed a hopeful sign that young men engaged in a traditionally masculine sport such as rugby are more open and welcoming to gay athletes. I wonder, however, if this really signifies a society-wide normative and behavioural shift. Work done in Canada on homophobia and transphobia in high schools paints a much darker and gloomy picture of bullying and violence (Haskell and Burtch 2010). Rachel O'Neill notes that Anderson's work, while it is optimistic and good news, requires more empirical support and, most worrisome, seems politically too close to the declared victory of post-feminist politics (2015: 106–107). Sam de Boise's (2015: 334) criticisms of the inclusive masculinity issue are more substantial on both theoretical and empirical grounds; however, the political implications are most salient:

> At best, an idea of inclusive masculinity is a catchall attempt to describe behaviors which do not fit within a cultural stereotype of machismo. At worst, however, it is actively dangerous in that it conflates the hard-fought legal rights won by gay rights activists with a mistaken belief that because homophobic speech and violence are less apparent in public contexts, we are nearing some historical end-point for gender and sexuality discrimination. This has the potential to close down discussions around how we should be continuing to change attitudes toward gender and sexuality.

It is important to remember that the concept of hegemonic masculinity, despite its importance for understanding what I am calling patriarchal, or perhaps more specifically Western capitalist patriarchal masculinity, was never meant to describe all or even most male gender practice. To the extent to which we, correctly, attribute much of the currency afforded the concept to the work of Connell, she always insisted that we need to pay attention to alternate masculinities, that is, alternate modes of practice that are available to boys and men. While no comprehensive classification or taxonomy of masculinities across gender orders may be possible, Connell (1995) has consistently pointed out several potential forms of masculine practice in addition to the hegemonic mode, including subordinate, complicit and marginal. The stories of the men she studies constantly refer to the diversities of each of these forms of masculinity, particularly when the analysis moves to the level of abstraction that involves the everyday lives of social actors. In speaking, for example, of the history of the gentry in Europe and the U.S. over the past two centuries, she notes the emergence of new hegemonic forms "and the emergence of an array of subordinate and marginalized masculinities" (1995: 191). Elsewhere she reminds us: "Seen close up, hegemonic and complicit masculinities are no more monolithic that are subordinate and marginal masculinities" (1995: 181).

In her discussion of the lives of boys and men Connell (2000) speaks of the fact that many men do not practise hegemonic masculinity. As she put it: "Indeed many men live in a state of some tension with, or distance from, the hegemonic masculinity of their culture or community" (2000: 11). Connell is unable to provide the details of how men who are not explicitly practising in the hegemonic mode go about their lives because her work often operates at a high level of abstraction, that of the gender order. Elsewhere she does provide some guidance noting the importance of subordination and complicity for some men (Connell 1995). The notion of complicity is important because as Connell and Messerschmidt (2005) point out, many men are able to reap some of the benefits of the patriarchal dividend by not actually having to engage in the systematic practice of hegemonic masculinity, but rather by living in a cultural, social and ideological environment that is structured on the basis of and accepts this form of masculinity. Some men are able to go about living their lives perhaps unconsciously accruing benefits without ever engaging in violence, overt domination or control, but rather just being men in patriarchy. The corollary is acceptance, complicity and never questioning their rights and privileges that just seem naturally theirs.

A particular form of masculine practice that Connell has consistently made an important part of her analysis is gay masculinity. A significant chapter in *Masculinities* titled "A Very Straight Gay" is based on Connell's interviews with eight gay men. The results are very likely bounded by the time of the study, now over twenty years ago, in that what Connell called the dominant cultural definition of gay men as effeminate was "obviously wrong as a description of the men … who mostly do 'act like a man,'" but these men are also an "outrage" to hegemonic masculinity because "their object-choice subverts the masculinity of their character and presence" (1995: 161–162). In the intervening years, changes to human rights and other legislation, public education by various groups and organizations, public demonstrations and the coming out of persons in virtually every walk of life have surely changed the overall situation in terms of the lives of gay men and lesbians and their ability to live freely. The variety of modes by which gay men practise their masculinities has been extensively documented and analyzed revealing what one would expect — a diversity of masculine practices. Luke Runyon began his National Public Radio special "In Changing America, Gay Masculinity Has 'Many Different Shades'" by noting:

> Life as a gay man in the U.S. has changed in the past decade — the law and cultural attitudes toward homosexuality have shifted. And those greater social and legal freedoms have also changed how some gay men choose to express their masculinity — and their femininity.

The potential options available for the expression of sexuality as sexual aesthetics is defined as the "cultural and stylistic distinctions utilized to delineate symbolic boundaries between gay and straight cultures and individuals" (Bridges 2014: 62). Sexual aesthetics involve taste (appearance and interests); behaviour (conduct, comportment, speech); and ideological stances (support for gay issues). One study finds cis men who employed the sexual aesthetics associated with gay tastes, behaviour and ideology in order to distance themselves from stereotypical masculinity in an effort to paint themselves as politically progressive (Bridges 2014). The notion of mixing and matching various modes of practising masculinity has received considerable attention over the past decade, including an important assessment of hybrid masculinities.

Such an understanding of masculinity informed Atkinson's (2011: 32) work as in his notion of a pastiche masculinity that incorporates "mixed and matched" elements of male performance possibilities. Other scholars speak of men appropriating "bits and pieces" of alternate cultures, such as gay masculinities, to "produce new hybrid configurations of gender practice that enable them to reproduce their domination over women in historically novel ways" (Demetriou 2001: 350–351). These hybrid masculinities involve "the selective incorporation of elements of identity typically associated with various marginalized and subordinated masculinities and — at times — femininities into privileged men's gender performance and identities" (Bridges and Pasco 2014: 246). Ethnographic documents in local settings the appropriation of elements of gay masculinities by men in homosocial settings in order to enhance the status and potential power of the men involved (Arxer 2011). While such flexibility, adaptation and incorporation of various forms of subordinate and marginalized masculinities point to the possibility of changes in male gender practices, the cases I have cited tend to cast cold water on the notion that this is a breakthrough in terms of a shift toward greater equity, as while hybridity has the potential for shifts in power relations it can also be used to consolidate with a different face the underlying dynamics of patriarchal relationship.

I have consistently argued that understanding the complexities of masculinity, as male social practice in all its dimensions and complexities, is a daunting task; however, we need not despair because the task is difficult. A founding figure of the discipline of sociology, German sociologist Max Weber (1968), set the task of sociology as understanding, explaining and interpreting human social action even in the face of the infinite complexity of the human social world. Given this daunting task, the question becomes, how do we proceed? The answer is quite simple — get the concepts right and it becomes possible to proceed to scratch away at the complexity and proffer explanations and suggestions to uncover what is really going on. A key element of developing and finding adequate concepts is understanding the role of concepts at various levels of abstraction and the intellectual work and creativity it takes to move across levels of abstraction.

There is a form of male gender practice that we can legitimately call hegemonic patriarchal masculinity, and there are some general and typical behaviours, ideologies and practices associated with this mode of doing gender. However, at the level of the gender order, patriarchy, we are not able to say much about how those practices unfold in, for example, 1920s Brisbane, or 1960s Chicago, or early twenty-first-century Calgary. However, since all of these social locations represent forms of gender practice in a patriarchal gender order, we can use our understanding of patriarchy to make sense of the complexities of how gender is practised in these historically, politically, culturally and economically contextualized social formations. That is, we can use our abstract concepts in more concrete analyses in order to make sense out of the complexities of masculinities in the everyday lives of girls and women and, of course, boys and men. The process of moving social analysis to a lower level of abstraction and the concretization of our concepts typically involves the refinement, elaboration and even recasting of our conceptual tools and never engaging in conformist dogma. The particular forms of hegemonic, subordinate, complacent and marginal masculinities in 1920s Brisbane, or 1960s Chicago, or early twenty-first-century Calgary will be different in many ways, but they will also exhibit certain commonalities. In a similar manner, the class structures and dynamics of 1920s Brisbane, or 1960s Chicago, or early twenty-first-century Calgary will differ in many ways; however, they will in some manner manifest the structural dynamics of class in a capitalist society.

In the light of this analytical reality it is not possible, given the level of abstraction at which I have typically operated in much of this book, to say much about specific forms of hegemonic, subordinate, complacent and marginal masculinities because such a project requires the application or utilization of these concepts in the context of a particular society or social formation, or the analysis of group and individual actions in a particular gender regime or institutional setting. I have conducted research, for example, on the gender practices of corporate executives at a certain moment in Canadian history, and found the employment of concepts such as hegemonic masculinity invaluable in making sense of the daily lives and concerns of business leaders. Similarly, my personal work life has involved a variety of positions including senior university leadership positions. Although some progress is being made, the world of senior university administration has traditionally tended to be a masculine world replete with gender practices that I would characterize as a variation on the theme in terms of hegemonic patriarchal masculinity.

That said, the analysis I have been developing has tended to operate at a certain level of abstraction that does not prevent me from making some comments about the implications and costs of how masculinity is practised in patriarchal capitalism.

THE COSTS OF THE DIVIDEND

A lot of work and effort goes into making boys into men and preparing them to practise hegemonic masculinity. For those practising hegemonic masculinity (or attempting to do so), much social effort goes into establishing, maintaining and sustaining that form of practice. As I have argued, systems of social control and dominance typically require mechanisms of power, including violence and the threat of violence, as well as ideological manipulation to maintain the order and attempt to ensure its legitimacy. The question that arises is: At what cost?

While it is clear that the practice and maintenance of hegemony and the patriarchal dividend come with high costs, I have not encountered an actual calculus of the costs of maintaining a patriarchal gender order and the patriarchal dividend. I suspect that, given our understanding of the complexities of the social world, such a calculus is impossible. Yet, we know that many of the social practices associated with patriarchal hegemonic masculinity come with individual and societal costs. It is time to consider a few of these costs.

I begin with boys, future men, by reconsidering the cost of manning up. I have made extensive use of the work of Judy Chu (2014) and Niobe Way (2011) because their data is gathered at the level of the daily lives of boys across various cultures and in various settings. The pattern I established was in variance with the "boys will be boys" cliché of boys willingly endorsing their status as just little men engaged in a little man's version of hegemonic masculinity. I have documented the emotional needs of boys who have close friends with whom they can confide, share secrets and love. However, Chu documents the dual worries of some fathers that their boys will lose their deep emotional capacities and their fears that retaining such emotional capacities past a certain age will have a negative impact in the world they will inevitably join. As one father put it, when it comes to meeting the expectations of conventional masculinity, boys need to "pretend that you can do it. Bluff your way. If you can't do it, bluff your way through it" (Chu 2014: 175).

Unfortunately boys do learn to not just bluff it, but to take action, not just the drastic actions of the school shooters and the unimaginable cost of their actions but in some cases everyday violence. Edward Morris's (2008: 738) interviews with a number of boys at a rural Ohio school disclosed a disturbing pattern. One of the boys noted:

> I mean in this school — it's all about football. Football, football, football. Not band. Band's gay! … The guys [in the band] act different too. They act kinda gay. So that's why they're picked on. But the girls [in the band] ain't really said nothin' to. You said they act kinda gay — now does that mean, do you think they're actually gay, or are they just acting in a certain way that kinda … They just don't act normal … So [other students] just make fun of them.

The issue is not just gay baiting but actual violence as two other boys noted after Morris explained he was writing a book about boys: "Well you'll have to put a lot in there about fighting." When questioned further one of the boys explains that there were three fights last week "But one was just a pussy fight." And another fight one of the boys was in because "He's tryin' to be somebody — he called me a rutter, so I got into it with him. … He's actin' like he's all somebody though — I'll fight him. He's a pussy. I saw a fight he was in and it was like a pussy fight" (2008: 743). Lastly, when asked why they fight so much and the problem with fighting:

> Not enough action. They get broke up too soon so you really … See you fight in school you get broke up too soon, you don't really get to express your actions you know? 'Cause the reason you fight is 'cause of anger. Well, that's the reason I fight, is 'cause of anger. And after you hit 'im four or five times, your anger gets released. But if it happens in school and you get pulled off of 'im before you can hit 'im then you end up getting into another fight with 'im. (2008: 745)

Morris's (2008: 746) conclusion is equally sobering:

> Fighting as a display of physical masculine dominance, or viewing academic work and striving as feminized and lower status, are examples. Such perceptions and behaviors operated within local, as well as regional and global, patterns of masculinity and social class. Local history meant that hegemonic masculinity in this context stemmed (partly) from maintaining a "breadwinner" role within the family through physically demanding labor.

It appears as if the culture of violence associated with this form of masculinity does not stop with school fights as, in 2014, among those under 26 years old, more people were killed by guns that in vehicle accidents (Diamond 2015).

It is obviously impossible to quantify the costs of manning up, but we can think critically about it. What is the cost to boys being pressured into athletics and away from academics, poetry and drama? What are the psychological and spiritual costs of feeling the need to be a bully in order to demonstrate your power and compensate for vulnerabilities, never mind the cost to the victims and their families?

What are the costs of the relentless pressure on boys to be sexual creatures? Survey data demonstrates that about two-thirds of teenaged boys think waiting to have sex is the preferred option; however, one in three 15- to 17-year-olds feels pressured by friends to engage in sex (Allen, Colin 2003). A major study published in *Pediatrics* also reported on the pressure factor, noting that "the majority (82 percent) of males 12 to 19 years of age reported feeling pressured by friends to have sex" (Marcell et al. 2011: e1661). Importantly, in terms of self esteem and self image, when they did engage in sexual activity, for many of these boys and young men the aftermath was not what they might have expected as demonstrated by the fact that "more than half (55%) wished that they had waited longer before having sex for the first time, and more than one-third (38%) of men 18 to 24 years of age reported that they really did not want sex to happen the first time that it did or had mixed feelings about it" (Marcell et al. 2011: e1661). I noted the importance of the various forms of the media as messengers of norms and social practice. The National Association of Social Workers in the U.S. has studied the various sources that pressure adolescent boys into sexual activity. They found that "more than half (56 percent) of all television shows contain sexual content — averaging more than three scenes with sex per hour" (NASW 2001). Although not the focus of this book, there is also, of course, the pressure on girls to engage in sexual activity. In addition to the assaults I discussed above, a study out of England found that of four out of ten girls report being pressured to engage in sexual activity (Doughty 2015).

Intimate partner violence is often related to the need to establish, assert, maintain and reinforce power, control, dominance and subordinate relations, and has obvious costs. The costs of physical, psychological, emotional and spiritual trauma, pain and acute and chronic suffering experienced by female victims are impossible to calculate; nevertheless they are real. Additionally, there is the loss of dignity, self-respect, autonomy and opportunity that visits victims and children over generations. Social costs include lost time at work and the real dollar costs in terms of health care and victim services as well. Although the appropriate focus is on victims as the bearers of the costs of violence geared to supporting, bolstering and maintaining patriarchy, male power and control, many men involved in the assaults experience guilt and other negative psychological and spiritual consequences. Such consequences, without doubt, are apparent in some of the unhealthy behaviours of some men.

While it may seem hard to estimate the actual costs of domestic violence, the Canadian Department of Justice undertook such a study in 2012. Using 2009 data they state: "The total economic impact of spousal violence in 2009 was $7.4 billion, amounting to $220 per Canadian" (Zhang et al. 2013: xiii). Their data is so shocking that it warrants further detail:

> The justice system bore 7.3% ($545.2 million) of the total economic impact, where $320.1 million was borne by the criminal justice system and $225.1 million was borne by the civil justice system. A breakdown of the total criminal justice system costs by specific cost items reveals that policing services accounted for the majority of expenditures (45.5%), followed by corrections (31.7%), courts (9.5%), prosecutions (7.9%), and legal aid (5.5%). For civil justice system costs, 80.8% was attributed to child protection systems, 18.2% to separations and divorces, and 1.0% to civil protection orders.
>
> The most direct economic impact is borne by primary victims. Of the total estimated costs, $6.0 billion was incurred by victims as a direct result of spousal violence for items such as medical attention, hospitalizations, lost wages, missed school days, and stolen/damaged property. The intangible costs of pain and suffering and loss of life accounted for 91.2% of the total victim costs. Of the remaining tangible costs ($525.0 million), other personal costs, including legal costs for divorce and separation, and moving expenses, represented 51.7%, followed by costs associated with mental health issues (34.2%), productivity losses (10.2%), and health care costs (4.0%). (2013: xiii)

In 2012 Kate McIntur of the Centre for Policy Alternatives also undertook a study of the actual costs of violence against women. Her conclusion was slightly higher. Making reference to her sources she found: "Based on these estimates, the combined cost of adult sexual assault and intimate partner violence is $334 per person in Canada" (McIntur 2013: 7).

The act of always being in control, dominant and powerful (or attempting to be) generates stress and anxieties that in turn have health consequences. In 1920–22 the average life expectancy for women in Canada was 61 years compared to 59 for men. By 2007–09 the average life expectancy for women had risen to 83 years, while for men to 79. Although both sexes experienced dramatic increases, comparatively men were doing worse, because on average they were dying two years earlier than women in the 1920s compared to four years earlier in this century

(Statistics Canada 2012). In 2012, 76 percent of the 3,926 suicides in Canada were males (Statistics Canada 2015e).

Perhaps men are dying earlier because males are more prone to "risky behaviour." One risky behaviour is heavy drinking. In 2012 over five million Canadians drank heavily, with men making up about 70 percent of the total (Statistics Canada 2015f). Males are also at much greater risk when it comes to dying in an auto accident: of the 2,158 auto-accident-related deaths in Canada, 72 percent were men. No data was available on the number of women killed in cars driven by men (Statistics Canada 2015g).

With unfortunate regularity, newspapers and television news report on the tragic outcomes of various male risky behaviours. For example, on December 28, 2009, tragedy struck in the small British Columbia town of Sparwood when eight local men died after a series of avalanches struck them while they were out riding their snowmobiles in the mountains. A memorial was held in the town, at which some of the victims were described as doing "anything with a thrill" and as "adventurous men" who "knew that the avalanche risk was elevated that day," but felt they were equipped for it (Komarnicki 2008). A poem on the back of a Memorial Program read: "We are men, feeling wild and free. Is this not the way it is supposed to be? We're like eagles, yet flying through the snow" (Graveland 2009). Both of the newspaper stories covering this tragedy featured pictures of grieving family and friends.

While behaving in a manner that does not display sissy stuff shows that one is a big wheel, always prepared to give 'em hell as befits a sturdy oak, it can be risky. We know men and boys are not invulnerable — quite the opposite. Most of the war films I noted in Chapter 7 represent men as virtually invulnerable and indestructible, both physically and psychologically. War heroes, cowboys and gunfighters, James Bonds, space explorers, police catching gangsters, the gangsters themselves — are all portrayed as hypermasculine and invulnerable to pain, suffering or emotion. However, in the world of real human beings there is pain and suffering. The aftermath of war is often just as ugly as the war itself. Canadian veterans have been much in the news, particularly since Canadian troops retuned from Afghanistan. The evidence is now clear that the costs of war often come down the road. A *Toronto Star* (September 16, 2014) headline says it all: "Suicide Claims More Soldiers Than Those Killed by Afghan Combat." Bruce Campion-Smith (2014: n.p.) describes the toll: "The latest statistics from the defence department reveal 160 personnel have committed suicide between 2004 and March 31, 2014 ... That compares to the 138 soldiers killed in combat between 2002 and 2014, when Canada's Afghan mission formally ended." Although the base numbers are higher, a similar pattern appears in data from the U.S. A mental health watchdog group, the Citizens Commission on Human Rights, reports: "In early 2013 ... the number of military suicides in 2012 had far exceeded the total of those killed in battle — an average of nearly one a day." A month later came an even more sobering statistic from the U.S. Department of Veterans Affairs: "veteran suicide was running at 22 a day — about 8000 a year" (CCHR n.p.). So much for the invulnerable, emotionless, Rambo killing-machine type.

In costing the patriarchal dividend and indirectly the negative impacts of practising hegemonic masculinity in a patriarchal gender order, it is important not to loose track of agency and individual volition. Some of the individual costs are directly attributable to individual decisions; however, we never only consider agency. What to make of the decision of lower-class boys to seek a career, if not fame and fortune in professional sports, even though the risks are apparent and known? The costs of the routine violence that is professional football in North America are, as I've noted, well known and mostly accepted. In fact, "current estimates are that nearly 30 percent of all NFL players will suffer some form of dementia by the time they are sixty-five" (Maraniss 2016: 17). Furthermore, "our allegiance to football legitimates and even fosters within us a tolerance for violence, greed, racism and homophobia" (16). Newspapers seem to carry endless stories about the high cost of violence in sports. The detailed story of a hockey player who suffered more than seventy-five concussions begins with a description of the player's constant pain and concludes by noting: "He still wakes up nauseous every day. He takes four or five hot baths daily to cope with the pain and admits to turning to alcohol when he can't afford medication" (Mirtle 2016: S11). Is this a personal problem or a public issue? It is clearly both.

Part of the difficulty of costing the patriarchal dividend is not just the problem of quantifying the qualitative or the lack of a calculus, but it is also the sheer number of indicators one could use. Without blaming every problem humanity faces on how hegemonic patriarchal masculinity is practised, there is much more we could consider. An argument could easily be made that the social practices of hegemonic masculinity ring the same bell as those described by Marxian notions of alienation from other humans and even one's own social species. How does a suite of gender practices focused on domination and control bear on the manner by which humanity seems hell-bent on destroying the environment? I documented some of the costs of bullying and homophobia in relationship to school shootings, but what of the millions of others who simply suffer in silence without taking dramatic action? How would their physical, psychological and spiritual pain and suffering be measured? Is it possible that the refusal to engage in equitable relationships with partners in simple life-going activities such as childcare and food preparation dull and blunt the potential for empathy and caring? What are the root causes of the loneliness and isolation that many men seem to feel? How do the natural drives associated with sexuality and intimacy turn to self-centred demands and even violence and brutality when entitlement and control are paramount? I have not addressed the omnipresence of the pornography industry and all its despicable and loathsome manifestations; however, given the role of male power, domination and control of the so-called industry, how do we measure the costs to children, girls, women, the justice system and the psychological and spiritual well being of men, consumers and others?

I have been suggesting that among the important factors in the lives of boys and particularly men are changes in the economic order that impact their capacity to practise their masculinity. Perhaps nowhere is this more apparent than in the current restructuring of agriculture and food production in places like Australia and Canada. The family farm has traditionally been a patriarchal social institution with land ownership an important marker of masculinity. The global restructuring of food production is increasingly rendering the family farm irrelevant and with it the class that prided itself on land ownership and independence. The cover of *Newsweek* (April 10, 2014) carried the banner headline, "Death on the Farm: Farmers are a Dying Breed in Part Because They're Killing Themselves in Record Numbers," with details in a story by Mat Kutner, while in July another media outlet ran a similar story under the headline "Why Farmer Suicide Rates Are the Highest of Any Occupation" and again in November 2014: "Too Many Farmers Are Committing Suicide" (Farkas 2014a; 2014b). A high cost indeed.

An interesting assessment of the costs of practising a typically hegemonic mode of masculinity emerges from Nora Vincent, a female journalist who spent eighteen months fully disguised and living as a man. Her reflections include, "It was *hard* being a guy. Really hard" (2006: 275, emphasis in original). Part of the reason it was hard had to do with her discomfort with the way she had to be in order to be accepted: "I don't like how wooden I felt I had to make myself in order to pass as a believable guy" (275). Further, as Ned, the man she pretended to be, she felt the need to be terse and in control, hardening to the point of what she calls ossification. Then there was the surveillance, not because she was in a guise but because she was a guy, "Somebody is always evaluating your manhood. Whether it's other men, other women, even children" (276). She refers to the constant need to conform because the other guys were "hypervigilant about the rules of manhood" (276). Her life as a man reminded her that "boys have the sensitivity routinely mocked and shamed and beaten out of them, and the treatment leaves scars for years" (286). The result is not a pretty picture: "a lot of men are in pain. That's evident" (286). The pain, however, is not because they have lost their bearings as men or are hapless victims of raging feminism — it is a direct result of how they practise masculinity and something they can change.

If the thousands of years of cross-cultural history of humanity tell us anything about humans, it is that we are amazingly adaptable; we have an adaptability that has produced the diversity and change that marks human history. Boys and men need not assume they are so special, entitled, powerful and need to be in control, that is, we need not practise hegemonic masculinity. We have agency and options, but we are also bound and bounded by structural dynamics and so when it comes to changing how we practise masculinity in the twenty-first century, the matter is more complicated than merely a series of individual decisions to do better, although these would help.

A COMPLICATION: CAPITALISM AND PATRIARCHY

As I have demonstrated, what I am calling patriarchal hegemonic masculinity emerged alongside, in conjunction with and as part of the emergence of capitalism as an economic order. While they can be understood as analytically distinct, as a gender order and as an economic order patriarchy and capitalism bear similarities that relate to the practice of hegemonic masculinity.

First, some simple comparisons:

- Capitalism is a class-divided system in which class differences are an inherent element. Patriarchy is a sex- and gender-divided system in which sex and gender differences are inherent features.
- Unequal relations of power and access to resources are inherent in capitalism. Unequal relations of power and access to resources are inherent in patriarchy.
- The nature of market relationships and the manner by which they impact the distribution of the social surplus mean that an unequal distribution of wealth is inherent in capitalism. Unequal distribution of wealth is inherent in patriarchy in part because of the patriarchal dividend.
- The dominant ideologies in capitalist society place emphasis on the naturalness of human competition, individualism and the necessary presence of the market relations. The dominant ideologies in patriarchy place emphasis on the naturalness of sex and gender difference and the inevitability of the rule of men.
- Success in the market accrues to those who are able to compete, be in control, thrive on dominance, make difficult decisions and so on. The successful patriarch is a man in control, a big wheel, a sturdy oak and one whom is prepared to give 'em hell.

Lastly, individual success and the overall functioning of a market-based society require human agents who are prepared to make difficult decisions, who are competitive, cool under pressure, ruthless when required and will put the interests of the company first. Said differently, market success requires leaders who will abide no sissy stuff, want to be the big wheel in a successful enterprise, want to be the sturdy oak, want to be in charge and, when necessary, are prepared to give 'em hell. These are the descriptors of how to practise hegemonic masculinity.

There is clearly an affinity between two institutional orders; there is congruence, resonance or a symbiotic relationship in which elements of each support and buttress the other. The affinity is not planned, but as I have demonstrated it did evolve historically as a result of deliberate individual and institutional dynamics, yet exists quite unconsciously, but its structural implications are real. I ask this last question: Could the characteristic behaviours of practising hegemonic masculinity be precisely those behaviours that are required for the successful operation of a capitalist economy?

THE FUTURE OF AND FOR MEN AND BOYS

While I have said a fair bit about men and boys, in reality I have only scratched the surface and much has been left unsaid. Numerous important aspects of the lives of men and boys require continued analytical attention, including the emotional lives of boys and men, and matters such as love, desire and intimacy. I have referred to the problem of misunderstanding the role of concepts when social analysis ranges, as it must, across different levels of abstraction. It is vital to explicitly acknowledge the distinction between analyses at such a high level of abstraction — when speaking of patriarchy or capitalism — as opposed to analyzing a particular social formation — such as capitalism in Canada or patriarchy in Australia. The concepts developed for analysis at higher levels of abstraction will serve as guides, sensitizing the analyst to essential features and dynamics; however, the complexities of concrete historical entities will typically require conceptual refinement and flexibility. For example, the specifics and particulars of profit-generating activities or the social practices of hegemonic masculinity will take on somewhat different forms and hues in Canada, Germany or Australia as we take culture, history and locale into consideration. Having said this, I must note that by using concepts from a higher level of abstraction it is possible to understand the historical and concrete particularities in their larger context, as expressions of some larger dynamics, structures and processes. The same obviously holds true when we push our analysis to an even more concrete level, such as the behaviours of particular boys or men, or groups of boys and men located in a specific place, time and context.

I am not interested in bashing men, although it may appear that I have been excessively critical of men and boys, particularly as they practise hegemonic masculinity. There is much about various masculinities that I admire and that has positive social impacts. While also important to various ways in which femininity is practised and to female social behaviours, masculinities are often predicated on behaviours that exhibit characteristics such as self reliance, goal directedness, caring, providing service, striving, responsibility, courage and confidence. To repeat, I am not suggesting that these are exclusively or even primarily characteristics of masculine social practice, but rather they represent descriptors of social behaviours that humans all need to practise. Having said this, perhaps encouraging these sorts of social practices as opposed to those associated with hegemonic masculinities can serve as one point of departure for those seeking opportunities for humans to explore and develop their full range of human possibilities and emotions.

If a man on a farm in Saskatchewan, in an office in Sydney, an oilrig offshore Newfoundland, a sawmill in Oregon, or a hospital in Atlanta can use what I have suggested about the nature and dynamics of capitalism and patriarchy to start to understand how his life intersects with history, then I am pleased. I am equally pleased if, having considered what I have suggested are key concepts historically, men can start to think about how they practise gender, who benefits from those practices and the costs to themselves, others around them and society as a whole. My pleasure has nothing to do with me personally, but rather it allows me to be hopeful that we are ready to reconsider how we practise masculinity.

REFERENCES

Aamoth, Doug. 2014. "Here's How Much Time People Spend Playing Video Games." *Time*, May 27. <http://time.com/120476/nielsen-video-games/>.

Abelson, Elaine S. 2003. "Women Who Have No Men to Work for Them: Gender and Homelessness in the Great Depression, 1930--1934." *Feminist Studies* 29.

Abraham, Carolyn. 2010. "Failing Boys and the Powder Keg of Sexual Politics." *Globe and Mail*, Oct. 15. <www.theglobeandmail.com/news/national/time-to-lead/part-1-failing-boys-and-the-powder-keg-of-sexual-politics/article4081751/?page=all>.

Addis, Michael E., Abigail K. Mansfield, and Matthew R. Syzdek. 2010. "Is "Masculinity" a Problem? Framing the Effects of Gendered Social Learning in Men." *Psychology of Men and Masculinity* 11, 2.

Ahuja, Masuma. 2013. "Teens Are Spending More Time Consuming Media, on Mobile Devices." *Washington Post Live*, March 13. <www.washingtonpost.com/postlive/teens-are-spending-more-time-consuming-media-on-mobile-devices/2013/03/12/309bb242-8689-11e2-98a3-b3db6b9ac586_story.html>.

Alix, Spiegel. 2012. "Teachers' Expectations Can Influence How Students Perform." National Public Radio. <www.npr.org/blogs/health/2012/09/18/161159263/teachers-expectations-can-influence-how-students-perform>.

Allen, Colin. 2003. "Peer Pressure and Teen Sex." *Psychology Today*, May 1. <www.psychologytoday.com/articles/200305/peer-pressure-and-teen-sex>.

Allen, Louisa. 2003. "Girls Want Sex, Boys Want Love: Resisting Dominant Discourses of (Hetero) Sexuality." *Sexualities* 6, 2.

Allport. Gordon. 1961. *Pattern and Growth in Personality*. New York: Holt, Rinehart, & Winston.

American Movie Classic Company. n.d. <www.filmsite.org/warfilms.html>.

Ammer, Christine. 2013. *The American Heritage Dictionary of Idioms*. Boston: Houghton Mifflin Harcourt.

Anderson, Eric. 2009. *Inclusive Masculinity: The Changing Nature of Masculinities*. New York: Routledge.

____. 2012. *Sport, Masculinities and Sexualities*. New York: Routledge.

____. 2014. *21st Century Jocks: Sporting Men and Contemporary Heterosexuality*. Palgrave-McMillian.

Anderson, Eric, and R. McGuire. 2010. "Inclusive Masculinity Theory and the Gendered Politics of Men's Rugby." *Journal of Gender Studies* 19, 3

Anderson, Paul H. 2007. Justice State of Minnesota Supreme Court. "State of Minnesota vs. John Jason McLaughlin." A05-2327 Filed: January 11, 2007. <mn.gov/law-library-stat/

archive/supct/0701/opa052327-0111.htm>.

Archer, Margaret. 1995. *Realist Social Theory: The Morphogenetic Approach.* Cambridge: Cambridge University Press.

____. 2000. *Being Human: The Problem of Agency.* Cambridge: Cambridge University Press.

____. 2007. *Making Our Way Through the World: Human Reflexivity and Social Mobility.* Cambridge: Cambridge University Press.

____. 2013. *Social Morphogenesis.* New York: Springer eBook.

Ariès, Philippe. 1962. *Centuries of Childhood: A Social History of Family Life.* New York: Vintage.

Armstrong, Pat. 1996. "Unravelling the Safety Net: Transformations in Health Care and Their Impact on Women." In Janine Brodie (ed.), *Women and Canadian Public Policy.* Toronto: Harcourt Brace & Company.

Armstrong, Pat, and Hugh Armstrong. 2010. *The Double Ghetto.* Toronto: Oxford University Press.

Arrighi, Barbara A., and David J. Maume, Jr. 2000. "Workplace Subordination and Men's Avoidance of Housework." *Journal of Family Issues* 21, 4 (May).

Arrighi, Giovanna. 2001. *The Long Twentieth Century.* London: Verso.

Arxer, Steven L. 2011. "Hybrid Masculine Power: Reconceptualizing the Relationship between Homosociality and Hegemonic Masculinity." *Humanity & Society November* 35, 4.

Atkinson, Michael. 2011. *Deconstructing Men & Masculinities.* Toronto: Oxford University Press.

Auster, Carol, and Claire Mansbach. 2012. "The Gender Marketing of Toys: An Analysis of Color and Type of Toy on the Disney Store Website." *Sex Roles* 67, 7/8.

Avila-Saavedra, Guillermo 2009. "Nothing Queer About Queer Television: Televized Construction of Gay Masculinities." *Media, Culture and Society* 31,1.

Aydt, Hilary, and William A. Corsaro. "Differences in Children's Construction of Gender Across Culture." *American Behavioral Scientist* 46, 10.

Backhouse, Constance. 1986. "'Pure Patriarchy': Nineteenth Century Canadian Marriage." McGill Law Journal 31. <www.constancebackhouse.ca/fileadmin/publicationlist/PurePatriarchy.pdf>.

Barlett, Peggy F. 2006. "Masculinities in Rural Small Business Ownership: Between Community and Capitalism." In Hugh Campbell, Michael Mayerfield Bell and Margaret Finney (eds.), *Country Boys: Masculinity and Rural Life.* University Park, PA: Pennsylvania State University Press.

____. 2011. "Three Visions of Masculine Success on American Farms." In Hugh Campbell, Michael Materfield Bell, and Margaret Finney (eds.), *Country Boys: Masculinity and Rural Life.* University Park, PA: Pennsylvania State University Press.

Baron-Cohen, Simon. 2003. "They Just Can't Help It." *The Guardian*, April 17. <www.theguardian.com/education/2003/apr/17/research.highereducation>.

Barrett, Michele. 1985. *Women's Oppression Today.* London: Verso.

Barrett, Michele, and Mary McIntosh. 1982. "The 'Family Wage': Some Problems for Socialists and Feminists." *Capital & Class* 4, 2.

BBC Report. 2014. "Men Get More Prize Money Than Women in 30% Of Sports." October 28. <www.bbc.com/sport/0/football/29744400>.

Beasley, Christine. 2008. "Rethinking Hegemonic Masculinity in a Globalizing World." *Men and Masculinities* 11, 1.

Bechdel, Allison. 2009. "The Bechdel Test for Women in Movies." <www.feministfrequency.com/2009/12/the-bechdel-test-for-women-in-movies/>.

Beighley, Chole, and Jeff Smith. 2013. "Normalizing Male Dominance: Gender Representation in 2012 Films." GRID. February 12. <https://griid.org/2013/02/12/normalizing-male-dominance-gender-representation-in-2012-films/>.

Bellamy, Foster John, Robert W. McChesney, and R. Jamil Jonna. 2011. "Monopoly and Competition in Twenty-First Century Capitalism." *Monthly Review* 62, 11.

Bem, Sandra. L. 1974. "The Measurement of Psychological and Androgyny." *Journal of Consulting and Clinical Psychology* 42.

Bennett, Judith M. 2006. *History Matters: Patriarchy and the Challenge of Feminism.* Philadelphia: University of Pennsylvania Press.

Benston, Margaret. 1969. "The Political Economy of Women's Liberation." *Monthly Review* 41, 7.

Berger, Peter. 1963. *Invitation to Sociology.* Garden City, NY: Doubleday & Company.

Berns, Nancy. 2001. "Degendering the Problem and Gendering the Blame: Political Discourse on Women and Violence." *Gender & Society* 15, 2.

Beverly A. Browne. 1998. "Gender Stereotypes in Advertising on Children's Television in the 1990s: A Cross-National Analysis." *Journal of Advertising* 27, 1.

Bieler, Andreas, Ian Bruff Adam, and David Morton. 2010. "Acorns and Fruit: From Totalization to Periodization in the Critique of Capitalism" *Capital and Class* 34.

Blank, Gary. 2011. "Gender, Production, and the 'Transition to Capitalism': Assessing the Historical Basis for a Unitary Materialist Theory." *New Proposals: Journal of Marxism and Interdisciplinary Inquiry* 4, 2.

Bly, Robert. 1990. *Iron John: A Book About Men.* Reading, MA: Addison-Wesley.

Boehm, Lisa Krissoff. 2004. "Women, Impact of the Great Depression on." *Encyclopedia of the Great Depression* (*Gale Virtual Reference Library*), Robert S. McElvaine (ed.). New York: Macmillan.

____. 2015. "Women, Impact of the Great Depression on." *Encyclopedia of the Great Depression*, Vol. 2. Robert S. McElvaine (ed.). New York: Macmillan. (Web. 2 Apr. 2015).

Bologna, Caroline. 2014. "What 9-Year-Old Boys Dislike About Masculinity." *Huffington Post* 11/20. <www.huffingtonpost.com/2014/11/20/what-9-year-old-boys-dislike-about-masculinity-_n_6193228.html>.

Branch, John. 2015. "Montador's Death Helps Put Concussions Back in the Spotlight." February 20. <http://torontostar.newspaperdirect.com/epaper/viewer.aspx>.

Brannon, Robert, and Deborah S. David. 1976. *The Forty-Nine Percent Majority: The Male Sex Role.* Reading, MA: Addison-Wesley.

Brannon, Robert, and Samuel Juni. 1984. "A Scale for Measuring Attitudes about Masculinity." *Psychological Documents* 14, 6–7.

Bridges, Tristan. 2014. "A Very 'Gay' Straight? Hybrid Masculinities, Sexual Aesthetics, and the Changing Relationship between Masculinity and Homophobia." *Gender & Society* 28, 1.

Bridges, Tristan, and C.J. Pasco. 2014. "Hybrid Masculinities: New Directions in the Sociology of Men and Masculinities." *Sociology Compass* 8, 3.

Brod, Harry. 1987. *The Making of Masculinities*. New York: Routledge.

____. 2002. "Studying Masculinites as Superordinate Studies." In Judith Kegan Gardiner (ed.), *Masculinity Studies and Feminist Theory: New Directions*. New York: Columbia University Press.

Brod, Harry, and Michael Kaufman (eds.). 1994. *Theorizing Masculinities*. Thousand Oaks: Sage Publications.

Brodie, Janne. 1996. *Women and Canadian Public Policy*. Toronto: Harcourt Brace and Company.

Brophy, Jere E. 1983. "Research on the Self-Fulfilling Prophecy and Teacher Expectations." *Journal of Educational Psychology* 75, 5.

Brophy, Jere E., and Thomas L. Good. 1970. "Teachers' Communication of Differential Expectations for Children's Classroom Performance: Some Behavioral Data." *Journal of Educational Psychology* 61, 5.

Brown, Ian. 2015. "Of Monsters and Men." *Globe and Mail*, January 31.

Brown, Lorne. 1987. *When Freedom Was Lost: The Unemployed, the Agitator, and the State*. Montreal: Black Rose Books.

____. 1996. *When Freedom Was Lost: The Unemployed the Agitator & the State*. Montreal: Black Rose Books.

Brush, Megan. 2014. "Shell Shock: The Culture of Cowardice in the First World War." *Esprit de Corps*, March 24. <http://espritdecorps.ca/in-history/2014/3/24/shell-shock-the-culture-of-cowardice-in-the-first-world-war>.

Bryson, Valerie. 1999. "Patriarchy: A Concept Too Useful to Lose." *Contemporary Politics* 5, 4.

Budgeon, Shelley. 2014. "The Dynamics of Gender Hegemony. Femininities, Masculinities and Social Change." *Sociology* 48, 2.

Burk, Linnea R., Barry R. Burkhart, and Jason F. Sikorski. 2004. "Construction and Preliminary Validation of the Auburn Differential Masculinity Inventory." *Psychology of Men & Masculinity* 5, 1.

Burke, Monte. 2011. "The PGA Tour's Biggest Purses." *Forbes*. <www.forbes.com/sites/monteburke/2011/06/15/the-pga-tours-biggest-purses/-2a2c21021186>.

Burnette, Joyce. 2008. *Gender, Work and Wages in Industrial Revolution Britain*. Cambridge: Cambridge University Press.

Burr, Christina. 1993. "Defending 'the Art Preservative': Class and Gender Relations in the Printing Trades Unions, 1850–1914." *Labour / Le Travail* 31.

Burstyn, Varda. 1985. "Masculine Dominance and the State." In Varda Burstyn and Dorothy Smith (eds.), *Women, Class, Family and the State*. Toronto: Garamond Press.

____. 1999. *The Rites of Men: Manhood, Politics and the Culture of Sport*. Toronto: University of Toronto Press.

Busby, Linda J. 1975. "Sex-Role Research on the Mass Media." *Journal of Communication* (Autumn).

Butler, Judith. 1988. "Performative Acts and Gender Constitution: An Essay in Phenomenology and Feminist Theory." *Theatre Journal* 40, 4.

____. 2004. "Bodily Inscriptions, Performance Subversions." In Sara Salih (ed.), *The Judith Butler Reader*. Malden, MA: Blackwell.

Cahill, Spencer E. 1986. "Language Practices and Self Definition: The Case of Gender Identity Acquisition." *Sociological Quarterly* 27, 3.

Cameron, Barbara. 1996. " Brave New World for Women: NAFTA and New Reproductive Technologies." In Janine Brodie (ed.), *Women and Canadian Public Policy.* Toronto: Harcourt Brace & Company.

Camphell, Hugh. 2011. "Real Men. Real Local, and Real Workers: Realizing Masculinity in Small-Town New Zealand." In Hugh Campbell, Michael Materfield Bell, and Margaret Finney (eds.), *Country Boys: Masculinity and Rural Life.* University Park, PA: Pennsylvania State University Press.

Campion-Smith, Bruce. 2014. "Suicide Claims More Soldiers Than Those Killed by Afghan Combat." *Thestar.com,* Sept. 6. <www.thestar.com/news/canada/2014/09/16/ suicide_claims_more_soldiers_than_those_killed_by_afghan_combat.html>.

Canada at War. <http://www.canadaatwar.ca/content-7/world-war-ii/ facts-and-information/>.

Caplan, Paula J., and Jeremy B. Caplan. 1994. *Thinking Critically about Research on Sex and Gender.* New York: HarperCollins.

Carrigan, Tim, Bob Connell, and John Lee. 1987. "Toward a New Sociology of Masculinity." In Harry Brod (ed.), *The Making of Masculinities.* New York: Routledge.

Caulfield, Philip. 2011. "Omaha School Shooter, Robert Butler Jr., Wrote Chilling Message on Facebook Before Deadly Attack." Daily News, January 6. <www.nydailynews. com/news/national/omaha-school-shooter-robert-butler-jr-wrote-chilling-message-facebook-deadly-attack-article-1.148674>.

CBC News Online. 2015. "Military Sexual Misconduct Due to 'Biological Wiring,' Gen. Tom Lawson Tells CBC News." June 16. <www.cbc.ca/news/politics/military-sexual-misconduct-due-to-biological-wiring-gen-tom-lawson-tells-cbc-news-1.3115993>.

CCHR (Citizens Commission on Human Rights). n.d. "The Hidden Enemy Documentary Exposes the Covert Operation Behind Military Suicides." <www.cchr.org/ documentaries/the-hidden-enemy.html>.

Chemaly, Soraya. 2014. "Fox, Feminism and the Boy Crisis: In the Beginning There Was Darkness." *Huffington Post Education.* Posted: 05/02. <www.huffingtonpost.com/ soraya-chemaly/fox-news-education-boy-crisis_b_5250448.html>.

Cherney, Isabelle D., and Kamala London. 2006. "Gender-Linked Differences in the Toys, Television Shows, Computer Games, and Outdoor Activities of 5- to 13-Year-Old Children." *Sex Roles* 54.

Chodorow, Nancy. 1976. *The Reproduction of Mothering: Psychoanalysis and the Sociology of Gender.* Berkeley: University of California Press.

____. 1989. *Feminism and Psychoanalytic Theory.* New Haven: Yale University Press.

____. 1995. "Gender as a Personal and Cultural Construction." *Signs* 20, 2.

Chomsky, Noam. 1988. *Language and Politics.* Montreal: Black Rose Books.

Chu, Judy Y. 2004. "A Relational Perspective on Adolescent Boys' Identity Development." In Niobe Way and Judy Chu (eds.), *Adolescent Boys: Exploring Diverse Cultures of Boyhood.* New York: New York University Press.

____. 2014. *When Boys Become Boys.* New York: New York University Press.

Clark, Alice. 1920. *Life of Women in the Seventeenth Century.* New York: Harcourt, Brace and Howe.

Clark, Anna. 1997. *The Struggle for the Breeches Gender and the Making of the British Working Class.* Berkeley: University of California Press.

Clatterbaugh, Kenneth. 1990. *Contemporary Perspectives on Masculinity: Men, Women, and Politics in Modern Society*. Boulder: Westview Press.

____. 1998. "What Is Problematic about Masculinities?" *Men and Masculinities* 1, 1.

Clearfield, Melissa W., and Naree M. Nelson. 2006. "Sex Differences in Mothers' Speech and Play Behavior with 6-, 9-, and 14-Month-Old Infants." *Sex Roles* 54.

Clegg, Sue. 2005. "Evidence-Based Practice in Educational Research: A Critical Realist Critique of Systematic Review." *British Journal of Sociology of Education* 26, 3.

Cohen, Michele. 2005. "'Manners' Make the Man: Politeness, Chivalry, and the Construction of Masculinity, 1750–1830." *Journal of British Studies* 44.

Collins, W. Andrew, Deborah P. Welsh, and Wyndol Furman. 2008. "Adolescent Romantic Relationships." *Annual Review of Psychology* 60.

Connell, R.W. 1987. *Gender and Power: Society, the Person and Sexual Politics*. Sydney: Allen and Unwin.

____. 1995. *Masculinities*. Berkley: University of California Press.

____. 2000a. "Making Gendered People: Bodies, Identities and Sexualities." In Myra Marx Feree, Judith Lober and Beth Hess (eds.), *Revisioning Gender*. New York: Rowman & Littlefield.

____. 2000b. *The Men and the Boys*. Berkley: University of California Press.

____. 2002. *Gender*. Cambridge: Polity.

Connell, R.W., and James W. Messerschmidt. 2005 "Hegemonic Masculinity Rethinking the Concept." *Gender and Society* 19, 6.

Connell, Raewyn. 2010. "Two Cans of Paint: A Transsexual Life Story, with Reflections on Gender, Change and History." *Sexualities* 13, 1.

Constantinople, Anne. 1973. "Masculinity–Femininity: An Exception to a Famous Dictum?" *Psychological Bulletin* 80, 5.

Cooley, Charles H. 1956. *Social Organization: A Study of the Larger Mind*. Glencoe, IL: Free Press.

Creighton, Donald. 1976. *The Forked Road: Canada 1939–1957*. Toronto: McClelland and Stewart.

Curry, Bill, and Barrie McKenna. 2014. "Stimulus Gamble: How Ottawa Saved the Economy – and Wasted Billions." *Globe and Mail*, Feb. 8. <www.theglobeandmail.com/report-on-business/stimulus-gamble-how-ottawa-saved-the-economy-and-wasted-billions/article16760149/?page=all>.

Dale, Maryclaire. 2015. "Judge Approves Concussion Settlement." *Globe and Mail*, April 23.

Daly, Martin, and Margo Wilson. 1988. "Evolutionary Social Psychology and Family Homicide." *Science*, New Series, 242.

Danermark, Berth, Mats Ekstrom, Liselotte Jakobsen, and Jan Ch. Karlsson. 2001. *Explaining Society: Critical Realism in the Social Sciences*. London: Routledge.

Daschuk, James. 2013. *Clearing the Plains: Disease, Politics of Starvation, and the Loss of Aboriginal Life*. Regina: University of Regina Press

de Beauvoir, Simone. 1973. *The Second Sex*. New York: Vintage Books.

de Boise, Sam. 2015. "I'm Not Homophobic, 'I've Got Gay Friends': Evaluating the Validity of Inclusive Masculinity." *Men and Masculinities* 18, 3.

Deaux, Kay. 1984. "From Individual Differences to Social Categories: Analysis of a Decade's Research on Gender." *American Psychologist* 39, 2.

DeKeseredy, Walter S. 2000. "Current Controversies on Defining Nonlethal Violence Against Women in Intimate Heterosexual Relationships; Empirical Implications." *Violence Against Women* 6, 7.

Delphy, Christine. 1988. "Patriarchy, Domestic Mode of Production, Gender, and Class." In Cary Nelson and Lawrence Grossberg (eds.), *Marxism and the Interpretation of Culture*. Urbana: University of Illinois Press.

____. 1993. "Rethinking Sex and Gender." *Women's Studies Int. Forum* 16, 1.

Demaree, Heath A.D., D. Eric Everhart, Eric A. Youngstrom, and David W Harrison. 2005. "Brain Lateralization of Emotional Processing: Historical Roots and a Future Incorporating 'Dominance'." *Behavioural and Cognitive Neuroscceicne Review* 4, 1.

Demetriou, Demetrakis M. 2001. "Connell's Concept of Hegemonic Masculinity: A Critique." *Theory and Society* 30, 3.

Dempsey, Kenneth C. 2000. "Men and Women's Power Relationships and the Persisting Inequitable Division of Housework." *Journal of Family Studies* 6, 1.

Dennis, Carina Dennis. 2004. "Brain Development: The Most Important Sexual Organ." *Nature* 427.

Deutsch, Francine M. 2007. "Undoing Gender." *Gender and Society* 21, 1.

Deutsch, Francine. 1999. *Having It All*. Cambridge, MA: Harvard University Press.

Di Novi, Will. 2014. "Skin in the Game." *The Walrus*, September 3.

Diamond, Dan. 2015. "More Young American Die from Guns than Cars." *Forbes*, August 26. <www.forbes.com/sites/dandiamond/2015/08/26/americas-gun-violence-problem-in-three-charts/ - 13260e1358b7>.

Diamond, Marian C. 2003. "Male and Female Brains." Summary of lecture for Women's Forum West Annual Meeting. <http://education.jhu.edu/PD/newhorizons/Neurosciences/ articles/Male%20and%20Female \%20Brains/>.

Dill, Karen E., and Kathryn P. Thill. 2007. "Video Game Characters and the Socialization of Gender Roles: Young People's Perceptions Mirrors Sexist Media Depictions." *Sex Roles* 57.

Dirks, Tim. n.d. "Filmsite: The Greatest Films." <www.filmsite.org/bestpics2.html>.

Dishion, Thomas J., and Jessica M. Tipsord. 2011. "Peer Contagion in Child and Adolescent Social and Emotional Development." *Annual Review of Psychology* 62.

Doidge, Norman. 2007. *The Brain That Changes Itself*. New York: Viking Press.

____. 2015. *The Brain's Way of Healing*. New York: Viking Press.

Donald, Ralph, and Karen MacDonald. 2011. *Reel Men at War: Masculinity and the American War Film*. Plymouth, UK: Scarecrow Press.

Donaldson, Mike. 1993. "What Is Hegemonic Masculinity." *Theory and Society* 22, 5.

Dos Santos, Theotonio. 1970. "The Concept of Social Classes." *Science and Society* 34, 2 (Summer).

Doughty, Eleanor. 2015. "Sexual Pressure: 'Who'd Want To Be a Teen Today?'" *The Telegraph*, Feb. 12. <www.telegraph.co.uk/education/educationopinion/11408182/Sexual-pressure-whod-want-to-be-a-teen-today.html>.

Dummitt, Christopher. 2007. *The Manly Modern: Masculinity in Postwar Canada*. Vancouver: UBC Press.

Dunk, Thomas W. 1991. *It's a Working Man's Town*. Montreal: McGill Queen's University Press.

Easton, Geoff. 2002. "Marketing: A Critical Realist Approach." *Journal of Business Research* 55, 2.

Edley, Nigel, and Margaret Wetherell. 1997. "Jockeying for Position: The Construction of Masculine Identities." *Discourse and Society* 8, 2.

Eliot, Lise. 2009. *Pink Brain Blue Brain*. Boston: Houghton Mifflin Harcourt.

Emihovich, Catherine A., Eugene L. Gaier, and Noreen C. Cronin. 1984. "Sex-Role Expectations Changes by Fathers for Their Sons." *Sex Roles* 11, 9/10.

Engels, Rutger C.M.E., and Tom ter Bogt. 2001. "Influences of Risk Behaviors on the Quality of Peer Relations in Adolescence." *Journal of Youth and Adolescence* 30, 6.

Epstein, Cynthia Fuchs. 1988. *Deceptive Distinctions*. New Haven: Yale University Press.

Erickson, Lesley. 2011. *Westward Bound: Sex, Violence, the Law, and the Making of a Settler Society*. Vancouver: UBC Press.

ERMResearch/Telefilm Canada/Show Canada. 2015. "Canadian Moviegoing Statistics 2015." <www.telefilm.ca/document/en/01/17/CanadaMoviegoing_2015_Summary. pdf>.

Falleti, Tulia, and Juylia Lynch. 2008. "From Process to Mechanisms: Varieties of Disaggregation." *Qualitative Sociology* 31.

Faludi, Susan. 1999. *Stiffed: The Betrayal of the American Man*. New York: William Morrow Co.

Farkas, Terezia. 2014a. "Why Farmer Suicide Rates Are the Highest of Any Occupation." *Huffington Post,* July 14. <www.huffingtonpost.com/terezia-farkas/why-farmer-suicide-rates-_1_b_5610279.html>.

____. 2014b. "Too Many Farmers Are Committing Suicide." *Huffington Post,* September 9. <www.huffingtonpost.ca/terezia-farkas/farmer-suicide_b_5798656.html>.

Fausto-Sterling, Anne. 1985. *Myths of Gender*. New York: Basic Books.

____. 1993 "The Five Sexes: Why Male and Female Are Not Enough." *The Sciences* March/April.

____. 2000a. *Sexing the Body*. Basic Books. New York.

____. 2000b. "The Five Sexes Revisited." *The Sciences* July/August.

____. 2012. *Sex/Gender: Biology in a Social World*. New York: Rutledge.

Fisher-Thompson, Donna, Angela Saus, and Terri Wright. 1995. "Toy Selection for Children: Personality and Toy Request Influences." *Sex Roles* 33, 3/4.

Fitzpatrick, Suzanne. 2005. "Explaining Homelessness: A Critical Realist Perspective." *Housing, Theory and Society* 22, 1.

Fortin, Nicole M., and Michael Huberman. 2002. "Occupational Gender Segregation and Women's Wages in Canada: An Historical Perspective." *Canadian Public Policy* 28 (Supplement: Occupational Gender Segregation: Public Policies and Economic Forces).

Foster, John Bellamy, Robert W. McChesney, and R. Jamil Jonna. 2011. "The Internationalization of Monopoly Capital." *Monthly Review* 63, 2.

Fox, Bonnie, and John Fox. 2008. "Occupational Gender Segregation of the Canadian Labour Force, 1931–1981." *Journal of Youth and Adolescence* 24, 3.

Freud, Sigmund. 1965 [1933]. "Lecture xxxi: The Dissection of the Psychical Personality." In James Stachey (ed.), *New Introductory Lectures on Psychoanalysis*. New York: W.W. Norton.

____. 1961. *Civilization and Its Discontents*. New York: W.W. Norton & Company.

____. 1982. *Civilization and Its Discontents.* London: Hogarth Press.

Fromm, Erich. 1941. *Escape from Freedom.* New York: Henry Holt and Company.

Gallagher, Kathryn E., and Dominic J. Parrott. 2011. "What Accounts for Men's Hostile Attitudes Toward Women? The Influence of Hegemonic Male Role Norms and Masculine Gender Role Stress." *Violence Against Women* 17, 5.

Gavigan, Shelley A.M. 2012. "Something Old, Something New? Re-Theorizing Patriarchal Relations and Privatization from the Outskirts of Family Law." *Theoretical Inquiries in Law* 13, 1.

Gayle, Rubin. 1975. "The Traffic in Women: Notes on the 'Political Economy' of Sex." In Rayna R. Reiter (ed.), *Toward an Anthropology of Women.* New York: Monthly Review Press.

Gerth, Hans, and C. Wright Mills. 1964. *From Max Weber: Essays in Sociology.* New York: Oxford University Press.

Giordano, Peggy C., Monica A. Longmore, and Wendy D. Manning. 2006. "Gender and the Meanings of Adolescent Romantic Relationships: A Focus on Boys." *American Sociological Review* 71, 2.

Good, Glen E., Don M. Dell, and Laurie B Mintz. 1989. "Male and Gender Role Conflict: Relations to Help Seeking Men." *Journal of Counselling Psychology* 36, 3.

Gordon, Neta. 2014. "White Masculinity and Civility in Contemporary Canadian Short Stories: The Fantasy of Reterritorialization and Return." *Men and Masculinities.* 17, 2.

Gosling, Samuel D., Peter J. Rentfrow, and William B. Swann. 2003. "A Very Brief Measure of the Big-Five Personality Domains." *Journal of Research in Personality* 37.

Gournelos, Ted. 2009. "Blasphemous Allusion Coming of Age in South Park." *Journal of Communication Inquiry* 33, 2.

Graveland, Bill. 2009. "A Small Town Mourns Eight Lost in Avalanches." *Globe and Mail,* January 5.

Greenhill, Pauline. 2012. "Men, Masculinities, and the Male in English-Canadian Traditional and Popular Cultures." In Jason A. Laker (ed.), *Canadian Perspectives on Men & Masculinities: An Interdisciplinary Reader.* Don Mills: Oxford University Press.

Gregory, Robert J. 2000. *Psychological Testing: History, Principles, and Applications.* Boston: Allyn and Bacon.

Greig, Christopher. 2014. *Ontario Boys: Masculinity and the Idea of Boyhood in Postwar Ontario, 1954–1960.* Waterloo: Wilfrid Laurier University Press.

Greig, Christopher J., and Susan Holloway. 2012. "Canadian Fatherhood." In Christopher J. Greig and Wayne J. Martino (eds.), *Canadian Men and Masculinities: Historical and Contemporary Perspectives.* Toronto: Canadian Scholars' Press.

Greven, David. 2016. *Ghost Faces: Hollywood and Post-Millennial Masculinity.* Albany, NY: State University of New York Press.

Hake, Laura, and Clare O'Connor. 2008. "Genetic Mechanisms of Sex Determination." *Nature Education* 1, 25. <www.nature.com/scitable/topicpage/genetic-mechanisms-of-sex-determination-314>.

Hall, Calvin S. 1979. *A Primer of Freudian Psychology.* New York: Mentor Books.

Hall, Calvin, and Gardner Lindzey. 1970. *Theories of Personality.* New York: John Wiley & Sons.

Hall, Stuart. 1997a. "The Work or Representing." *Representation: Cultural Representations and Signifying Practices.* London: Sage Publications.

____. 1997b. "Representations and the Media." Northampton, MA: Media Education Foundation. Transcript of videos found at <www.mediaed.org/assets/products/409/transcript_409.pdf>.

Hamilton, Roberta. 2004. *Gendering the Vertical Mosaic: Feminist Perspectives on Canadian Society.* Toronto: Copp Clark.

Hansen, Phillip. 1993. *Hannah Arendt: Politics, History and Citizenship.* Cambridge: Polity Press.

Harding, David J., Cybelle Fox, and Jal D. Mehta. 2002. "Studying Rare Events Through Qualitative Case Studies: Lessons from a Study of Rampage School Shootings" *Sociological Methods & Research* 31.

Hareven, Tamara K. 1991. "The History of the Family and the Complexity of Social Change." *The American Historical Review* 96, 1.

Hartley, Ruth E. 1959. "Sex-Role Pressures and the Socialization of the Male Child." *Psychological Reports* 5.

Hartmann, Heidi. 1976. "Capitalism, Patriarchy and Job Segregation by Sex." *Signs* 1, 3.

____. 1981. "The Unhappy Marriage of Marxism and Feminism: Towards a More Progressive Union." In Lynda Sargent (ed.), *The Unhappy Marriage of Marxism and Feminism: A Debate of Class and Patriarchy.* London: Pluto Press. <http://web.ics.purdue.edu/~hoganr/SOC%20602/Hartmann_1979.pdf>.

Harvey, David. 1989. *The Condition of Postmodernity.* Cambridge: Blackwell. <www.nytimes.com/2014/11/09/magazine/how-one-lawyers-crusade-could-change-football-forever.html>.

____. 2002. "Agency and Community: A Critical Realist Paradigm." *Journal for the Theory of Social Behaviour* 32, 2.

Harvey, Karen, and Alexandra Shepard. 2005. "What Have Historians Done with Masculinity? Reflections on Five Centuries circa 1500–1950." *The Journal of British History* 44: 2

Haskell, Rebecca, and Brian Burtch. 2010. *Get That Freak: Homophobia and Transphobia in High Schools.* Halifax: Fernwood Publishing.

Hatty, Suzanne E. 2000. *Masculinities, Violence and Culture.* Thousand Oaks: Sage Publications.

Havas, Eva. 1995. "The Family as Ideology." *Social Policy & Administration* 29, 1.

Hearn, Jeff. 2004. "From Hegemonic Masculinity to the Hegemony of Men." *Feminist Theory* 5, 1.

Hedstrom, Peter, and Richard Swedenberg. 2001. "Social Mechanisms." ACTA *Sociologica* 39.

Heilbroner, Robert. 1968. *The Making of Economic Society.* Englewood Cliffs, NJ: Prentice Hall.

____. 1992. *Twenty-First-Century Capitalism.* Concord, ON: Anansi.

Held, David. 1980. *Introduction to Critical Theory.* Berkley: University of California Press.

Herrmann, Esther, Josep Call, María Victoria Hernàndez-Lloreda, Brian Hare and Michael Tomasello. 2007. "Humans Have Evolved Specialized Skills of Social Cognition: The Cultural Intelligence Hypothesis." *Science* 317.

Hesketh, Anthony, and Steve Fleetwood. 2006. "Beyond Measuring the Human Resources Management-Organizational Performance Link: Applying Critical Realist

Meta-Theory." *Organization* 13.

Hickey, Walt. 2014. "The Dollar-And-Cents Case Against Hollywood's Exclusion of Women." *FiveThirtyEight*. <fivethirtyeight.com/features/the-dollar-and-cents-case-against-hollywoods-exclusion-of-women/>.

Hinckley, David. 2014. "Average American Watches 5 Hours of TV Per Day, Report Shows." *New York Daily News*. <www.nydailynews.com/life-style/average-american-watches-5-hours-tv-day-article-1.1711954>.

Hobsbawm, Eric. 2013. "The Myth of the Cowboy." *The Guardian*, March 20.

Hobson, Barbara (ed.). 2002. *Making Men Into Fathers*. Cambridge: Cambridge University Press.

Hochschild, Arlie. 1983. *The Managed Heart: Commercialization of Human Feeling*. Berkeley: University of California Press.

Hochschild, Arlie, and Anne Machung. 1989. *The Second Shift: Working Parents and the Revolution at Home*. New York: Viking Penguin.

Hogg, Robert. 2012. *Men and Manliness on the Frontier*. London: Palgrave Macmillan.

Honey, Maureen. 1984. *Creating Rosie the Riveter: Class, Gender, and Propaganda During World War II*. Boston: University of Massachusetts Press.

hooks, bell. n.d. *Understanding Patriarchy*. <http://imaginenoborders.org/pdf/zines/UnderstandingPatriarchy.pdf>.

Horkheimer, Max. 1972. "Authority and the Family." In *Critical Theory: Select Essays*. New York: Herder and Herder.

Howson, Richard. 2006. *Challenging Hegemonic Masculinity*. London: Routledge.

Hoyenga, Katherine Blick, and Kermit T. Hoyenga. 1979. *The Question of Sex Difference*. Boston: Little Brown and Co.

Hull, John H., Debra B. Hull, and Christina Knopp. 2011. "The Impact of Color on Ratings of 'Girl' and 'Boy' Toys." *North American Journal of Psychology* 13, 3.

Humphries, Jane. 1977. "The Working Class Family, Women's Liberation, and Class Struggle: The Case of Nineteenth Century British History." *Review of Radical Political Economics* 9, 3.

Hunt, Emery Kay. 1981. *Property and Prophets: The Evolution of Economic Institutions and Ideologies*. New York: Harper & Row.

Hussey, Mark (ed.). 2003. *Masculinities: Interdisciplinary Readings*. Upper Saddle, NY: Prentice Hall.

Hywel Bishop, and Adam Jaworski. 2003. "'We Beat 'em': Nationalism and the Hegemony of Homogeneity in the British Press Reportage of Germany versus England during Euro 2000." *Discourse Society* 14, 3.

Ingle, Sean. 2014. "American Football Can No Longer Ignore Dangers of Trauma." *The Guardian*, Sept. 21. <www.theguardian.com/sport/blog/2014/sep/21/research-shows-american-football-can-ignore-dangers-of-trauma-no-longer>.

Irigaray, Luce. 1993. "Women: Equal or Different." In Stevi Jackson and Jane Prince (eds.), *Women's Studies: Essential Readings*. New York: New York University Press.

Irish Examiner. 2014. "Pressure on Teen Girls to Be Sexually Active Is Intrusive, Unfair and Damaging." October 25. <www.irishexaminer.com/lifestyle/healthandlife/relationships/pressure-on-teen-girls-to-be-sexually-active-is-intrusive-unfair-and-damaging-293684.html>.

Jeffries, Elena D. 2004. "Experience of Trust with Parents." In Noibe Way and Judy Y. Chu (eds.), *Adolescent Boys: Exploring Diverse Culture of Boyhood*. New York: New York University Press.

Jenson, Jane. 1986. "Gender and Reproduction: Or, Babies and the State." In M. Patricia Connelly and Pat Armstrong (eds.), *Feminism in Action*. Toronto: Canadian Scholars' Press.

Jessop, Bob. 2015. "What Follows Fordism? On the Periodisation of Capitalism and Its Regulation." <http://bobjessop.org/2014/01/03/what-follows-fordism-on-the-periodisation-of-capitalism-and-its-regulation/>.

Johnson, Holly, and Myrna Dawson. 2011. *Violence Against Women in Canada*. Don Mills: Oxford University Press.

Jones, Susan, and Debra Myhill. 2004. "'Troublesome Boys' and 'Compliant Girls': Gender Identity and Perceptions of Achievement and Underachievement." *British Journal of Sociology of Education* 25, 5.

Kane, Emily. 2006. "'No Way My Boys Are Going to Be Like That!': Parents' Responses to Children's Gender Nonconformity." *Gender & Society* 20, 2.

Kansaku, K., A. Yamaura, and S. Kitazawa. 2000. "Sex Differences in Lateralization Revealed in the Posterior Language Areas." *Cerebral Cortex* 10, 9.

Karin, A. Martin. 1989. "Becoming a Gendered Body: Practices of Preschools." *American Sociological Review* 63, 4.

Katz, Jackson. 2014. "Rice Video Accelerates Cultural Shift on Men's Violence." *Huffington Post*, Sept. 12. <www.huffingtonpost.com/jackson-katz/rice-video-accelerates-cu_b_5812366.html>.

Kaufman, Scott Barry. 2012. "Men, Women, and IQ: Setting the Record Straight — What James Flynn's Data Actually Shows." In *Beautiful Minds*. <www.psychologytoday.com/blog/beautiful-minds/201207/men-women-and-iq-setting-the-record-straight>.

Kelly, Jeffrey A., and Judith Worell. 1977. "New Formulations of Sex Roles and Androgyny: A Critical Review." *Journal of Consulting and Clinical Psychology* 45, 6.

Kilpatrick, Dean G. 2004. "What Is Violence Against Women? Defining and Measuring the Problem." *Journal of Interpersonal Violence* 19, 11 (November).

Kimmel, Michael. 1991. "From Separate Spheres to Sexual Equality: Men's Responses to Feminism at the Turn of the Century." In Laura Krammer (ed.), *The Sociology of Gender*. New York: St. Martin's Press.

____. 1994. "Masculinity as Homophobia." In Harry Brod and Michael Kaufman (eds.), *Theorizing Masculinities*. Thousand Oaks: Sage Publications.

____. 2002. "Introduction." In Juddith Kegan Gardner (ed.), *Masculinity Studies and Feminist Theory: New Directions*. New York: Columbia University Press.

____. 2004. *The Gendered Society Reader*. New York: Oxford University Press.

____. 2005. *The History of Men*. Albany: State University of New York Press.

____. 2008. *Guyland: The Perilous World Where Boys Become Men* New York: Harper Collins.

____. 2010. *Manhood in America*. New York: Oxford University Press.

____. 2013. *Angry White Men*. New York: Nation Books.

Kimmel, Michael, and Amy Aronson. 2004. *The Gendered Society Reader*. New York: Oxford University Press.

Kimmel, Michael, and Michael Kaufman. 1994b. "Weekend Warriors: The New Men's

Movement." In Harry Brod and Michael Kaufman (eds.), *Theorizing Masculinities*. Thousand Oaks: Sage Publications.

Kimmel, Michael S., and Matthew Mahler. 2003. "Adolescent Masculinity, Homophobia, and Violence: Random School Shootings, 1982–2001. *American Behavioral Scientist* 46, 10.

Kimmel, Michael, and Michael Messner. 2004. *Men's Lives*. Boston: Pearson Educational Inc.

Kimura, Doreen. 2002. "Sex Differences in the Brain." *Scientific American* May 13.

Klein, Jonathan D., Jane D. Brown, Carol Dykers, Kim Walsh Childers, Janice Oliveri, and Carol Porter. 1993. "Adolescents' Risky Behavior and Mass Media Use." *Pediatrics* 92, 1.

Klosterman, Chuck. 2014. "Is It Wrong to Watch Football?" *New York Times Sunday Magazine*, Sept. 7. <ww.nytimes.com/2014/09/07/magazine/is-it-wrong-to-watch-football.html>.

Knuttila, K. Murray, and Wendee Kubik. 2000. *State Theories: Classical, Global and Feminist Perspectives* third edition. Halifax, NS: Fernwood Publishing.

Knuttila, Murray, and Andre Magnan. 2012. *Introducing Sociology*. Toronto: Oxford University Press.

Kohlberg, Lawrence. 1966. "A Cognitive-Developmental Analysis of Children's Sex-Role Concepts and Attitudes." In E. Maccoby (ed.), *The Development of Sex Differences*. London: Tavistock.

Kohlberg, Lawrence, and Richard H. Hersh. 1977. "Moral Development: A Review of the Theory." *Theory into Practice* 16, 2.

Komarnicki, Jamie. 2008. "B.C. Avalanche Survivor Describes Ordeal." *Calgary Herald*, December 31. <www.canada.com/avalanche+survivor+describes+ordeal/1130770/story.html>.

_____. 2009. "Here's to the Boys." *Regina Leader Post*, January 5.

Kristen, Myers. 2012. "'Cowboy Up!' Non-Hegemonic Representations of Masculinity in Children's Television Programming." *Journal of Men's Studies* 20, 2.

Kuhn, Steven L., and Mary C. Stiner. 2006. "What's a Mother to Do? The Division of Labor among Neandertals and Modern Humans in Eurasia." *Current Anthropology* 47, 6.

Kutner, Max. 2014. "Death on the Farm: Farmers Are a Dying Breed in Part Because They're Killing Themselves in Record Numbers." *Newsweek*, April 10.

Laker, Jason A. (ed.). 2012. *Canadian Perspectives on Men & Masculinities: An Interdisciplinary Reader*. Don Mills, ON: Oxford University Press.

Lang, Brent. 2015. "Is Hollywood Making Too Many Movies?" *Variety*, June 23. <http://variety.com/2015/film/news/hollywood-making-too-many-movies-1201526094/>.

Lanier, Christina, and Michael O. Maume. 2009. "Intimate Partner Violence and Social Isolation Across the Rural/Urban Divide." *Violence Against Women* 15, 11.

Leacock, Eleanor. 1978. "Women's Status in Egalitarian Society: Implications for Social Evolution." *Current Anthropology* 19, 2.

Leacock, Eleanor, and Richard Lee (eds.). 1982. "Relations of Production in Band Societies." In *Politics and History in Band Societies*. Cambridge: Cambridge University Press.

Lerner, Gerda. 1986. *The Creation of Patriarchy*. New York: Oxford University Press.

Levant, Ronald. 1992. "Toward the Reconstruction of Masculinity." *Journal of Men's Studies* 5, 3/4.

Levant, Ronald F., and Katharine Richmond. 2007. "A Review of Research on Masculinity Ideologies Using the Male Role Norms Inventory." *Journal of Men's Studies* 15, 2.

Levin, Jack, and Eric Madfis. 2009. "Mass Murder at School and Cumulative Strain: A Sequential Model." *American Behavioural Scientist* 52, 9.

Lewontin, Richard. 1991. *Biology as Destiny.* Toronto: Penguin Books.

LFN. n.d. "What Is Patriarchy?" <http://londonfeministnetwork.org.uk/home/patriarchy>.

Lovgren, Stefan. 2006. "Sex-Based Roles Gave Modern Humans an Edge, Study Says." *National Geographic News,* December 7. <http://news.nationalgeographic.com/news/2006/12/061207-sex-humans.html>.

Low, Sabina, Joshua R. Polanin, and Dorothy L. Espelage. 2004. "The Role of Social Networks in Physical and Relational Aggression Among Young Adolescents." *Journal of Youth and Adolescence* 33, 6.

Lowe, Graham S. 1982. "Class, Job and Gender in the Canadian Office." *Labour/Le Travail* 10.

____. 1987. *Women in the Administrative Revolution: The Feminization of Clerical Work.* Toronto: University of Toronto Press.

LPGA Homepage. <www.lpga.com/news/2015-lpga-schedule>.

Lusher, Dean, and Garry Robins. 2009. "Hegemonic and Other Masculinities in Local Social Contexts." *Men and Masculinities* 11, 4.

Maccoby, Eleanor E. 1998. *The Two Sexes.* Harvard University Press Cambridge

MacKinnon, Catharine A. 1989. "Toward a Feminist Theory of the State." Cambridge, MA: Harvard University Press.

Macpherson, Crawford Brough. 1962. *The Political Theory of Possessive Individualism: Hobbes to Locke.* London: Oxford University Press.

Madfis, Eric. 2014. "Triple Entitlement and Homicidal Anger: An Exploration of the Intersectional Identities of American Mass Murderers." *Men and Masculinities* 17.

Mahalik, J.R., B.D. Locke, and L.H. Ludlow. 2003. "Development of the Conformity to Masculine Norms Inventory." *Psychology of Men and Masculinity* 4, 1.

Mak, Geertje. 2006. "Doubting Sex from Within: A Praxiographic Approach to Late Nineteenth-Century Case of hermaphroditism" *Gender and History* 18, 2.

Mangan, James Anthony, and James Walvin (eds.). 1987. *Manliness and Morality: Middle-Class Masculinity in Britain and America, 1800–1940.* New York: St. Martin's Press.

Mannino, Clelia Anna, and Francine M. Deutsch. 2007. "Changing the Division of Household Labor: A Negotiated Process Between Partners." *Sex Roles* 56.

Maraniss, David. 2016. "The Collision of Sport on Trial." *New York: New York Review of Books,* February 11.

Marcell, Arik V., Charles Wibbelsman, and Warren M. Seigel. 2011. "Male Adolescent Sexual and Reproductive Health Care." *Pediatrics* 128, 6. <http://pediatrics.aappublications. org/content/pediatrics/128/6/e1658.full.pdf>.

Maroney, Heather Jon, and Meg Luxton (eds.). 1988. *Feminism and Political Economy: Women's Work, Women's Struggles.* Toronto: Methuen.

Martin, Hale, and Stephen E. Finn. 2010. *Masculinity and Femininity in the MMPI-2 and MMPI-A.* Minneapolis: University of Minnesota Press.

Martin, Joe. 2013. "The Great Depression Hit Canada the Hardest." *The Record.com,* March 28. <www.therecord.com/ opinion-story/2628477-the-great-depression-hit-canada-the-hardest/>.

Martin, Patricia Yancey. 2004. "Gender as a Social Institution." *Social Forces* 82, 4.

Martino, Wayne. 1999. "'Cool Boys,' 'Party Animals,' 'Squids' and 'Poofters': Interrogating the Dynamics and Politics of Adolescent Masculinities in School." *British Journal of Sociology of Education* 20, 2.

Maslow, Abraham Harold. 1943. "A Theory of Human Motivation." *Psychological Review* 50.

Maxwell, Kimberly A. 2002. "Friends: The Role of Peer Influence Across Adolescent Risk Behaviors." *Journal of Youth and Adolescence* 31, 4.

May, Martha. 1982. "The Historical Problem of the Family Wage: The Ford Motor Company and the Five Dollar Day." *Feminist Studies* 8, 2.

McAdam, Doug, Sidney Tarrow, and Charles Tilly. 2008. "Methods for Measuring Mechanisms of Contention." *Qualitative Sociology* 31.

McCabe, Janice, Emily Fairchild, Liz Grauerholz, Bernice A. Pescosolido, and Daniel Tope. 2011. "Gender in Twentieth-Century Children's Books Patterns of Disparity in Titles and Central Characters." *Gender and Society* 25, 2.

McCallum, Todd. 1998. "'Not a Sex Question'? The One Big Union and the Politics of Radical Manhood." *Labour/Le Travail* 42.

McCrae, Robert R., and Antonio Terracciano. 2005. "Universal Features of Personality Traits from the Observer's Perspective: Data From 50 Cultures." *Journal of Personality and Social Psychology* 88, 3.

McDonald, Melissa M., Carlos David Navarrete, and Mark Van Vugt. 2012. "Evolution and the Psychology of Intergroup Conflict: The Male Warrior Hypothesis." *Philosophical Transactions of the Royal Society B.* 367

McGillis, Roderick. 2009. *He Was Some Kind of Man: Masculinities in B Westerns*. Waterloo, ON: Wilfrid Laurier University Press.

McGloin, Jean Marie, Christopher J. Sullivan, and Kyle J. Thomas. 2014. "Peer Influence and Context: The Interdependence of Friendship Groups, Schoolmates and Network Density in Predicting Substance Use." *Journal of Youth and Adolescence* 43.

McIntur, Kate. 2013. *The Gap in the Gender Gap: Violence Against Women in Canada*. Ottawa: Canadian Centre for Policy Alternatives. <www.policyalternatives.ca/sites/default/files/uploads/publications/National%20Office/2013/07/Gap_in_Gender_Gap_VAW.pdf>.

McKegney, Sam. 2014. *Mascuindians*. Winnipeg: University of Manitoba Press.

McQuarie, Donald. 1978. "Marx and the Method of Successive Approximations." *The Sociological Quarterly* 19.

Mead, George Herbert. 1962. *Mind, Self and Society*. Chicago: University of Chicago Press.

Mead, Margaret. 1971. *Sex and Temperament in Three Primitive Societies*. New York: William Morrow.

Medick, Hans. 1976. "The Proto-Industrial Family Economy: The Structural Function of Household and Family during the Transition from Peasant Society to Industrial Capitalism." *Social History* 1, 3.

Merton, Robert K. 1948. "The Self-Fulfilling Prophecy." *The Antioch Review* 8, 2.

Messner, Michael A. 2000. "Barbie Girls versus Sea Monsters: Children Constructing Gender." *Gender and Society* 14, 6.

Metrics 2.0. n.d. "Video Game Addiction: 81% of American Youth Play; 8.5% Are Addicted." <http://www.metrics2.com/blog/2007/04/04/video_game_addiction_81_of_american_youth_play_85.html>.

Mielach, David. 2014. "Americans Spend 23 Hours Per Week Online, Texting." *Business News Daily.* <www.businessnewsdaily.com/4718-weekly-online-social-media-time.html>.

Milestone, Katie, and Anneke Meyer. 2011. *Gender and Popular Culture.* Cambridge, UK: Polity.

Mileva-Seitz, Viara R., Akhgar Ghassabian, Marian J. Bakermans-Kranenburg, Jessica D. van den Brink, Marielle Linting, Vincent W.V. Jaddoe, Albert Hofman, Frank C. Verhulst, Henning Tiemeier, and Marinus H. van IJzendoorn. 2015. "Are Boys More Sensitive to Sensitivity? Parenting and Executive Function in Preschoolers." *Journal of Experimental Child Psychology* 130.

Miller, Eleanor M., and Carrie Yang Costello. 2001. "The Limits of Biological Determinism." *American Sociological Review* 66, 4.

Milojev, Petar, and Chris G. Sibley. 2014. "The Stability of Adult Personality Varies Across Age: Evidence From a Two-Year Longitudinal Sample of Adult New Zealanders." *Journal of Research in Personality* 51.

Mirtle, James. 2016. "One Last Fight." *Globe and Mail*, February 27.

Mitchell, Juliet. 1967. "Women: The Longest Revolution." *New Left Review* 40.

____. 1974. *Psychoanalysis and Feminism.* New York: Allen Lane.

Monrad, Merete. 2013. "On a Scale of One to Five, Who Are You? Mixed Methods in Identity Research." *Acta Sociologica* 56, 4.

Morandi, Emmanuele, and Riccardo Prandini (eds.). 2011. *Sociological Realism.* London: Routledge.

Morris, Edward W. 2008. "'Rednecks,' 'Rutters,' And 'Rithmetic: Social Class, Masculinity, and Schooling in A Rural Context." *Gender and Society* 22, 6.

Morton, Desmond. 1999. *A Military History of Canada.* Toronto: McClelland and Stewart.

Morton, Peggy. 1970. "Women's Work Is Never Done." *Women Unite.* Toronto: Women's Press.

Murdock, George Peter. 1949. *Social Structure.* New York: The MacMillan Company.

Murdock, George, and Caterina Provost. 1973. "Factors in the Division of Labor by Sex: A Cross-Cultural Analysis." *Ethnology* 12, 2.

Muschert, Glenn W. 2007. "Research in School Shootings." *Sociology Compass* 1, 1.

Myers Kristin. 2012. "Cowboy Up!" Non-Hegemonic Representations of Masculinity in Children's Television Programming." *Journal of Men's Studies* 20, 2.

Nadelhaft, Matthew. 1993. "Metawar: Sports and the Persian Gulf War." *Journal of American Culture* 16, 4.

Nash Information Services. 2015. "The Numbers." <www.the-numbers.com/market/>.

NASW (National Association of Social Workers). 2001. "Parents, Peers, and Pressures: Identifying the Influences on Responsible Sexual Decision-Making." <www.naswdc.org/practice/adolescent_health/ah0202.asp>.

Nathanson, Paul, and Katherine K. Young. 2001. *Spreading Misandry: The Teaching of Contempt for Men in Popular Culture.* Montreal: McGill-Queen's University Press.

Nauright, John, and Kimberly S. Schimmel (eds.). 2005. *The Political Economy of Sport.* New York: Palgrave Macmillan.

NCFM (National Coalition for Men). <http://ncfm.org/ncfm-home/>.

Nelson, Adie. 2010. *Gender in Canada,* fourth edition.Toronto: Pearson.

New York Film Academy. n.d. "Gender Inequality in Film." <www.nyfa.edu/

film-school-blog/gender-inequality-in-film/>.

Newman, Katherine, and Cybelle Fox. 2009. "Repeat Tragedy: Rampage Shooting in American High School and College Settings, 2002–2008." *American Behavioural Scientist* 52, 9.

Newman, Katherine S., Cybelle Fox, David J. Harding, Jal Mehta, and Wendy Roth. 2013. "Adolescent Culture and the Tragedy of Rampage Shootings." In Nils Boeckler, Thorsten Seeger, Peter Sitzer, and Wilhelm Heitmeyer (eds.), *School Shootings: International Research, Case Studies, and Concepts for Prevention.* EBook.

Newsday. 2014. "Recent Domestic Incidents by NFL Players." September 14. <www.newsday.com/sports/football/recent-domestic-incidents-by-nfl-players-1.9308197>.

Nicholas, Jane. 2012. "Representing the Modern Man: Beauty, Culture, and Masculinity in Early-Twentieth-Century Canada." In Christopher J. Greig and Wayne J. Martino (eds.), *Canadian Men and Masculinities Historical and Contemporary Perspectives.* Toronto: Canadian Scholars' Press.

NPR. 2012. "Teachers' Expectations Can Influence How Students Perform." September 17. <www.npr.org/blogs/health/2012/09/18/161159263/teachers-expectations-can-influence-how-students-perform>.

O'Neill Rachel. 2015. "Whither Critical Masculinity Studies: Notes on Inclusive Masculinity Theory, Postfeminism, and Sexual Politics." *Men and Masculinities* 18, 1.

O'Toole, Mary Ellen. 1999. *The School Shooter: A Threat Assessment Perspective.* Washington, DC: National Center for the Analysis of Violent Crime.

Oakley, Ann. 1972. *Sex, Gender and Society.* London: Temple Smith.

Olfret, Rose M., and Dianne M. Moebis. 2006. "The Spatial Economy of Gender-Based Occupational Segregation." *The Review of Regional Economics* 36, 1.

Oliffe, John L., John S. Ogrodniczuk, Joan L. Bottorff, Joy L. Johnson, and Kristy Hoyak. 2010. "'You Feel Like You Can't Live Anymore': Suicide from the Perspectives of Canadian Men Who Experience Depression." *Social Science and Medicine* 74.

Oliveira, Michael. 2013a. "Canadians Watch 30 Hours of TV But for Many the Web Dominates Free Time." *Thestar.com.* <www.thestar.com/life/technology/2013/04/26/canadians_watch_30_hours_of_tv_but_for_many_web_dominates_free_time.html>.

____. 2013b. "Average Canadian Watches 30 Hours of TV a Week, Spends More Time Online." CTV News, Kitchener, April 25. <http://kitchener.ctvnews.ca/average-canadian-watches-30-hours-of-tv-a-week-spends-more-time-online-1.1253812>.

Oransky, Matthew, and Celia Fisher. 2009. "The Development and Validation of the Meanings of Adolescent Masculinity Scale." *Psychology of Men & Masculinity* 8, 1.

Orr, Amy J. 2011 "Gendered Capital: Childhood Socialization and the 'Boy Crisis' in Education." *Sex Roles* 65.

Owen, Judith E. Blakemore, and Renee E. Centers. 2005. "Characteristics of Boys' and Girls' Toys." *Sex Roles* 53, 9/10.

Pappas, Nick T., Patrick C. McKenry, and Beth Skilken Catlett. 2004. "Athlete Aggression On the Rink and Off the Ice: Athlete Violence and Aggression in Hockey and Interpersonal Relationships." *Men and Masculinities* 6, 3.

Parsons, Amy, and Nina Howe. 2013. "'This Is Spiderman's Mask.' 'No, It's Green Goblin's': Shared Meanings During Boys' Pretend Play With Superhero and Generic Toys." *Journal of Research in Childhood Education* 27.

Parsons, Talcott. 1965a. "The American Family: Its Relation to Personality and the Social System." *Family Socialization and Interaction Process.* New York: Free Press.

____. 1965b. "The Normal American Family." In Bert Adams and Thomas Weirath (eds.), *Readings in the Sociology of Family.* Chicago: Markham.

Pascoe, C.J. 2003. "Multiple Masculinities? Teenage Boys Talk About Jocks and Gender." *American Behavioral Scientist* 46, 10.

Perry, Tony. 2002. "Youth Gets 50 to Life for Shootings." *Los Angles Times,* August 16. <http://articles.latimes.com/2002/aug/16/local/me-andy16>.

Phan, K. Luan, Tor Wager, Stephan F. Taylor, and Israel Liberzon. 2002. "Functional Neuroanatomy of Emotion: A Meta-Analysis of Emotion Activation Studies in PET and fMRI1" *NeuroImage* 16.

Pike, Jennifer J., and Nancy A. Jennings. 2005. "The Effects of Commercials on Children's Perceptions of Gender Appropriate Toy Use." *Sex Roles* 52, 1/2.

Pleck, Joseph. 1984. *The Myth of Masculinity.* Cambridge: MIT Press.

____. 1992. "The Theory of Male Sex-Role Identity: Its Rise and Fall, 1936 to the Present." In Harry Brod (ed.), *The Making of Masculinities.* London: Routledge.

____. 1995. "The Gender Role Strain Paradigm: An Update." In Robert F. Levant and William S. Pollack (eds.), *New Psychology of Men.* New York: Basic Books.

Pleck, Joseph, and Jack Sawyer (eds.). 1974. *Men and Masculinity.* Englewood Cliffs, NJ: Prentice Hall.

Pleck, Joseph, Freya L. Sonenstein, and Leighton C. Ku. 1993. "Masculinity Ideology: Its Impact on Adolescent Males' Heterosexual Relationships." *Journal of Social Issues* 49, 3.

____. 2004. "Adolescent Boys' Heterosexual Behaviour." In Niobe Way and Judy Chu (eds.), *Adolescent Boys: Exploring Diverse Cultures of Boyhood.* New York: New York University Press.

Polanyi, Karl. 1944. *The Great Transformation.* Boston: Beacon Press.

Pollack, William S. 2000. *Real Boys' Voices.* New York: Penguin Books.

Pollert, Anna. 1996. "Gender and Class Revisited; or, The Poverty of 'Patriarchy'." *Sociology* 30, 4.

Potter, Troy. 2007. "(Re)constructing Masculinity: Representations of Men and Masculinity in Australian Young Adult Literature." *Papers: Explorations into Children's Literature* 17, 1. <http://search.informit.com.au/documentSummary;dn=235644908525486; res=IELHSS>.

Prinz, Jesse. 2012. "Why Are Men So Violent? Are Men Warriors by Nature? History, Not Evolution, May Explain Male Violence." *Psychology Today,* February 3. <www.psychologytoday.com/blog/experiments-in-philosophy/201202/ why-are-men-so-violent>.

Rabelo, Laura Z., Renato Bortoloti and Debora H. Souza. 2014. "Dolls Are for Girls and Not for Boys: Evaluating the Appropriateness of the Implicit Relational Assessment Procedure for School-Age Children." *Psychological Record* 64.

Ramsay, Christine (ed.). 2011. *Making It Like a Man: Canadian Masculinities in Practice.* Waterloo: WIlfrid Laurier Press.

Reich, Wilhelm. 1946. *The Mass Psychology of Fascism.* New York: Orgone Institute Press.

Renold, Emma. 2001. "Learning the 'Hard' Way: Boys, Hegemonic Masculinity and the

Negotiation of Learner Identities in the Primary School." *British Journal of Sociology of Education* 22, 3.

____. 2004. "'Other' Boys: Negotiating Non-Hegemonic Masculinities in the Primary School." *Gender and Education* 16, 2.

Rhode, Deborah (ed.). 1990. *Theoretical Perspectives on Sexual Difference*. New Haven: Yale University Press.

Richard Lewontin, Richard, and Steven Rose. 1984. *Not in Our Genes*. Harmondsworth, UK: Penguin Books.

Richard, Lynn. 1994. "Sex Differences in Intelligence and Brain Size: A Paradox Resolved." *Personality and Individual Differences* 17, 2.

Rico, Johnny. n.d. "The Different Genres of War Movies." <http://warmovies.about.com/od/FilmReviewsbyGenre/tp/Types-of-War-Films.htm>.

Ridgeway, Cecilia L., and Shelley J. Correl. 2004. "Unpacking the Gender System: A Theoretical Perspective on Gender Beliefs and Social Relations."*Gender & Society* (August).

Ridgeway, Cecilia L., and Lynn Smith-Lovin. 1999. "The Gender System and Interaction." *Annual Review of Sociology* 25.

Risman, Barbara J., and Georgiann Davis. 2013. "From Sex Roles to Gender Structure." *Current Sociology Review* 61, 5–6.

Risman, Barbara, and Pepper Schwartz. 2002. "After the Sexual Revolution: Gender Politics in Teen Dating." *Contexts* (Spring).

Rist, Ray C. 1970. "Student Social Class and Teacher Expectations: The Self-Fulfilling Prophecy in Ghetto Education." *Harvard Educational Review* 40, 3.

Rivers Caryl, and Rosalind Chait Barnett. 2006. "The Myth of the Boys Crisis." *The Washington Post*, April 9. <www.washingtonpost.com/wp-dyn/content/article/2006/04/07/AR2006040702025.html>.

Robertson, Ian. 1981. *Sociology*. New York: Worth.

Robidoux, Michael A. 2012. "Male Hegemony or Male Mythology? Uncovering Distinctions through Some of Canada's Leading Men: The Coureurs de Bois and Professional Hockey Players." In Jason A. Laker (ed.), *Canadian Perspectives on Men & Masculinities: An Interdisciplinary Reader*. Don Mills, ON: Oxford University Press.

Roper, Michael. 2005. "Between Manliness and Masculinity: The 'War Generation' and the Psychology of Fear in Britain, 1914–1950." *The Journal of British Studies* 44, 02.

Roper, Michael, and J. Tosh. 1991. *Manful Assertions: Masculinities in Britain since 1800*. New York: Taylor & Francis.

Rosbech, Malise. 2013. "What Is Patriarchy." New Left Project. <www.newleftproject.org/index.php/site/article_comments/what_is_patriarchy>.

Rose, Sonya O. 1988. "Gender Antagonism and Class Conflict: Exclusionary Strategies of Male Trade Unionists in Nineteenth-Century Britain." *Social History* 13, 2.

Rose, Steven, and Hilary Rose. 2000. *Alas, Poor Darwin: Arguments against Evolutionary Psychology*. London: Vintage.

Rosenthal, Robert, and Lenore Jacobson. 1968. *Pygmalion in the Classroom*. New York: Holt, Rinehart and Winston.

Roth, Melanie A., and Jeffrey G. Parker. 2001. "Affective and Behavioral Responses to Friends Who Neglect Their Friends for Dating Partners: Influences of Gender, Jealousy and

Perspective." *Journal of Adolescence* 24.

Rothman, Lily. 2013. "FYI, Parents: Your Kids Watch a Full-Time Job's Worth of TV Each Week." *Time*, Nov. 20. <http://entertainment.time.com/2013/11/20/fyi-parents-your-kids-watch-a-full-time-jobs-worth-of-tv-each-week/>.

Royko, Mike. 1991. "War as Seen Through the Slo-Mo Lens of NFL Films." *Baltimore Sun*. April 08. <http://articles.baltimoresun.com/1991-04-08/features/1991098176_1_nfl-films-football-war>.

Rubin, Gayne. 1975. "The Traffic in Women: Notes on the 'Political Economy' of Sex." In Rayna Reiter (ed.), *Toward an Anthropology of Women*. New York: Monthly Review Press.

Ruggles, Steven. 1994. "The Transformation of American Family Structure." *The American Historical Review* 99, 1.

Runyon, Luke. 2014. "In Changing America, Gay Masculinity Has 'Many Different Shades.'" National Public Radio, August 22. <www.npr.org/2014/08/22/339831032/in-changing-america-gay-masculinity-has-many-different-shades>.

Rush, Curtis. 2015. "Sports Giant Angelo Mosca Copes with Alzheimer's." *Toronto Star*, Feb. 27. <www.thestar.com/sports/football/2015/02/27/sports-giant-angelo-mosca-copes-with-alzheimers.html>.

Rush, Curtis. 2015. "Years in CFL Have Taken Toll on Former Star Receiver." *Toronto Star*, Dec. 6.

Rutherdale, Robert. 2012. "Fathers in Multiple Roles: Assessing Modern Canadian Fatherhood as a Masculine Category." In Christopher J. Greig and Wayne J. Martino (eds.), *Canadian Men and Masculinities: Historical and Contemporary Perspectives*. Toronto: Canadian Scholars' Press.

Ruyle, Eugene E. 1975. "Mode of Production and Mode of Exploitation: The Mechanical and the Dialectical." *Dialectical Anthropology* 1, 1.

Sargent, Lynda (ed.). 1981. *The Unhappy Marriage of Marxism and Feminism: A Debate of Class and Patriarchy*. London, Pluto Press.

Scharrer, Erica. 2012. "More Than 'Just the Facts'? Portrayals of Masculinity in Police and Detective Programs Over Time." *Howard Journal of Communications* 23.

Schick, Laurie. 2014. "Hit Me Baby": From Britney Spears to the Socialization of Sexual Objectification of Girls in a Middle School Drama Program." *Sexuality and Culture* 18.

Schoppe-Sullivan, Sarah J., Letitia E. Kotila, Rongfang Jia, Sarah N. Lang, and Daniel J. Bower. 2013. "Comparisons of Levels and Predictors of Mothers' and Fathers' Engagement with Their Preschool-Aged Children." *Early Child Development and Care* 183, 3/4.

Schultz, Duane P. 1975. *A History of Modern Psychology*. New York: Academic Press.

Schwalbe, Michael. 2005. "Identity Stakes, Manhood Acts, and the Dynamics of Accountability." *Studies in Symbolic Interaction* 28.

____. 2014. *Manhood Acts: Gender and the Practices of Domination*. Boulder, CO: Paradigm.

Scott, Joan W. 1986. "Gender: A Useful Category of Historical Analysis" *American Historical Review* 91, 5.

____. 2010. "Gender: Still a Useful Category of Analysis." *Diogenes* 225.

Sellers, Jennifer Guinn, Matthias R. Mehl, and Robert A. Josephs. 2007. "Hormones and Personality: Testosterone as a Marker of Individual Differences." *Journal of Research in*

Personality 41.

Sharar, Shulamith. 1990. *Childhood in the Middle Ages.* London: Routledge.

Sheftall, Mark. 2015. "Mythologising the Dominion Fighting Man: Australian and Canadian Narratives of the First World War Soldier, 1914–39." *Australian Historical Studies* 46, 1.

Sherman, Aurora M., and Eileen L. Zurbriggen. 2014. "Boys Can Be Anything: Effect of Barbie Play on Girls Career Cognitions." *Sex Roles* 70.

Shugart, Helene A. 2003. "The New (Gay) Man in Contemporary Popular Media." *Critical Studies in Media Communication* 20, 1.

Sims, Christo. 2014. "Video Game Culture, Contentious Masculinities, and Reproducing Racialized Social Class Divisions in Middle School." *Signs* 39, 4.

Singleton, Andrew, and Jane Maree Maher. 2004. "The 'New Man' Is in the House: Young Men, Social Change, and Housework." *The Journal of Men's Studies* 12, 3.

Sinha, Marie (ed.). 2013. "Measuring Violence Against Women: Statistical Trends." Statistics Canada Catalogue no. 85-002-X. <www.statcan.gc.ca/pub/85-002-x/2013001/article/11766-eng.pdf>.

Smiler, Andrew P. 2008. "'I Wanted to Get to Know Her Better': Adolescent Boys' Dating Motives, Masculinity Ideology, and Sexual Behavior." *Journal of Adolescence* 31.

Smith, Lois J. 1994. "A Content Analysis of Gender Differences in Children's Advertising." *Journal of Broadcasting & Electronic Media* 38, 3.

Smith, Stacey, and Crystal Allene Cook. 2008. "Gender Stereotypes: An Analysis of Popular Films and TV." <http://seejane.org/wp-content/uploads/GDIGM_Gender_Stereotypes.pdf>.

Snell, William E. 1986. "The Masculine Role Inventory: Components and Correlates." *Sex Roles* 15, 7/8.

_____. 1989. "Development and Validation of the Masculine Behavior Scale: A Measure of Behaviors Stereotypically Attributed to Males vs. Females." *Sex Roles* 21, 11/12.

Sokolovenov, Michael. 2014. "How One Lawyer's Crusade Could Change Football Forever." *New York Times Sunday Magazine*, Nov. 6. <www.nytimes.com/2014/11/09/magazine/how-one-lawyers-crusade-could-change-football-forever.html>.

Sommer, Iris E.C., André Aleman, Anke Bouma, and René S. Kahn. 2004. "Do Women Really Have More Bilateral Language Representation Than Men? A Meta-Analysis of Functional Imaging Studies." *Brain* 127, 8.

Sommers, Christina Hoff. 2000. *The War Against Boys: How Misguided Feminism Is Harming Our Young Men.* New York: Simon and Schuster.

Staggenborg, Suzanne. 2008. "Seeing Mechanisms in Action." *Qualitative Sociology* 31. <http://link.springer.com/article/10.1007/s11133-008-9101-5?LI=true#page-1>.

Statistics Canada. 2006a. "Experienced Labour Force 15 Years and Over by Occupation and Sex, by Province and Territory (2006 Census)" <http://www.statcan.gc.ca/tables-tableaux/sum-som/l01/cst01/labor45a-eng.htm>.

_____. 2006b. "Population 15 Years and Over by Hours Spent Doing Unpaid Housework, by Sex, by Province and Territory (2006 Census) Newfoundland and Labrador, Prince Edward Island, Nova Scotia, New Brunswick)." Census of Population. <www.statcan.gc.ca/tables-tableaux/sum-som/l01/cst01/famil56a-eng.htm>.

_____. 2010. "Time Spent on Household Domestic Work, by Working Arrangement, Canada, 2010." General Social Survey. <www.statcan.gc.ca/pub/89-503-x/2010001/

article/11546/tbl/tbl007-eng.htm>.

____. 2012. "Life Expectancy at Birth, by Sex, by Province." <www.statcan.gc.ca/tables-tableaux/sum-som/l01/cst01/health26-eng.htm>.

____. 2013. "Average Earnings by Sex and Work Pattern (All Earners)." <www.statcan.gc.ca/tables-tableaux/sum-som/l01/cst01/labor01a-eng.htm>.

____. 2015a. "Time Spent on Unpaid Care of a Child in the Household, by Working Arrangement and Age of Youngest Child, Canada, 2010." <www.statcan.gc.ca/pub/89-503-x/2010001/article/11546/tbl/tbl006-eng.htm>.

____. 2015b. "Victims and Persons Accused of Homicide, by Age and Sex." <www.statcan.gc.ca/tables-tableaux/sum-som/l01/cst01/legal10a-eng.htm>.

____. 2015c. "Victims of Police-Reported Violent Crime, by Relationship of Accused to Victim and Sex of Victim, Canada, 2010." <www.statcan.gc.ca/pub/85-002-x/2012001/article/11643/tbl/tbl2-1-eng.htm>.

____. 2015d. "Victims of Police-Reported Violent Crime, by Intimate and Non-Intimate Partners, Type of Offence and Sex of Victim, Canada, 2010." <www.statcan.gc.ca/pub/85-002-x/2012001/article/11643/tbl/tbl2-4-eng.htm>.

____. 2015e. "Suicides and Suicide Rate, by Sex and by Age Group." <www.statcan.gc.ca/tables-tableaux/sum-som/l01/cst01/hlth66a-eng.htm>.

____. 2015f. "Heavy Drinking, by Age Group and Sex." <www.statcan.gc.ca/tables-tableaux/sum-som/l01/cst01/health79a-eng.htm>.

____. 2015g. "Motor Vehicle Accidents Causing Death, by Sex and by Age Group." <www.statcan.gc.ca/tables-tableaux/sum-som/l01/cst01/health112a-eng.htm>.

____. 2016. "Full-Time and Part-Time Employment by Sex and Age Group." <www.statcan.gc.ca/tables-tableaux/sum-som/l01/cst01/labor12-eng.htm>.

Steinem, Gloria. 1999. "Supremacy Crimes." *Ms. Magazine* (Aug./Sept.).

Stephens, John (ed.). 2002. *Ways of Being Male: Representing Masculinities in Children's Literature and Film*. New York: Routledge.

Stix, Gary. 2014. "The 'It' Factor." *Scientific American* September 1. <www.nature.com/scientificamerican/journal/v311/n3/full/scientificamerican0914-72.html>.

Struthers, James, and Richard Foot. 2013. "Great Depression." *The Canadian Encyclopedia*. <www.thecanadianencyclopedia.ca/en/article/great-depression/>.

Super, Donald E. 1982. "The Relative Importance of Work: Models and Measures for Meaningful Data." *The Counseling Psychologist* 10, 4.

Sweet, Elizabeth. 2014. "Toys Are More Divided by Gender Now Than They Were 50 Years Ago." *The Atlantic*, Dec. 12. <www.theatlantic.com/business/archive/2014/12/toys-are-more-divided-by-gender-now-than-they-were-50-years-ago/383556/>.

Sweezy, Paul M., and Harry Magdoff. 1974. "Keynesian Chickens Come Home to Roost." *Monthly Review* 25, 11.

Synnott, Anthony. 2009. *Re-thinking Men, Heroes, Villains and Victims*. Burlington, ON: Ashgate.

Tavris, Carol. 1984. *The Longest War: Sex Differences in Perspective*. New York: Harcourt Brace Jovanovich.

The Telegraph. 2014. "'Not Suppost to Cry': What I Hate About Being a Boy." *The Telegraph*, Nov. 14. <www.telegraph.co.uk/men/the-filter/11246279/Not-suppost-to-cry-what-I-hate-about-being-a-boy.html>.

Theocarakis, Nicholas J. 2010. "Metamorphoses: The Concept of Labour in the History of Political Economy." *The Economic and Labour Relations Review* 20, 2.

Thompson, Anna, and Aimee Lewis. 2014. "Men Get More Prize Money Than Women in 30% of Sports." BBC Sport. <http://www.bbc.com/sport/football/29744400>.

Thompson, Edward H., and Joseph H. Pleck. 1986. "The Structure of the Male Role Norms." In Michael Kimmer (ed.), *Changing Men: New Directions in Research on Men and Masculinities*. Newbury Park, CA: Sage.

Thompson, Edward H., Joseph H. Pleck, and David L. Ferrera. 1992. "Men and Masculinities: Scales for Masculinity Ideology and Masculinity-Related Constructs." *Sex Roles* 27, 11/12.

Tillotson, Shirley. 1991. "We May All Soon Be 'First-Class Men': Gender and Skill in Canada's Early Twentieth Century Urban Telegraph Industry." *Labour/Le Travail* 27.

Tjaden, Patricia. 2004. "What Is Violence Against Women? Defining and Measuring the Problem: A Response to Dean Kilpatrick." *Journal of Interpersonal Violence* 19, 11.

Tolmie, Jane, and Karis Shearer. 2012. "Masculinities in Canadian Literature." In Jason A. Laker (ed.), *Canadian Perspectives on Men & Masculinities: An Interdisciplinary Reader*. Don Mills: Oxford University Press.

Torgrimson, Britta N., and Christopher Minson. 2005. "Sex and Gender: What Is the Difference." *The Journal of Applied Physiology* 99.

Tosh, John. 2005. *Manliness and Masculinities in Nineteenth-Century Britain: Essays on Gender, Family, and Empire*. New York: Pearson Longman.

Tracy L. Dietz. 1998. "An Examination of Violence and Gender Role Portrayals in Video Games: Implications for Gender Socialization and Aggressive Behavior." *Sex Roles* 38, 5/6.

Tyre, Peg. 2006. "Education: Boys Falling Behind Girls in Many Areas." *Newsweek*, Jan. 29. <www.newsweek.com/education-boys-falling-behind-girls-many-areas-108593>.

U.S. Treasury. 2012. *The Financial Crisis Response in Charts April*. <www.treasury.gov/resource-center/data-chart-center/Documents/20120413_FinancialCrisisResponse.pdf>.

Udry, Richard J. 1994. "The Nature of Gender." *Demography* 31, 4.

____. 2000. "Biological Limits of Gender Construction." *American Sociological Review* 65, 3.

Unger, Rhoda Kesler. 1979. "Towards a Redefinition of Sex and Gender." *The American Psychologist* 34.

United States Department of the Treasury. 2012. "The Financial Crisis Response in Charts." <www.treasury.gov/resource-center/data-chart-center/Documents/20120413_FinancialCrisisResponse.pdf>.

Vacante, Jeffery. 2012. "Quebec Manhood in Historical Perspective." In Christopher J. Greig and Wayne J. Martino (eds.), *Canadian Men and Masculinities: Historical and Contemporary Perspectives*. Toronto: Canadian Scholars' Press.

Vaillancourt, Roxan. 2010. "Gender Differences in Police-Reported Violent Crime in Canada, 2008." Ottawa: Statistics Canada, Canadian Centre for Justice Statistics. <www.statcan.gc.ca/pub/85f0033m/85f0033m2010024-eng.pdf>.

van Hooffa, Jenny H. 2011. "Rationalising Inequality: Heterosexual Couples' Explanations and Justifications for the Division of Housework along Traditionally Gendered Lines." *Journal of Gender Studies* 20, 1.

Vandello, Joseph A., and Jennifer K. Bosson. 2013. "Hard Won and Easily Lost: A Review and Synthesis of Theory and Research on Precarious Manhood." *Psychology of Men & Masculinity* 14, 2.

Vandello, Joseph A., and Jennifer K. Bosson, Dov Cohen, Rochelle M. Burnaford and Jonathan R. Weaver. 2008. "Precarious Manhood." *Journal of Personality and Social Psychology* 95, 6.

Vanier Institute. 2013. "Video Gaming In Canada." <http://vanierinstitute.ca/wp-content/uploads/2015/10/FS_2013-12-12_Video-gaming.pdf>.

Venker, Suzanne. 2013. *The War on Men*. Washington: WND Books. Kindle Edition.

Verlinden Stephanie, Michel Hersen, and Jay Thomas. 2000. "Risk Factors in School Shootings." *Clinical Psychology Review* 20, 1.

Vincent, Nora. 2006. *Self Made Man*. New York: Viking Press.

Vossekuil, Bryan, Robert Fein, Maria Reddy, Randy Borum, and William Modzeleski. 2004. *The Final Report and Findings of the Safe School Initiative: Implications for the Prevention of School Attacks in the United States*. Washington, DC: The United States, United States Secret Service, and United States Department of Education.

Wagera, Tor D., K. Luan Phan, Israel Liberzona, and Stephan F. Taylora. 2003. "Valence, Gender, and Lateralization of Functional Brain Anatomy in Emotion: A Meta-Analysis of Findings from Neuroimaging." *NeuroImage* 19.

Wannamaker, Anna. 2009. *Boys in Children's Literature and Popular Culture: Masculinity, Abjection and the Fictional Child*. New York: Routledge.

Ward, Lisa. 2013. "The New Science of Sex Difference." *Sociology Compass* 7, 4.

Ware, Susan. 2009. "Women and the Great Depression." *Journal of the Gilder Lehrman Institut.* <www.gilderlehrman.org/history-by-era/great-depression/essays/women-and-great-depression>.

Warwick, Jason. 2016. "La Loche Shootings 'a Call for Action' Vice-Chief Says." *Saint Catharines Standard,* January 26.

Watson, J.B. 1924. *Behaviorism*. New York: People's Institute.

Way, Niobe. 2011. *Deep Secrets: Boys' Friendships and the Crisis of Connection*. Cambridge: Harvard University Press.

Way, Niobe, and Judy Chu. 2003. *Adolescent Boys*. New York: New York University Press.

Way, Niobe, Jessica Cressen, Samuel Bodian, Justin Preston, Joseph Nelson, and Diane Hughes. 2014. "'It Might Be Nice to Be a Girl, Then You Wouldn't Have to Be Emotionless': Boys' Resistance to Norms of Masculinity During Adolescence." *Psychology of Men and Masculinity* 15, 3.

Weber, Max. 1946. "Politics as a Vocation." In Hans Gerth and C. Wright Mills (eds.), *From Max Weber: Essays in Sociology*. New York: Oxford University Press.

____. 1948. *The Methodology of the Social Sciences* (E. Shils and H. Finch, eds.). Glencoe, IL: Free Press.

____. 1968. *Economy and Society: An Outline of Interpretative Sociology* (Guenther Roth and Claus Wittich, eds.). Berkley: University of California Pres.

Wedgwood, Nikki. 2009. "Connell's Theory of Masculinity – Its Origins and Influences on the Study of Gender." *Journal of Gender Studies* 18, 4.

West, Candice, and Don Zimmerman. 1987. "Doing Gender." *Gender and Society* 1, 2.

Westbrook, Laurel, and Kristen Schilt. 2014. "Transgender People, Gender Politics, and the

Maintenance of the Sex/Gender/Sexuality System." *Gender and Society* 28, 1.

Wester, Stephen R., David L. Vogel, James M. O'Neil, and Lindsay Danforth. 2012. "Development and Evaluation of the Gender Role Conflict Scale Short Form." *Psychology of Men & Masculinity* 13, 2.

Whitehead, Stephen. 2002. *Men and Masculinities*. Cambridge: Polity.

Wilkinson, Ross B. 2004. "The Role of Parental and Peer Attachment in the Psychological Health and Self-Esteem of Adolescents." *Journal of Youth and Adolescence* 33, 6.

Williams, Simon J. 2003. "Beyond Meaning, Discourse and the Empirical World: Critical Realist Reflections on Health." *Social Theory & Health* 1, 1.

Wilson, Arron. 2015. "Ray Rice Seeks End to Exile from NFL." *Baltimore Sun*, Feb. 28. <www.baltimoresun.com/sports/bs-sp-ray-rice-speaks-20150228-story.html>.

Withers, Bethany P. 2015. "Without Consequence: When Professional Athletes Are Violent Off the Field." *Harvard Journal of Sports and Entertainment Law*. <http://harvardjsel.com/2015/07/bethany-withers-without-consequence/>.

Wood, Eileen, Serge Desmarais, and Sara Gugula. 2002. "The Impact of Parenting Experience on Gender Stereotyped Toy Play of Children." *Sex Roles* 47, 1/2.

Wood, Ellen Meiksins. 2002. *The Origins of Capitalism*. London. Verso.

Woods, Rich, Elizabeth Goodman, S. Jean Emans, and Robert H. DuRant. 1998. "Aggressors or Victims: Gender and Race in Music Video Violence." *Pediatrics* 101.

Wright, Michelle F., and Yan Li. 2013. "The Association Between Cyber Victimization and Subsequent Cyber Aggression: The Moderating Effect of Peer Rejection." *Journal of Youth and Adolescence* 42.

Zaretsky, Eli. 1986. *Capitalism, the Family and Personal Life*. New York: Harper and Row.

Zhang, Ting, Josh Hoddenbagh, Susan McDonald, and Katie Scrim. 2009. *An Estimation of the Economic Impact of Spousal Violence in Canada, 2009*. Ottawa: Government of Canada, Department of Justice Canada. <www.justice.gc.ca/eng/rp-pr/cj-jp/fv-vf/rr12_7/>.

Zosuls, Kristina M., Cynthia F. Miller, Dianne N. Ruble, Carole L. Martin, and Richard A. Fabes. 2011. "Gender Development Research in Sex Roles: Historical Trends and Future Directions." *Sex Roles* 64, 11/12.

Acts of Legislation

The Canadian Bill of Rights, Canadian Human Rights Act of 1977, and the Canadian Human Rights Employment Equity Act of 1995

INDEX